BESTSELLING BOOK SERIES

Photo Retouching & Restoration For Dummies

Cheat Sheet

P9-DEB-636

Universal Keyboard Shortcuts

Press these key combinations to perform basic operations in most image-editing programs.

Operation	Windows Shortcut	Macintosh Shortcut
Open an existing image	Ctrl+O	⌘+O
Create a new image	Ctrl+N	⌘+N
Save an image	Ctrl+S	⌘+S
Cut a selection to the Clipboard	Ctrl+X	⌘+X
Copy a selection to the Clipboard	Ctrl+C	⌘+C
Paste the contents of the Clipboard into an image	Ctrl+V	⌘+V
Select the entire image	Ctrl+A	⌘+A
Undo the last thing you did	Ctrl+Z	⌘+Z
Quit the program	Ctrl+Q	⌘+Q

Input Resolution Guide

Use the scanner or digital camera setting that captures the number of pixels shown below if you want the minimum resolution required for good print output (200 ppi). For even better prints and or to allow for cropping away part of the image, capture the pixels shown in the third column (300 ppi).

Final print size	Pixels needed for 200 ppi	Pixels needed for 300 ppi
4 x 6 inches	800 x 1200	1200 x 1800
5 x 7 inches	1000 x 1400	1500 x 2100
8 x 10 inches	1600 x 2000	2400 x 3000

File Format Guide

Stick with these file formats when saving your photos.

Format	Description
PSD	The Adobe Photoshop file format. If you're using Photoshop or Photoshop Elements, save works-in-progress in this format to preserve special image features, such as layers, and enable faster processing by the software.
Your photo editor's native format	In programs other than Photoshop and Photoshop Elements, save photos in the program's own format, for the same reasons just stated, until you need to open the photo in some other program.
TIFF	Save a copy of your finished image in the TIFF format if you need to use the photo in a print publication, such as a newsletter. Files saved in this format can be opened on both PC and Macintosh computers and in all page layout programs, but not in Web browsers or e-mail programs.
JPEG	Save your image in JPEG only after doing all editing work and only to use the picture on a Web page, send it with an e-mail message, or for some other on-screen use. JPEG can compress images so that files are significantly smaller, but too much compression reduces image quality.

For Dummies: Bestselling Book Series for Beginners

Photo Retouching & Restoration For Dummies®

Cheat Sheet

Photoshop Elements Shortcuts

The following shortcuts apply to Adobe Photoshop Elements 1.0 and 2.0.

Selection Tricks

To do this	Windows shortcut	Macintosh shortcut
Select everything on active layer	Ctrl+A	⌘+A
Deselect everything	Ctrl+D	⌘+D
Invert the selection outline	Shift+Ctrl+I	Shift+⌘+I
Feather a selection outline	Alt+Ctrl+D	Option+⌘+D
Nudge a selection outline one pixel	Arrow key with selection tool active	Arrow key with selection tool active
Select non-transparent areas of layer	Ctrl+click layer in Layers palette	⌘+click layer in Layers palette

Layer Tricks

To do this	Windows shortcut	Macintosh shortcut
Make layer active	Click layer in Layers palette	Click layer in Layers palette
Copy selection to new layer	Ctrl+J	⌘+J
Merge layer with underlying layer	Ctrl+E	⌘+E
Merge all visible layers	Shift+Ctrl+E	Shift+⌘+E
Create new layer	Shift+Ctrl+N	Shift+⌘+N

Painting and Editing Tricks

To do this	Windows shortcut	Macintosh shortcut
Paint or apply edit in a straight line	Shift+drag with tool	Shift+drag with tool
Return to default foreground and background colors	D	D
Swap current foreground and background colors	X	X
Access Eyedropper while working with paint tool	Alt	Option
Display Hue/Saturation dialog box	Ctrl+U	⌘+U
Display Levels dialog box	Ctrl+L	⌘+L
Choose Free Transform command	Ctrl+T	⌘+T

Zoom/View Tricks

To do this	Windows shortcut	Macintosh shortcut
Zoom in	Ctrl+plus key	⌘+plus key
Zoom out	Ctrl+minus key	⌘+minus key
Fit entire image in window	Ctrl+0	⌘+0
Display actual-pixels size	Alt+Ctrl+0	Option+⌘+0
Show/hide rulers	Ctrl+R	⌘+R
Display Preferences dialog box	Ctrl+K	⌘+K

Wiley Publishing, For Dummies, the For Dummies Bestselling Book Series logo and all related trade dress are trademarks or registered trademarks of Wiley Publishing, Inc. All other trademarks are the property of their respective owners.

For Dummies: Bestselling Book Series for Beginners

Photo Retouching & Restoration
FOR DUMMIES®

by Julie Adair King

Wiley Publishing, Inc.

Photo Retouching & Restoration For Dummies®

Published by
Wiley Publishing, Inc.
909 Third Avenue
New York, NY 10022
www.wiley.com

Copyright © 2002 Wiley Publishing, Inc., Indianapolis, Indiana

Published simultaneously in Canada

For general information on our other products and services or to obtain technical support, please contact our Customer Care Department within the U.S. at 800-762-2974, outside the U.S. at 317-572-3993, or fax 317-572-4002.

Wiley also publishes its books in a variety of electronic formats. Some content that appears in print may not be available in electronic books.

Library of Congress Cataloging-in-Publication Data:

Library of Congress Control Number: 2002106039

ISBN: 0-7645-1662-0

Manufactured in the United States of America

10 9 8 7 6 5 4 3 2

1B/SX/QZ/QS/IN

About the Author

Digital imaging and photography expert Julie Adair King is the author of *Digital Photography For Dummies, Adobe PhotoDeluxe For Dummies, Microsoft PhotoDraw 2000 For Dummies,* and other books about computer graphics. She is a graduate of Purdue University and lives in Indianapolis, Indiana.

Dedication

This book is dedicated to my incredible grandmother, Irene Harris, whose courage and humor are a continual source of inspiration. Thank you for a lifetime of love and support.

Author's Acknowledgments

I would like to express my sincere gratitude to everyone at Wiley Publishing who helped make this book possible, especially project editor Andrea Boucher; acquisitions editor Steve Hayes; and Erin Smith and Shelley Lea in the Composition department.

I am also grateful to technical editor Sibylle Jennett for sharing her expertise and to Dale King and Seta Frantz for reviewing my rough manuscript. Thanks also to Mark Dahm at Adobe and to the folks at Hewlett-Packard and Wacom Technology.

Finally, many hugs and kisses to the friends and family members who graciously allowed me to show their wonderful selves in the pictures featured in this book.

Publisher's Acknowledgments

We're proud of this book; please send us your comments through our online registration form located at www.dummies.com/register.

Some of the people who helped bring this book to market include the following:

Acquisitions, Editorial, and Media Development

Project Editor: Andrea C. Boucher

Acquisitions Editor: Steven H. Hayes

Technical Editor: Sibylle Jennett

Editorial Manager: Constance Carlisle

Permissions Editor: Laura Moss

Media Development Specialists: Marisa Pearman, Travis Silvers

Media Development Manager: Laura VanWinkle

Media Development Supervisor: Richard Graves

Editorial Assistant: Amanda Foxworth

Production

Project Coordinator: Erin Smith

Layout and Graphics: Scott Bristol, Brian Drumm, Stephanie D. Jumper, Jackie Nicholas, Brent Savage, Jacque Schneider, Bette Schulte, Mary J. Virgin, Erin Zeltner

Proofreaders: John Greenough, Andy Hollandbeck, Susan Moritz, Angel Perez, TECHBOOKS Production Services, Inc.

Indexer: TECHBOOKS Production Services, Inc.

Publishing and Editorial for Technology Dummies

Richard Swadley, Vice President and Executive Group Publisher
Andy Cummings, Vice President and Publisher
Mary C. Corder, Editorial Director

Publishing for Consumer Dummies

Diane Graves Steele, Vice President and Publisher
Joyce Pepple, Acquisitions Director

Composition Services

Gerry Fahey, Vice President of Production Services
Debbie Stailey, Director of Composition Services

Cartoons at a Glance

By Rich Tennant

"Well, well! Guess who just lost 9 pixels?"

page 85

ATTEMPTING TO SAVE MONEY ON FAMILY PHOTOS, THE DILBRANTS SCAN THEIR NEWBORN INTO A PHOTO IMAGING PROGRAM WITH PLANS OF JUST DITHERING THE CHILD INTO ADOLESCENCE.

Nope! She must have moved again! Run the scanner down her one more.

page 9

"I THINK YOU'VE MADE A MISTAKE. WE DO PHOTO RETOUCHING, NOT FAMILY PORTRAI....OOOH, WAIT A MINUTE-I THINK I GET IT!"

page 241

"THAT'S A LOVELY SCANNED IMAGE OF YOUR SISTER'S PORTRAIT. NOW TAKE IT OFF THE BODY OF THAT PIT VIPER BEFORE SHE COMES IN THE ROOM."

page 333

"...and here's me with Cindy Crawford. And this is me with Madonna and Celine Dion..."

page 313

Cartoon Information:
Fax: 978-546-7747
E-Mail: richtennant@the5thwave.com
World Wide Web: www.the5thwave.com

Table of Contents

· ·

Introduction

Think back to the last time you browsed through your photo collection. You probably didn't get very far before you thought to yourself, "This picture would have been great if only . . . ." If only the exposure had been better. If only that big plant, sign, or other distracting object wasn't cluttering up the background. If only the print hadn't been sitting for 30 years in the basement being attacked by mildew, dirt, and paper-munching bugs.

In years past, you either had to live with lousy or damaged photos or pay big bucks to have them professionally repaired. Today, thanks to the development of consumer-friendly photo-editing software, you can use your computer to do the job yourself.

Whether you want to fix a 100-year-old family photo or a business shot you took yesterday, *Photo Retouching & Restoration For Dummies* shows you how. Here are just some of the things that you can do by following the simple, easy-to-understand instructions provided in this book:

- Bring new life to old, faded photographs
- Adjust colors throughout the picture or in a certain object
- Improve exposure and contrast
- Sharpen focus
- Cover up flaws such as negative scratches, scanner dust, and dirt
- Remove unwanted elements from the scene
- Get rid of red-eye, soften wrinkles, and do other facial retouching
- Replace a busy background with one that compliments the subject

In other words, you can cure just about whatever ails your photographs, whether they need minor retouching or major restoration. And you don't need a Ph.D. in photography or computers to get the job done, either. All you need is the willingness to spend an hour or two in front of the computer with this book by your side.

Is This Stuff Hard to Do?

As you flip through this book, you may spot many terms that you don't know — *pixels, resolution, layer blending mode,* and the like. Some of the example images may look pretty complicated, too.

Don't worry. You *do not* need any prior experience with the terminology or the tools featured in this book to be successful. Even though some of the techniques may seem complex at first, when you try them, you'll discover that they're actually very easy. I explain everything you need to know as I walk you through each retouching and restoration process, and Chapter 11 provides a handy reference guide to photo-editing lingo.

If you're brand-new to computers, however, you may find it helpful to pick up one of the *For Dummies* guides to your operating system to use as a companion to this book. So that I can provide you with as much photo-related information as possible, I don't spend much time covering basic operating instructions, such as how to launch programs and locate files stored on your computer's hard drive.

What Software Do I Need?

To do the types of projects discussed in this book, you need a photo-editing program that offers a few advanced features that I won't get into here because they probably won't mean anything to you yet. Suffice it to say that you can use almost any intermediate or professional-level software, including the following programs:

- Adobe Photoshop Elements
- Adobe Photoshop
- Jasc Paint Shop Pro
- Ulead PhotoImpact

In order to provide step-by-step guidance for certain techniques, however, I had to pick one program to feature. I selected Photoshop Elements, for three reasons. One, it's available for both the Windows and Macintosh platforms. Two, it provides all the tools you need to restore even seriously damaged photos. And three, it retails for less than $100. (You can often find it on sale for significantly less than $100, in fact.)

Note: As I was writing this book, Adobe was preparing to release a new version of Elements. I cover the original Version 1.0 and the new Version 2.0. However, because the new version wasn't officially complete by the time this book went to press, a few things in that version may be slightly different than described here. Check your software's manual if you need help finding or using a particular feature.

If you are fortunate enough to own Adobe Photoshop, the more powerful, higher-priced cousin of Photoshop Elements, you will find that most of the instructions in this book also work perfectly for your software. A table in Appendix A indicates the few commands that are found in different places in Photoshop than they are in Photoshop Elements.

You can easily adapt the information in this book to other programs as well, assuming that it offers a feature set similar to or greater than the one offered by Photoshop Elements. If you selected Paint Shop Pro or PhotoImpact as your photo editor, be sure to see Appendix A, which provides information to help you translate my instructions to those programs.

If you don't own *any* photo editing software yet, the CD attached to the back cover of this book offers a great way to find a program that suits your needs. The CD includes try-before-you-buy versions of all the aforementioned programs plus a few others.

One more word about photo-editing software: If you're working with an entry-level program such as Adobe PhotoDeluxe, you can use many of the techniques that I discuss. But if you get serious about photo retouching and restoration, I encourage you to move up to a more sophisticated program. Surprisingly, many tasks are much easier to do with the more advanced tools found in the higher-level programs than they are with the more-limited features available in the entry-level programs.

Sneak Preview

The chapters to come provide the A-to-Z story on photo retouching and restoration. You'll find detailed descriptions to help you put your photo editor's tools to their best use plus background information you need to know to get professional, high-quality results. In addition, full-color examples of important concepts are provided in the 16-page color section in the middle of the book.

To give you a clearer idea of where to find topics that may be of special interest to you, the following sections offer a quick preview of each chapter.

Part 1: First Steps

As the name implies, chapters in this part provide the information you need to get your photo repair off to a good start.

✔ Chapter 1 helps you evaluate your pictures and figure out the best way to tackle a photograph that has a multitude of problems. I also provide recommendations for hardware and software tools that can help you get the job done more quickly.

✔ Chapter 2 discusses the fine art of scanning, explaining such tricky issues as what input resolution to select. You can find instructions for saving and protecting your original photo files here as well.

✔ Chapter 3 shows you how to create a selection outline, which tells the program what areas of the picture you want to alter. This crucial initial step in the editing process can have a dramatic impact on your picture, so I include professional tricks that enable you to get better results than you can achieve with basic selection techniques.

Part II: Makeover Magic

This part of the book is filled with quick, easy techniques that you can use to dramatically improve your photos.

✔ Chapter 4 covers color-related issues, such as removing ugly color casts and restoring faded colors.

✔ Chapter 5 shows you how to solve focus and exposure problems.

✔ Chapter 6 offers simple tricks for hiding flecks of dirt, scratches, and other small flaws. In addition, this chapter explains how to create a seamless patch to cover larger defects.

✔ Chapter 7 explores ways to create a better image by cropping out extraneous background areas, fixing tilting horizon lines, and even rearranging subjects within the scene.

✔ Chapter 8 spotlights special problems you may encounter when retouching portraits. Look here for information about such topics as removing red eye, toning down wrinkles, and dealing with reflections caused by eyeglasses.

Part III: Finishing Touches

This two-chapter section of the book presents ideas for giving your pictures some additional creative flair and for sharing the results of your efforts.

✔ Chapter 9 provides recipes for creating a photo collage, applying special effects, slipping a new background behind the subject, and replacing one color with another.

✔ Chapter 10 guides you through the steps involved in preparing your pictures for printing or for use in a Web page, e-mail message, or multi-media presentation. This chapter also offers some tips on buying a photo printer and for getting printed colors to better match what you see on your computer screen.

Part IV: The Part of Tens

As is the tradition in *For Dummies* books, this part presents three "top ten" lists, each of which offers short, but important, bits of information.

✔ Chapter 11 provides a quick reference to the ten most important technical terms you'll encounter during your photo editing adventures.

✔ Chapter 12 offers ten pointers to help you get more professional results from the minute you first fire up your photo software.

✔ Chapter 13 discusses ten steps that you can take to protect your images from being damaged in the future.

Part V: Appendixes

I really should name this part something like, "Wait, still more good stuff here." Despite its lackluster name, this part of the book contains some very useful information.

✔ As I mentioned earlier, Appendix A provides charts that help you translate the Photoshop Elements-specific instructions I give to three other leading photo-editing programs: Adobe Photoshop, Jasc Paint Shop Pro, and Ulead PhotoImpact.

✔ Appendix B contains information about the CD found in the back of this book. The CD contains some sample photos plus trial versions of photo-editing software, image-cataloging programs, photo-album programs, and specialty software such as printing and scanning utilities.

Notes about Using This Book

Like other titles in the *For Dummies* series, this book uses special formatting in some step-by-step instructions. The following list explains these features and discusses a few other issues about how information is presented:

- **Menu commands:** When I mention an item that you're supposed to select from a menu at the top of the program window, I separate the menu name and menu item with an arrow. For example, "Choose File⇨Print" means to click the File menu and then click the Print command on that menu.

- **Keyboard shortcuts:** For some tasks, you can press one or two keys on your keyboard instead of clicking your way through menus. I list these so-called *keyboard shortcuts* by listing each key in the sequence, separated by a plus sign. So if you see something like "Press Ctrl+C," you should press the Ctrl key and then the C key.

- **Windows or Macintosh?:** Although the figures in this book feature the Windows version of Photoshop Elements, everything works the same way in the Macintosh version unless I specifically provide alternate instructions.

  Most keyboard shortcuts *are* different on a Macintosh computer than they are on a Windows-based PC, however. I list the PC shortcut first, followed by the Macintosh version in parentheses, like so: "Press Ctrl+C (⌘+C).

- **Key-click shortcuts:** Some shortcuts involve clicking a mouse button while pressing a particular key. Again, I list the Windows key, followed by the Macintosh key in parentheses — for example, "Alt (Option)+click with the tool." In some cases, you press the same key on both Windows and Macintosh computers, in which case you see only one instruction, such as "Shift+click with the tool."

- **Dialog boxes:** When I refer to a *dialog box,* I mean a box of options that appears when you choose a particular command. Some dialog boxes contain drop-down lists or menus, which you typically display by clicking a little triangle on the list or menu.

- **Photoshop Elements 1.0 and 2.0:** For instructions that are specific to Photoshop Elements, I provide information for both Version 1.0 and 2.0. However, I don't waste time (or insult your intelligence) by spelling out minimal differences — for example, a menu command that is Window⇨Show Layers in Version 1.0 and Window⇨Layers in Version 2.0.

In addition, little pictures — known as *icons* in the computer-book biz — appear next to some paragraphs. These icons flag information that I think is especially important. Each icon has a different meaning:

Tip icons mark a trick that enables you to do something better, faster, or with less hassle — or all three.

Remember icons highlight a detail that I may present elsewhere in the book but think is so vital that I'm mentioning it again.

Think of this icon as a big red light. Stop, before you hurt yourself or your photo, and pay close attention to what the warning paragraph has to say.

 If you want to sound like a photo-editing pro, take a minute or two to read paragraphs marked with this icon, which I use when defining a technical term.

 Text marked with this icon tells you where to find more details about a particular subject.

When I mention a program that's included on the bonus CD at the back of the book, I attach this icon to the text. You can install the program on your computer and see if you agree with my evaluation.

Where Should I Start?

This book is designed so that you can either read it from cover to cover, starting with Chapter 1, or just dive into whatever section interests you at the moment. So where you begin is completely up to you.

Wherever you start, however, I want to emphasize that you shouldn't feel like a, well, dummy, if you don't understand everything right away or get perfect results on the first try. That's *normal*. Everyone feels a little overwhelmed and incapable when they try something new, especially if that something involves a computer.

With each page you read and each picture you tackle, you'll acquire new skills and a better understanding of what techniques offer the best solutions in particular situations. Before long, you'll build up a repertoire of skills that you can use to improve any photograph, no matter how badly damaged.

Above all, don't take any of this too seriously. Enjoy remembering the occasion or subject of your pictures and take pleasure in reclaiming an image that otherwise might have been lost. Let me guide you through the technical parts of your project — you concentrate on having fun!

Part I
First Steps

In this part . . .

*I*f you're like most people making their first foray into photo retouching and restoration, you already have a problem photo or two in hand. And you have a clear idea about what changes you want to make to those pictures. But other than switching on your computer and assembling a supply of computer-friendly snacks, you're not quite sure how to get started.

Well, this part of the book answers that question along with a few others that probably haven't occurred to you yet, but will. Chapter 1 helps you figure out what tools you need to repair your pictures and which problems you should tackle first, second, and last. Chapter 2 explains how to get your pictures into the computer and safeguard your picture files after you create them. To wrap things up, Chapter 3 shows you how to take the critical first step in every photo-editing project: selecting the area of the picture that you want to alter.

Chapter 1

Can This Picture Be Saved?

• •

In This Chapter

▶ Taking a look at what's possible — and what's not

▶ Evaluating your pictures to determine how much work is needed

▶ Planning your photographic repair job

▶ Outfitting your digital studio

• •

*I*n many ways, fixing a problem photograph is like tackling a household repair. In both cases, the first step is to assess the damage and determine whether the solution involves a minor tweak or a major renovation. You may be able to make your photo shine with a few mouse clicks, just as you sometimes can stem a dripping faucet by simply swapping out a washer. Rescuing other pictures may involve the photographic equivalent of a complete plumbing overhaul, requiring patience, effort, and expertise with some sophisticated tools.

To help you understand what level of work your photographs need, this chapter shows you some examples of minor, moderate, and major restoration and retouching projects. In addition, the pages to come offer advice about planning your project and introduce you to hardware and software tools that make the job easier.

As you read through this chapter, don't be alarmed if you come across terms that are unfamiliar to you. This chapter is intended just to get you thinking about what changes you may want to make to your photos — later chapters explain all the terminology and other technical stuff in detail.

Tweaking Exposure

Proper lighting is key to a good photograph — and, unfortunately, one of the more challenging aspects of picture-taking. Even with today's auto-exposure cameras, you can easily wind up with a picture that's *underexposed* (too dark) or *overexposed* (too light).

Correcting a too-dark image typically is easier than darkening a too-light image because an underexposed image tends to retain more original color information than an overexposed one. In a seriously overexposed image, colors toward the light end of the color spectrum may go completely white, a problem that you usually can't fix with exposure-correction tools.

Figure 1-1 shows an example of an exposure problem that's easily remedied. In this photo, I was able to use an exposure tool called a *Levels filter* to brighten up my skating nephew without changing the already light area at the top of the image. You can see the corrected image on the right in Figure 1-1. (I also improved the focusing a little; see the next section for more on that topic.) Although the bright regions at the top of the picture are probably still a little hot, they're not integral to the scene, so I left them alone.

For a more challenging exposure problem, take a look at the "before" image in Color Plate 3-1. That's my grandmother sitting by the window, with me on her lap and big sister looking on. The strong bands of sunshine streaming through the window created an uneven lighting situation, resulting in some areas that were seriously dark and others that were much too bright.

Figure 1-1:
To fix this too-dark image (left), I lightened the foreground without altering the bright areas at the top of the scene (right).

Fixing the underexposed areas wasn't a problem; as I did with my nephew's picture, I just used the Levels filter to bring some light into the darkness. The overexposed regions of my grandmother's skin, though, were completely washed out. Unlike the overexposed regions in Figure 1-1, these too-hot areas are important to the image and need to be fixed. But darkening them with exposure tools only made the skin gray — gray is a darker shade of white, after all.

Abandoning the exposure tools, I toned down the brightest areas of the skin by using my photo editor's painting tools to subtly tint the skin with color. I opted not to go too far with this digital tanning session because I wanted to retain the interplay of shadows and highlights, which I think adds interest to the scene.

For the full story on the Levels filter and other exposure-correction tools, see Chapter 5. Also check out Chapter 8, which explains the painting technique that I used to fix the skin areas in Color Plate 3-1.

Correcting Colors

Many old photographs suffer from color problems. Over time, colors shift and fade as the chemicals used to produce the image break down. Prints typically take on a red or amber cast, while slides tend to exhibit a blue or green tint. The left image in Color Plate 4-4 shows a 1950s color print of my great-grandmother that has shifted almost completely into the red zone; the too-blue "before" example in Color Plate 9-1 shows a color slide from the early 1960s.

Getting images like the one in Color Plate 4-4 back to their original color condition isn't terribly difficult because the color cast is consistent throughout the image and the original shadows, highlights, and midtones (areas of medium brightness) remain mostly intact. You can do the job using any image-editing program that has a decent color balancing feature. Most programs also offer features that make simple work of restoring faded colors.

The image in Color Plate 9-1 presents a more difficult challenge. In addition to a serious blue cast, the picture is underexposed, and dark blotches — possibly caused by mold — mar the subjects' skin. Toward the bottom of the picture, very little of the original image information remains. With pictures like this, don't expect miracles — although you can significantly improve the image, you likely won't be able to completely restore it. In fact, I wouldn't have tackled this photo at all except for the fact that it's one of the few images showing my father and my toddler-aged self. (Apparently when you're the middle child, as I was, nobody gets too excited about taking your picture, an oversight that I whine about to my parents on a regular basis.)

In this case, my first editing decision was to *crop* — cut away — the outer edges of the picture. Although I probably could have recreated the areas at the bottom of the photo, I opted not to do so because they don't really add much interest (and, okay, I'm a little lazy). After working on this picture for several weeks, using every exposure and color-correction technique I knew, I managed to achieve the results shown in the example labeled *Best-effort correction* in the color plate. The image remains really grainy and poorly focused.

When it became clear that I'd never be able to make this image into a sharp, perfectly exposed photo, I decided to apply some special effects that would make the soft focus and excess grain look like an artistic choice instead of flaws. Starting with my best-effort correction image, I created two variations on the picture, which you can see in the color plate.

For the center-right example, I applied the Sponge effect filter in Photoshop Elements. To create the hand-tinted photo look in the lower-right example, I first removed all the original colors from the image, resulting in the grayscale image shown in the lower-left example. Then I painted in new colors using a special technique that I cover in Chapter 9.

Grayscale is the professional's term for what most people call *black-and-white* images. In the imaging world, *black-and-white* refers to a picture that contains only black and white — no intermediate shades of gray.

Modern photographs, too, may need some color tweaking; for example, photographs shot in office buildings sometimes have a greenish tint due to the fluorescent lighting. Fortunately, taking care of these color casts is a quick and painless process.

To find out how to make these and other types of color corrections, visit Chapter 4. Chapter 9 introduces you to special effects and other creative techniques.

Shifting Focus

If you've spent any time at all with image-editing software, you've no doubt discovered something called a *sharpening filter*. You can use a sharpening filter on a blurry image to create the illusion of better focus.

Sharpening filters can improve an image that's slightly off in the focus department, but they can't take a really blurry image and make it perfectly sharp. For an example of the results you can expect, take another look at Figure 1-1. In addition to being too dark, the original image is a little soft. I used a special filter called an *Unsharp Mask filter* to sharpen the image. Note, however, that my nephew's arms, which he moved at the time I pressed the shutter button, remain blurry, especially around the hands. No amount of sharpening will fix that kind of blur. (In this image, the blurred area adds to the feeling of motion and shouldn't be eliminated, anyway.)

The opposite of sharpening filters, *blur filters,* create the appearance of softer focus. Why would you want to make a picture look less sharp? Any aging model can give you one answer: to make wrinkles less prominent. Blurring the edges between a wrinkle and the surrounding skin works more facelift magic than any miracle cream. In addition, you can blur the background of a picture to make the foreground subject more prominent, mimicking the look of a photograph that was taken using a lens that has a short depth of field. This technique works well for diminishing a distracting background, as illustrated by the photo in Color Plate 5-2.

To get familiar with sharpening and blur filters, check out Chapter 5. For more information about softening wrinkles and other facial flaws, see Chapter 8.

Removing Crud

By *crud,* I'm not referring to the slimeball ex-boyfriend or devious ex-girlfriend who you'd just as soon didn't appear in your last family photo — the next section discusses that sort of image renovation. I'm speaking of small-scale crud, the kind caused by scratches in negatives, dust on a scanner bed, wrinkles and holes in old prints, and the like. The photo in Figure 1-2 contains two such flaws. Toward the bottom of the picture, you can see a thin white line, the result of a negative scratch. The curly white thing in the hair is another remnant left by a careless photo-finishing lab.

Figure 1-2:
Dust,
scratches,
and other
minor image
flaws mar
what would
otherwise
be a
wonderful
image.

Fortunately, you usually can eliminate these sorts of flaws by a careful application of something called a Clone tool, which is found in most photo-editing programs. This tool enables you to copy — clone — a good area of your picture and use the copy to cover up a damaged area. To fix the image in Figure 1-2, for example, I cloned some of the unblemished hair over the squiggly line and then cloned areas just above and below the scratch onto that blemish. I also decided to clone away the bright highlight that swoops from just above the mouth up to the ear. Although the swoop was a natural highlight caused by a reflection from a nearby mirror, it was distracting in this shot. Figure 1-3 shows the corrected image.

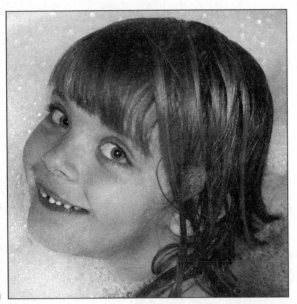

Figure 1-3:
Getting this picture into perfect shape required less than 15 minutes of retouching work.

All told, fixing up Figure 1-2 took less than 15 minutes. Of course, the more garbage littering your picture, the longer your editing session. But even in the worst cases, getting rid of small flaws like these isn't difficult, just time consuming.

Chapter 6 explains basic crud elimination. Be sure to also investigate Chapter 8, which discusses special techniques for removing flaws from faces and other skin areas.

Recomposing the Picture

Technically, *retouching* refers to covering up small image flaws and making other minor corrections, and *restoring* means bringing a photograph back to its original condition. But you also can use your photo-editing software to go a step beyond restoring or retouching and actually improve upon what the photographer saw through the viewfinder.

Case in point: The picture in Figure 1-4 shows my grandmother's childhood home in Ohio. To put it mildly, this photo's a wreck. The image is faded, small holes mar the area near the roof, and some sort of grunge is eating away at the photograph along the upper-right and entire left sides. (In real life, the grunge has a yellowish-brown tint.) After correcting the exposure, I used the Clone tool, introduced in the preceding section, to cover up the grunge with still-untouched surrounding areas. Those fixes comprised the restoration of the image. I then took the liberty of rotating the image slightly so that the house no longer appears to be sliding off a hillside. I also cropped away some of the lawn and tree areas to create a better composition. Figure 1-5 shows the final product.

Purists may turn up their noses at this type of change, but to me, compositional changes are perfectly valid as long as you're not making them with malicious intent. For example, if the house in Figure 1-4 really *were* sliding off a hill, I wouldn't advocate using the "after" image in a real-estate advertisement.

In addition to cropping and rotating a photo — both of which are easy, one- or two-click operations — you can get rid of distracting background objects and even move people and objects closer together or farther apart. How much work and expertise such changes require depends on the complexity of the original scene. In the example shown in Figure 1-6, eliminating the distracting plants and tree behind the subjects' heads was a fairly easy job. I just cloned some of the surrounding lawn area over the unwanted objects. Because a lawn is by nature irregular, it's easy to make the cloned areas blend in with the original grass areas.

Figure 1-4: In addition to needing some repairs, this image could use some compositional help.

Figure 1-5:
After covering up blemishes and tweaking exposure, I cropped and rotated the picture.

Figure 1-6:
Plants and a tree in the background distract from the subjects (left); I used surrounding lawn areas to alter the landscape.

For a look at another way you can deal with a distracting background, see Color Plate 9-2. In this image, there really wasn't anything I could use to cover up the clutter behind the mother and child in a natural way. So I replaced the background entirely with a pattern of clouds for a fun effect that isn't supposed to look like real life. As I mentioned earlier in this chapter, you also can blur distracting backgrounds to make them less intrusive; again, see Color Plate 5-2 for an example of this approach.

Repositioning subjects within a picture presents more of a challenge. First off, whenever you move something in a photo, you create a hole that you must fill in with something else — just as you would if you used a pair of scissors and glue to move an object in a photographic print. Sometimes, you can move the surrounding areas together to fill the hole, as I did when recomposing the scene featured in Color Plate 7-2. In this image, I cut out a Christmas-party Santa who was sitting between the man and woman. The white areas in the top image show the hole that Santa's removal created. I was able to slide the woman into the position previously occupied by Santa, making it appear that she and her husband had been sitting next to each other all along. I then slipped an entirely new background behind the couple to fill the remaining holes and get rid of the distracting Christmas tree.

In addition to finding a suitable way to fill any holes that you create, you also have to pay attention to the lighting and shadows to successfully recompose a picture. As an example, take another look at Color Plate 3-1. If I wanted to move my older sister from her current position to the other side of my grandmother, I'd have to reorient the stripes of light and shadow that currently fall on my grandmother and shift them onto my sister. That's way beyond what I have the patience or talent to do — heck, I'd just as soon crop my sister out of the picture entirely — but if you are a skilled artist with an understanding of such compositional matters, there's no end to what you can achieve.

You can find out how to crop, rotate, and otherwise alter composition in Chapter 7. For information on how I made the composite cloud image in Color Plate 9-2 and the new background for Color Plate 7-2, see Chapter 9.

Working with Product, Travel, and Nature Shots

Although the majority of images used as examples in this book feature people, you can use all the techniques covered here to improve your travel, nature, and product photographs as well. In Figure 1-7, for example, I adjusted exposure and focus and then darkened just the sign lettering to make the irony in this image easier to see. (Apparently the jet-skiing teens who zoomed past the signs seconds before I took this shot don't yet understand the meaning of "no wake" or "dead slow." Or perhaps the harbor master just needs to add a third sign to drive home the point!)

I caution you again, however, to use discretion when altering product shots, whether you're a publications manager retouching images for a company catalog or an antiques dealer preparing photos of goods you want to list in an online auction. Correcting flaws related to the photographic technique, such as brightening exposure and sharpening focus, is fine. Changing insignificant details such as the color of a backdrop, as I did in Color Plate 9-3, is also acceptable. But intentionally making the product itself look different to hide manufacturing defects and other inherent problems is absolutely not okay. Such image manipulation is not only unethical, but also dangerous from a legal standpoint.

Figure 1-7: In my original shot (left), the sign was difficult to read. Darkening just the letters (right) makes the point of the image clearer.

Planning the Job

After assessing what's wrong with your picture and how you may be able to improve it, you need to plan the order in which you'll make the changes you have in mind. Certain image-editing moves need to be made late in the game because they can limit your ability to make other corrections. For best results, do your retouching and restoration work using the following ten-step approach:

1. **Level the horizon line.**

   If your image has a tilt problem like the one shown in Figure 1-4, use your software's rotation tools to shift the scene as needed. (Chapter 7 shows you how.)

2. **Correct convergence problems.**

   Convergence refers to a phenomenon that sometimes occurs when you shoot with a wide-angle lens, which can cause vertical lines to tilt toward the center of the image. You can fix the problem using perspective or distortion tools.

   For an example of convergence, see Color Plate 7-1. For help with correcting the problem, see Chapter 7.

3. **Crop (trim away) unwanted areas around the edges of the picture.**

Cropping at this stage reduces the size of the image file that your computer system needs to process when you make your remaining changes. The smaller the image file, the faster your system can work. If you're not certain how tightly you want to crop the picture, leave a little excess.

4. **Adjust color and exposure.**

Don't worry about areas that you plan to cover up later, such as scratches, dust, and other unwanted objects. Concentrate on the main subject for now.

5. **Do retouching and recomposing work.**

Clean away the gunk from your picture, fix red-eye problems, and move elements from here to there as needed.

6. **Check color and exposure again.**

Depending on what you changed in Step 5, you may need to tweak color and exposure in altered areas again to make your edits blend in with the untouched regions.

7. **Apply creative filters, if desired.**

Most image-editing programs offer special-effects filters that you can use to give your picture the look of a watercolor painting, a charcoal sketch, antique photograph, and the like. Chapter 9 shows you some of these filters.

8. **Set the final image size and resolution.**

Chapter 2 explains the subject of resolution, which is one of the most vital issues in producing the highest quality prints and in preparing pictures for online use. Chapter 10 walks you through the process of establishing your final image size and resolution.

9. **Sharpen as needed.**

As your last editing move, use a sharpening filter to tighten up soft-focus areas. Why wait until this point to sharpen or blur? Because the preceding steps can affect how much you need to adjust the image sharpness. For example, after reducing image resolution to prepare an image for online distribution, you often need to sharpen the image to bring back details that get lost during that process.

10. **Do a final close-up inspection for dust and scratches.**

Sharpening often brings dust and scratches that you previously didn't see into view. Chapter 6 shows you how to take care of any remaining flaws.

As you complete each of these steps, be sure to save a copy of the image file under a name that's different from the original. That way, if you don't like what happens in the next editing step, you can return to the last version of the picture and try again. Within each step, save after you make a significant editing change, for the same reason.

Flip ahead to the end of the next chapter for details on the file-saving process.

Outfitting Your Digital Studio

As with a household renovation or repair, having the right tools makes your photo-editing work easier and can even affect your odds of success. A well-equipped digital photo studio includes a few essential hardware and software tools, as outlined in the next few sections.

Computer system

Photo-editing makes significant demands on a computer's memory (RAM), processor, hard drive, and video card. If you want to edit photos for output as 5 x 7-inch or larger pictures, you're going to be working with fairly large data files, and the larger the file, the more power and memory your system needs to do your bidding. I recommend the following specifications:

- ✔ **Processor speed:** On a Windows-based system, a Pentium-class processor; on a Macintosh, a PowerPC processor. Naturally, the faster the processor, the better.

- ✔ **RAM:** At bare minimum, 64MB. The more, the merrier.

- ✔ **Free hard drive space:** You need at about twice as much free hard drive space as you have system RAM. Why? Because your computer uses that free space as additional temporary memory as you process pictures.

  In geekspeak, this temporary memory area is known as a *scratch disk* or *virtual memory.*

  If your hard drive is cramped, you need to delete some existing files or add a second hard drive to free up space for your image-editing projects.

- ✔ **Video card:** The video card, sometimes called a *graphics card* or *display adapter,* determines how many different colors your monitor can display at its highest screen resolution. When you're working with digital images, you need a setup that enables you to display *24-bit color,* also known as *true color,* which translates to about 16.7 million colors.

  Chapter 2 explains screen resolution and how it affects the pictures you see on your monitor.

Digital input options

Of course, if you want to use your computer to edit photographs, you need a way to get your pictures into digital form. If you're working with images from a digital camera, you're all set — just follow the camera manual's instructions for transferring the pictures to your computer.

If you want to work on film photographs, you can have the prints, slides, or negatives scanned to a CD at a photo lab or invest in a scanner and do the job yourself. Chapter 2 explores scanners and scanning options in detail.

Image storage

You also need somewhere to store your image files. Because a computer's hard drive is subject to failure — it's rare, but it happens — you should make backup copies of important pictures on some sort of auxiliary storage device.

A floppy disk typically won't do the trick because most image files are too big to fit on a floppy, which can hold only about 1.4MB of data. Products such as the Iomega Zip drive, which stores data on 100MB and 250MB disks, work swell for temporary backup storage space. However, for long-term, archival protection, you should copy your images to a CD. CD burners today are inexpensive and easy to use, but if you don't have your own CD recorder, you should be able to find an imaging lab nearby that can transfer the images to disc for you.

Be sure that you put your archival images on a CD-R disc, not a CD-RW disc. You can erase files from a CD-RW disc, just as you can from your hard drive. But after you put data on a CD-R disc, it can't be altered, which is a quality you want in an archival storage medium.

For more tips on protecting your photographs, see Chapter 13.

Graphics tablet and pen

Returning to the household repair analogy I used to kick off this chapter, doing photo editing with a computer mouse can be like trying to paint a room using only a 9-inch roller — doable, but more difficult than it needs to be. For areas where little precision is needed, the mouse works fine. But for detail work, a graphics tablet gives you better control, just as a trim brush gives you an advantage when you're painting windowsills and other woodwork.

A graphics tablet enables you to work with a pressure-sensitive stylus instead of a mouse. To click, you tap the tablet with the end of the stylus or press a button on the side of the stylus. To drag, you simply drag the stylus across the pad, as if you were drawing with a pencil. For some operations, you can alter the impact of your edits by simply pressing down harder as you drag. For example, when you're painting with the Paintbrush tool in Photoshop Elements, you can set the tool to paint a line that varies in opacity, size, or color depending on the stylus pressure.

When making changes that affect your entire image — for example, cropping or adjusting the exposure — you don't get much benefit from a tablet. But when you want to do detail work to specific areas of your photo, a tablet and stylus give you much better control. You also don't wind up with that "mouse claw" hand you get from wrapping your paw around a mouse for hours.

The best news is that you don't have to spend much to enjoy the benefits of a graphics tablet. Wacom, long the industry leader in this type of product, makes a $99 consumer model called the Graphire 2, shown in Figure 1-8. The Graphire includes a wireless mouse that you can use interchangeably with the pen stylus.

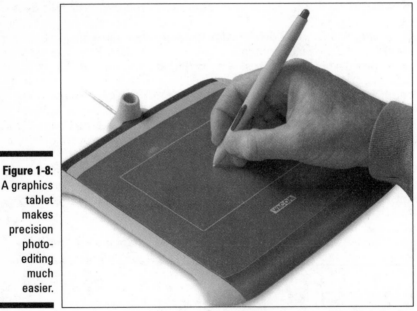

Figure 1-8:
A graphics
tablet
makes
precision
photo-
editing
much
easier.

Courtesy Wacom Technology Corp.

I recommend that whatever tablet you buy, you get one that allows you to easily switch between mouse and pen; although working with a pen is great for image-editing, the mouse is a more natural choice for other computing activities, such as surfing the Internet and using a word processor.

The active input area of the Graphire is 4 inches by 5 inches, but if you want a larger working surface, you can buy professional drawing tablets as large as 12 by 18 inches. Keep in mind that with a larger tablet, you have to move your pen a greater distance to travel from one area of your image to another. For that reason, I prefer a smaller tablet when doing image editing — I'm all for any concept that requires less movement on my part.

Photo-editing software

One of the most vital parts of any digital retouching studio is the photo-editing software. You can find a wide variety of photo-editing programs, but some products are more capable than others.

At the high-end, professional level, the leading software has long been Adobe Photoshop. This program is so prevalent in studio circles, in fact, that some people use the product name as a verb, as in "I Photoshopped the picture to correct the exposure." If you have Photoshop already, congratulations; you have the cream of the crop. Corel Photo-Paint also offers high-level tools and is another favorite among graphics professionals. Unfortunately, both products are as pricey as they are powerful. Photoshop retails for about $600; Photo-Paint, $479. (*Note:* Prices given in this chapter reflect the suggested retail for in-the-box products; you may be able to save money through rebates and upgrade offers or by purchasing a downloadable version of the product direct from the vendor.)

If you're not ready to make such a substantial investment in software, don't worry. Unless you plan on making retouching and restoration your full-time job, you can get by nicely with much less. In this book, for example, I feature a $99 program called Adobe Photoshop Elements, which offers many, though not all, of the same sophisticated editing tools as its more expensive cousin. Elements is a good program to use when you're starting out not only because of its price, but also because it provides some on-screen help features to guide you through various tasks. For example, a Recipes palette provides guidance for handling some editing jobs, as shown in Figure 1-9.

Two other products that give you some nice power-user tools for your software buck include Jasc Paint Shop Pro ($109) and Ulead PhotoImpact ($99). Both programs are geared more to the intermediate-to-advanced user, though, so don't expect much in the way of on-screen handholding. (If you're working with either of these programs, be sure to check out Appendix A, which contains information to help you translate the Photoshop Elements instructions I give in the rest of this book to your software.)

For even less money, you can find a number of programs that do cater to the novice photo-editing enthusiast, including Adobe PhotoDeluxe ($49), Ulead PhotoExpress ($50), and Jasc After Shot ($50). If you're not sure how much photo-editing you'll really do, you may want to start with one of these lower-priced offerings. You can always move up to something more sophisticated if you get serious about image-editing. However, keep in mind that some editing tasks can be more difficult in an entry-level program because the tools aren't as capable as they are in a higher-level product.

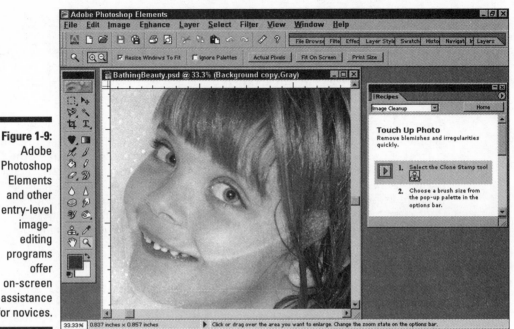

Figure 1-9:
Adobe
Photoshop
Elements
and other
entry-level
image-
editing
programs
offer
on-screen
assistance
for novices.

If you haven't yet invested in editing software or are interested in changing programs, check out the CD that's packaged into the back of this book. The CD contains try-before-you-buy versions of several editing programs, including Photoshop Elements.

Catalog and album software

In addition to image-editing software, I recommend that you also invest in some sort of image-cataloging or album software to help you organize all your digital photo files. Otherwise, finding a particular image amid the mass of pictures you store on your computer or on removable media can be a nightmare.

Cataloging programs such as ThumbsPlus (Cerious Software, $80), ACDSee (ACD Systems, $50), and Picture Information Extractor (PicMeta, $20) enable you to view thumbnails of your image files in a Windows Explorer-style interface, as shown in Figure 1-10. If you shoot with a digital camera that stores capture information (such as the shutter speed, date, and so on) along with the image file, you can view that data with these programs.

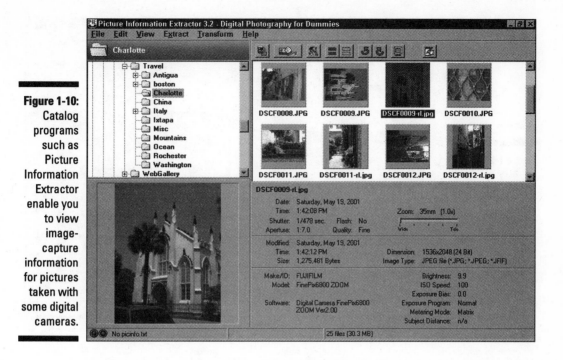

Figure 1-10:
Catalog
programs
such as
Picture
Information
Extractor
enable you
to view
image-
capture
information
for pictures
taken with
some digital
cameras.

For a great way to share your finished pictures electronically, consider a photo-album program such as FlipAlbum Suite (E-Book Systems, $80). These programs enable you to arrange your images on photo-album like pages, as shown in Figure 1-11. With FlipAlbum, you can burn an entire album to a CD-ROM so that your friends and family members need only slip the CD into a computer's CD-ROM drive to view your pictures. I especially like this option for times when I want to present someone with a particular collection of images. For example, I took pictures of my friends' newborn baby boy, put them together in an album, and then copied the whole thing to a CD for them. Even though my friends aren't very computer savvy, they can easily click through the pages of this digital album.

You can try out ThumbsPlus, ACDSee, Picture Information Extractor, FlipAlbum, and other cataloging software by installing the versions found on the CD at the back of this book.

Figure 1-11:
With programs such as FlipAlbum Suite, you can create digital photo albums featuring your favorite images.

Chapter 2

Creating and Protecting Your Digital "Negatives"

• •

In This Chapter

▶ Getting your photos into digital form

▶ Figuring out what input resolution to use

▶ Choosing the right home or office scanner

▶ Getting the best results from your scanner

▶ Selecting a professional scanning service

▶ Safeguarding your image files

▶ Undoing mistakes you make while editing photos

• •

*B*efore you can use your computer's power to retouch or restore a picture, you need to transform the photo into computer data — to create a digital "negative," if you will. You can turn almost any photographic medium — print, slide, negative, whatever — into a digital image by using a device known as a *scanner.*

A few years ago, I would have recommended that you take your pictures to a professional imaging lab for scanning because quality scanners cost several hundred dollars and were complicated to use. Today, scanners are not only more affordable but also much simpler to operate, making do-it-yourself scanning a viable option.

Even though newer scanners are more user-friendly, however, getting good scans isn't a brainless operation. Make the wrong pre-scan moves, and you can wind up with a crummy, undersized digital version of your picture. And just as you can't make a silk purse out of a sow's ear, you can't turn a lousy scan into a wonderful image.

This chapter explores the ins and outs of scanning, touching on such topics as buying a scanner, getting the best results from your scanner, and exploring professional scanning options. At the end of the chapter, you find instructions for saving your image files and undoing mistakes that you make while editing your photos.

If you're working with photos from a digital camera, your pictures are already in digital form, of course, and you can skip the scanning discussion. (Follow the camera manual's instructions for transferring the image files to your computer.) But be sure to check out the first part of this chapter, which explains how many pixels you need in your original image to wind up with a good-quality print or, if you're putting your pictures on a Web page, an appropriately sized screen image. Keep these guidelines in mind when you choose the resolution setting on your camera. Also review the file-saving information at the end of the chapter; you need to know that stuff to safeguard your pictures.

Determining Input Resolution

When you sew a pair of curtains from scratch, you need to start with a certain amount of fabric to adequately cover your windows. Similarly, you need to begin your photo retouching or restoration project with enough *pixels*.

Pixels are the tiny squares of color that make up any digital image, whether it comes from a digital camera or a scanner. If you open an image in your photo-editing program and zoom in for a close-up view, you can see the individual pixels, as shown in Figure 2-1.

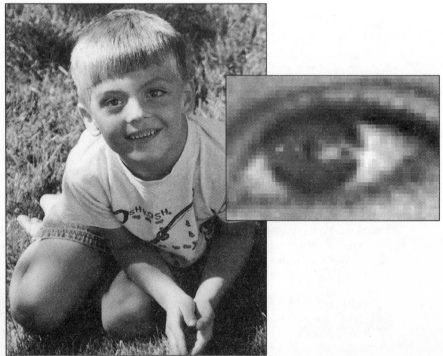

Figure 2-1:
Zoom in on a digital image to see the individual pixels.

Although viewing pixels in your image editor is interesting — and sometimes necessary when doing detailed retouching work — you *don't* want individual pixels to be discernable in your final, edited prints, as they are in Figure 2-2. Although the pixels aren't as big as they are in the outset area in Figure 2-1, they're big enough to give the picture a blocky look.

How do you get undetectable pixels? By making sure that your digital image contains plenty of those little squares. The more pixels you have, the smaller they become, and the harder it becomes for the eye to make out the individual pixels. As a point of comparison, the photo in Figure 2-1 contains roughly 1.5 million pixels, while the version in Figure 2-2 has about 25,000.

The next two sections explain how to figure out the appropriate *input resolution* — how many pixels you want your scanner or digital camera to manufacture when you scan or shoot a picture. If you're working with a digital camera, you determine this value by using the camera's resolution control, usually labeled something vague like "Quality" or "Size." (Check your camera manual for this information.) If you're scanning an existing picture, you set the input resolution using the scanner software. In both cases, the formula is different depending on whether you plan to print your picture or display it on a computer monitor or television screen.

Figure 2-2:
Too few
pixels
results in a
jagged
appearance.

Always capture the pixels you need at the scanning or shutter-pressing stage. Although you can add pixels in your photo-editing program, doing so typically reduces image quality. You usually can eliminate extra pixels without harming the image, so having too many pixels in your original is far better than having too few. That said, don't go way overboard when gathering pixels. You don't gain anything in image quality by exceeding the optimum resolution required by your printer or display screen. And because each added pixel increases the image's file size, you wind up with a file that's needlessly bloated, straining your computer's resources.

For specifics on how to change the number of pixels in an existing digital image, see Chapter 10.

Determining input resolution for prints

To wind up with enough pixels to produce a high-quality print, you need to know two things:

- ✔ The largest size at which you want to print the picture
- ✔ The image output resolution the printer needs in order to make the best reproduction of your image

To avoid confusion, I want to stop here to stress the difference between *input resolution* and *output resolution*:

- ✔ *Input resolution* refers to the number of original pixels you capture with your scanner or digital camera.

- ✔ *Output resolution* refers to the number of *pixels per linear inch* in your final, printed picture. This value is stated in terms of *ppi* (pixels per inch). A 2-inch wide by 3-inch tall image with an output resolution of 200 ppi has 400 pixels across and 600 pixels down. You establish this value in your image-editing program before sending the picture to the printer.

See Chapter 10 for details on setting the output resolution.

Most consumer photo printers require an image output resolution of 200 to 300 ppi to do their best work; check your printer's manual for advice relevant to your model. If the manual doesn't offer any guidance, do some test prints with the output resolution set to 200, 250, and 300 ppi. You should be able to settle on one of those three values as optimum for your printer. If you're having your picture professionally printed, talk with the lab's technician to find out the best resolution.

Another important point of emphasis here: Don't confuse output resolution — the number of pixels per inch in your image — with *printer resolution*. In the world of home and small business printers, resolution is measured in *dots per inch*, or *dpi*, which refers to how many dots of ink your printer can lay down per inch. Many printers use several dots to print a single image pixel. Also note that even though many scanner manufacturers refer to scanner resolution in terms of dpi, that's an improper use of the term. Scanners, like digital cameras, produce images made up of square pixels, not dots. (Makes you think there's a conspiracy to keep you confused, doesn't it?)

At any rate, when you know your print size and the optimum output resolution, figuring out how many original pixels you need is a simple math problem:

- To determine the number of horizontal pixels, multiply the desired print width by the suggested output resolution.

- To determine the number of vertical pixels, multiply the print height by the suggested output resolution.

For example, say that you want to end up with a 5 x 7-inch print, and your printer manual states that your photos should have an output resolution of 300 ppi. You calculate the pixel requirements as follows:

5 (print width) x 300 (ppi) = 1500 pixels across

7 (print height) x 300 (ppi) = 2100 pixels down

When setting up your scan job or digital camera, choose the setting that gets you closest to that number of pixels. In most cases, you won't find a setting that exactly matches both the horizontal and vertical pixel numbers, so pick the setting that delivers the larger of the two pixel counts.

To save you some mathematical effort, Tables 2-1, 2-2, and 2-3 offer quick reference guides to input resolution. Which table you should use depends on how you're getting your picture into digital form:

- Refer to Table 2-1 if you're taking pictures with a digital camera. The table shows you how many pixels you need to print quality photos at standard sizes, using 200 ppi and 300 ppi as the desired output resolutions.

  You can also use Table 2-1 as a guide if your scanner software enables you to specify the input resolution in terms of pixels.

- Refer to Table 2-2 if your scanner software requires you to set up the scan by specifying a desired output resolution (pixels per inch) and a *scaling factor.* The scaling factor sets the dimensions of the scanned image as a percentage of the original photo dimensions.

  For example, if you're scanning a 4 x 6-inch print and want to wind up with an image that you can output at 5 x 7 inches at 300 ppi, you enter 300 ppi as the resolution value and 125 percent as the scaling factor (4 x 125% = 5; 6 x 125% = 7.5). Table 2-2 provides approximate scale values for outputting photos from a variety of original photo sizes.

  To figure out the scale factor for yourself, just divide the desired output width by the original width and multiply the result by 100. Or do the same thing with the photo heights. When you're working with traditional photo sizes, the scale value usually won't be the same for both the width and height; use the larger of the two values to make sure you're not short of pixels along one dimension. You then can crop your image to the desired dimensions in your photo editor.

✔ As an alternative, you can leave the scaling factor at 100 percent and just adjust the resolution value as needed to come up with the right number of pixels. Table 2-3 shows the approximate resolution settings to use if you go this route. You can also use these values if your scanner requires you to specify a desired resolution but doesn't offer a scaling factor. (In other words, the software assumes a scaling factor of 100 percent.)

Keep in mind that Tables 2-2 and 2-3 assume that you're scanning the entire original. If you use your scanner's software to limit the scan to a particular part of the picture, you'll have to do your own calculations based on the dimensions of the area you want to scan.

Table 2-1	How Many Pixels Are Enough?	
Final Print Size	*Pixels Needed for 200 ppi*	*Pixels Needed for 300 ppi*
4 x 6 inches	800 x 1200	1200 x 1800
5 x 7 inches	1000 x 1400	1500 x 2100
8 x 10 inches	1600 x 2000	2400 x 3000

Table 2-2	Scale Values to Achieve Print Sizes at Specified Resolution	
Original	*Desired Output Size*	*Scale Percentage**
35mm slide or negative**	4 x 6	455%
	5 x 7	570%
	8 x 10	925%
4 x 6-inch print	4 x 6	100%
	5 x 7	125%
	8 x 10	200%

Original	Desired Output Size	Scale Percentage*
5 x 7-inch print	4 x 6	86%
	5 x 7	100%
	8 x 10	150%
8 x 10-inch print	4 x 6	60%
	5 x 7	70%
	8 x 10	100%

*Assumes that your software enables you to set the final output resolution (200 ppi, 300 ppi, etc.)

**Assumes approximate scannable image area of ⅞ inch x 1⅜ inches.

Table 2-3 Input Resolution Values for Scale Factor of 100 Percent

Original	Desired Output Size	Input Resolution Needed for Output Resolution of 200 ppi/300 ppi
35mm slide or negative*	4 x 6	910 ppi/1370 ppi
	5 x 7	1140 ppi/1710 ppi
	8 x 10	1820 ppi/2730 ppi
4 x 6-inch print	4 x 6	200 ppi/300 ppi
	5 x 7	250 ppi/375 ppi
	8 x 10	400 ppi/600 ppi
5 x 7-inch print	4 x 6	170 ppi/260 ppi
	5 x 7	200 ppi/300 ppi
	8 x 10	320 ppi/480 ppi
8 x 10-inch print	4 x 6	120 ppi/180 ppi
	5 x 7	140 ppi/210 ppi
	8 x 10	200 ppi/300 ppi

*Assumes approximate scannable image area of ⅞ inch x 1⅜ inches; required input values rounded up to nearest tenth.

Determining input resolution for screen display

If you plan on using your image for a Web page, multimedia presentation (such as a Microsoft PowerPoint show), or other on-screen use, you need to calculate input resolution differently than you do when your goal is a printed photo.

Computer monitors, televisions, and other electronic displays use pixels to create images, just like digital cameras. The term *screen resolution* refers to how many pixels the monitor or other device uses to display what you see on the screen. This value is typically stated in terms of pixels across by pixels down rather than pixels per inch.

With most computer monitors, the user can choose from several screen resolution settings. For example, on my 17-inch monitor, I can choose from screen resolution settings including 640 x 480 pixels, 800 x 600 pixels, and 1024 x 768 pixels.

When you display a photo on-screen, the display device devotes one screen pixel to every image pixel. So to determine the right input resolution for your image, you simply match image pixels to screen pixels according to how much screen real-estate you want your picture to consume.

For example, if you're taking a picture with your digital camera and want the photo to completely fill a monitor that's set to a screen resolution of 640 x 480, you set your camera to capture 640 pixels across and 480 pixels down. (This setting, 640 x 480, is available on almost all digital cameras.)

If you're scanning your picture and your scanner software requires that you set up the scan in terms of resolution (pixels per inch) and scaling factor instead of a pure pixel count, you have to do some math to figure out the settings that will give you the appropriate number of pixels. (See the preceding section to find out what I mean by *scaling factor*.)

Some people advocate using a scan resolution in the neighborhood of 72 to 96 ppi and setting the scaling factor as you normally would. Although this approach may get you close to where you want to be, it's not terribly accurate. See the sidebar titled "But the guy on the Internet said 72 ppi!" in Chapter 10 to dig into this thorny issue and other aspects of preparing pictures for screen display.

If you think that you someday may want to print your image as well as share it electronically via the Web or other on-screen means, use the input resolution guidelines provided in the preceding section. Then duplicate the image file and delete pixels as necessary to make an appropriately sized image for screen display. As I mentioned earlier, you don't get good prints when you start out with too few pixels, but you can dump excess pixels without doing much damage.

Making Your Own Scans

If you need only a few photos digitized, your best option is to take them to a professional imaging lab for scanning. (See the upcoming section "Letting the Pros Do It" for details on professional scanning options.) But if you plan on scanning lots of pictures, purchasing a scanner makes better sense. Doing your own scanning is more convenient, can save you money over the long haul, and gives you better control over how your pictures are scanned.

The following sections tell you how to choose a scanner (if you don't already own one) and how to get the best possible scans from your machine.

Choosing a scanner type

Scanners for the consumer and small-office market fall into two categories:

- ✔ Print scanners digitize paper materials — photographic prints, newspapers, books, and the like.
- ✔ Film scanners digitize slides, transparencies, and film negatives.

Most serious digital imaging enthusiasts prefer option number two because film scanners typically produce better, higher resolution scans that are truer to the original image. When you scan a photographic print, you get the image as it was developed and printed by the film lab, which may or may not have done a bang-up job with color and exposure. When you scan the film negative or slide, you see the image as your camera originally captured it. (The process that turns slide film into positive slides doesn't involve the same image manipulation by the lab as the process of printing film negatives.) In many cases, a photographic print that comes back from the lab too dark or with funky colors looks just fine when you scan the negative.

The down side to film scanners is that they cost more than print scanners. You can buy a decent print scanner for as little as $100, while good film scanners cost from about $400 to $1600. Only you can decide whether your scanning work justifies that additional expense. I personally have both a print scanner and a film scanner, but use the print scanner only when I don't have access to the original negative or slide.

A few scanner models, such as the Hewlett-Packard ScanJet 5490c pictured in Figure 2-3, can handle all types of originals. With this scanner, which retails for $399, you use a special transparency adapter, shown in the upper-right corner of Figure 2-3, to scan negatives and slides. The scanner also has a document feeder, not shown, for scanning multiple print documents.

Figure 2-3:
Hybrid
scanner
models like
this ScanJet
5490c from
Hewlett-
Packard
can scan
prints,
slides, and
negatives.

Hybrid models like the ScanJet 5490c can be a good solution if you can afford only one scanner and need to scan a variety of original materials. However, make sure that the scanner's resolution is high enough to enable you to capture the appropriate number of pixels when scanning slides and negatives that you want to print at large sizes. (See Tables 2-1 through 2-3 for guidance.) The ScanJet model shown in Figure 2-3 can achieve an input resolution of 2400 ppi, which is enough to turn a slide or negative into an acceptable 8 x 10-inch print.

Deciphering scanner specs

After you decide what type of scanner fits your needs, you can narrow your options further by reviewing some important scanner specifications. Look for this information either on the scanner box, if you're shopping at your local electronics or computer outfit, or at the manufacturer's Web site. The following list explains the most important specifications to help you sort out the technobabble.

Resolution

Scanner resolution, as explained earlier, indicates how many pixels the scanner can generate when scanning your original. This value should be stated in terms of *ppi* (pixels per linear inch), but some scanner manufacturers mistakenly use the term *dpi* (dots per inch) instead of ppi.

When looking at resolution specs, pay attention only to the *optical* resolution. This value tells you the true capabilities of the machine. Most scanner marketing materials also state an *interpolated* or *enhanced* resolution value. This second value indicates a resolution that can be achieved through some manipulation by the scanner's software, which produces lower image quality than you get through the optical resolution.

Bit depth

A *bit* is a chunk of computer data. The *bit depth* of a scanner indicates how much color data the machine can capture, which is why this value is sometimes called *color depth.*

Today's scanners typically offer anywhere from 24-bit color to 48-bit color. For most purposes, 24 bits is plenty. A higher bit depth is supposed to mean better color accuracy, but most image-editing programs either can't open images with the extra bits, simply whittle the image down to 24 bits upon opening the file, or limit the editing changes you can make to a higher-bit image.

Be aware, too, that some scanners don't send the extra bits to the image file but instead convert the file down to 24 bits. So while the scanner specs may boast of an *internal bit depth* of 48 bits, the resulting image file doesn't contain all those bits. In addition, some scanner specs reference an *interpolated* or *enhanced* bit depth, which, like interpolated or enhanced resolution, is achieved through software manipulation. With these scanners, the specification called the *hardware, external,* or *converter* bit depth represents the meaningful measurement.

Dynamic range

Dynamic range indicates the difference between the brightest tone and the darkest tone that the scanner can "see." This value is commonly stated as the scanner's *Dmax* rating. The brightness values used to calculate dynamic range are based on a scale of 0 to 4, with 0 representing pure white and 4 representing pure black. For example, if a scanner can pick up a maximum brightness value of 0.4 and a maximum shadow value of 3.5, the dynamic range is 3.1. With a higher dynamic range, you theoretically capture more details in the darkest and lightest areas of the image — in other words, better reproduction of the shadows and highlights. Of course, a higher dynamic range usually means a higher-priced scanner.

Unfortunately, some scanner marketing folks play with the dynamic range numbers a little in an attempt to make their models look better than the competition's. Without getting into the science that's used to justify this "tweaking," let me just say that you should take the dynamic range spec with at least a tiny grain of salt. Although you may see a noticeable difference between a scanner that has a dynamic range of, say, 2.4, and a scanner with a dynamic range of 3.6, you may or may not see any improvement going from 3.4 to 3.6.

So what's a smart consumer to do? The best answer is to read reviews done by the high-tech imaging gurus who have developed real-world testing to measure a scanner's actual dynamic range. You can find such reviews in digital imaging magazines, both print and online.

Also keep in mind that whatever the scanner's dynamic range may be, you can't capture a broader range of brightness values than are present in the original photo that you're scanning.

Flatbed versus sheetfed

If you opt for a print scanner, you have to choose between a *sheetfed* or *flatbed* model.

- *Sheetfed scanners* work similarly to a traditional fax machine. You feed the original into a roller mechanism, which winds the picture past a stationary scanning head. You can probably guess that this type of scanner isn't great for scanning photos because the journey the picture makes through the scanner rollers can bend and wrinkle the photo.

- *Flatbed scanners* look much like copy machines. You place your original face down on a glass bed, and the scanning head passes underneath the glass to "read" and digitize the photo. This is the way to go if your primary use of the scanner is for digital imaging projects.

Computer connection

One final but crucial specification to consider is the scanner *interface* — the type of cable you use to connect the scanner to your computer. Make sure that the interface of the model you're considering is appropriate for your computer setup.

Most consumer scanners now offer a USB (Universal Serial Bus) interface, which is a standard connection on newer PCs and Macintosh computers. If you're running Windows 95 or Windows 98 First Edition, however, you can't use USB devices, even if your computer has a USB port. You need to upgrade to Windows 98 Second Edition or a later version of the operating system to take advantage of USB. And if your system's available USB ports are already being used by other devices, such as a drawing tablet or printer, you may need to buy a USB hub, which enables you to plug multiple devices into a single port.

Some scanners also offer the option of a parallel or a serial port interface. Again, other computer devices may already be using those ports, so you may have to buy a port switching device that enables the scanner to "share" the port. More important, parallel and serial connections transfer data more slowly than USB connections.

For the fastest data transfer between scanner and computer, high-end film scanners may also offer the option of a SCSI (pronounced *scuzzy)* or Firewire connection. In most cases, you have to buy a compatible SCSI or Firewire card and cable in order to use this option.

Improving scan quality

All scanners ship with some sort of software that you use to set up the scanning job. Because each scanner's software offers different types of scanning controls, I can't give you detailed instructions on using those controls to their best advantage — I'm afraid you need to consult your owner's manual for that. But the following list provides some general tips to improve the quality of your scans.

✔ **Start with a clean original.** If fingerprints or dirt mar your original, give it a *gentle* cleaning before scanning. You can blow away dust with a can of compressed air or wipe it off with a soft cloth. Be careful not to rub very hard, though, as you can wind up scratching the surface of the photo. For best (and safest) cleaning results, head to your local camera store and look for special cleaning cloths and sprays that are designed to clean photographic materials without damaging the image.

Always test the cleaning solution on an inconspicuous area of the photo first. For safety's sake, you may want to go ahead and scan the image before cleaning, just in case you do irreparable harm to the original.

✔ **Use the appropriate input resolution.** For details, read the section "Determining Input Resolution" earlier in this chapter. Don't use interpolated resolution settings — that is, don't set the resolution higher than the scanner's optical resolution.

✔ **Take advantage of correction tools not found in your photo-editing software.** Most scanning utilities offer at least basic controls for adjusting exposure, color balance, and contrast. Imaging experts debate whether you're better off doing image correction pre-scan, via the scanner software tools, or post-scan, in your photo editor. I opt for the latter in most cases. Yes, it makes sense to do what corrections you can via the scanning software — why waste time scanning in bad data? But many scanner utilities don't offer very capable correction tools. In addition, you typically must make changes to the entire image if you use the scanner software, while photo-editing software enables you to alter just certain areas. I leave it to you to determine whether your scanner software or photo-editing program has the better correction capabilities for the kind of problems you need to fix.

The scanner's manual should explain how to use all the correction tools in the scanner software. For more background about image correction in general, skim through the chapters in Part II.

✔ **For sharper scans, turn off dust removal filters.** Some scanners include dust-removal filters that are supposed to make the scanner overlook specks of dust on the surface of the original, resulting in less post-scan clean-up work for you. Sounds great, but in many cases the dust-removal filters also soften the focus of the image. If you're not happy with the sharpness of your scanned image, try scanning again with the dust-removal option turned off.

Chapter 6 shows you how to cover up any dust that may remain in your scanned photo.

✔ **Don't use scanner sharpening filters.** The one correction you don't want to make during the scanning stage is image sharpening. Sharpening should always be done near the very end of the retouching or restoration process.

You can read more about the order in which you should make various changes to your pictures in Chapter 1. For details about sharpening, see Chapter 5.

✔ **Save your scanned image immediately.** Some scanning software automatically saves the scanned image file to your hard drive or other storage vault that you specify. But if you're scanning directly into your photo-editing software, you usually don't get this file-saving protection. So as soon as your scanner finishes its work, save the image file, following the guidelines set out later in this chapter, in the section "Protecting Your Image Files." Be sure to save the image in a format that retains all image data — TIFF and the Adobe Photoshop format (PSD) are two such formats.

Most image-editing programs enable you to scan directly into the program via a technology known as TWAIN, which is simply a piece of code that enables your scanner to talk to your editing programs. Check your software and scanner manual to find out how to set up this scanner/software communication.

However, be aware that some photo editing programs, including Photoshop Elements, refuse to let you work on your scanned photo until you close the scanner software. That stubbornness can be a hassle when you want to scan a batch of images. For those jobs, you may find it more convenient to scan using the scanner's own utilities, save the images to disk, and then fire up your image editor when you're all done scanning. As an alternative, some image cataloging programs, such as Cerious Software's ThumbsPlus, work happily alongside scanner software. So you can scan a batch of images, organize them in the cataloging program, and then scan some more without shutting down either program.

If you want to give ThumbsPlus a whirl, check out the CD at the back of this book. The CD contains a trial version of that cataloging program as well as a few others. In addition, you can try out two scanning utilities, VueScan, from Hamrick Software, and SilverFast SE, from LaserSoft Imaging. Both programs provide advanced scanning options that your scanner's own software may lack.

Letting the Pros Do It

If you need only the occasional image scanned, don't bother buying your own scanner. Instead, find a local photo or imaging lab that can do the job for you. You also may want to go the professional route if your scanner doesn't offer a high enough resolution for special photos that you want to print at a large size.

Most retail photo labs now offer to scan your photos to a CD or other storage media at the time you have a roll of film processed and printed. This option typically costs about $5 to $10 extra for a 24-exposure roll of film. Although this service is convenient, it has two drawbacks. First, you're paying to scan all the images on a single roll, and you may want digital copies of only a few of the best photos. Second, the scan resolution isn't always high enough to produce decent print quality at anything but snapshot size.

Refer to the section "Determining Input Resolution," earlier in this chapter, for help figuring out your resolution needs.

Many corner-store photo labs also offer scanning of existing prints, sometimes at do-it-yourself kiosks. Again, the convenience factor is there, but the quality isn't a certainty. For one thing, the scanner bed may be less than clean, given all the traffic the device attracts. For another, the store employees probably won't be able to give you much assistance if you have difficulty getting a decent scan.

For scans of prints and slides, your best bet is to turn to a professional imaging lab or to a camera store that also offers imaging services. In most cases, you can choose from two types of professional scans:

✔ **Photo CD:** Photo CD is a special file format developed by Eastman Kodak expressly for professional scanning. Each Photo CD image file contains the same scanned image at several different resolutions, ranging from very low to high. Expect to pay about $1 per image scanned, plus an initial cost of about $10 for the CD. You can bring the CD back to the lab to add more scanned images if you don't have enough pictures to fill it with your initial order.

Don't confuse *Photo* CD with Kodak *Picture* CD — the latter refers to the aforementioned service that gives you scanned images on CD when you process and print a roll of film.

Note that you may need to install a special file utility to open Photo CD files in some image-editing programs. So before you decide on this option, check your imaging software to find out whether it can handle the format.

Although I've had good results from most Photo CD scans, I have been disappointed with scans of some very dense slide films, such as Fujifilm Velvia. If you're working with slides, be sure to ask the scanner operator whether the film type presents any unusual scanning challenges and, if so, what other scanning option may give you better results.

✔ **Drum scanning:** For the ultimate in scan quality, professional graphic artists rely on a high-end piece of equipment known as a *drum scanner.* Unfortunately, drum scanning isn't cheap; you can expect to pay about $40 per scan at minimum. So unless you're having the scan made for a very special purpose — or a client who doesn't mind the expense — Photo CD is a more reasonable option.

Whichever professional scanning choice you make, be sure to inspect your image files closely after you get them from the lab. Assuming that the original you provided was in good shape, you shouldn't see any dust, scratches, or other flotsam in the scanned image. Do be aware that you may see some color variations between your original and the digital version you see on-screen. These differences likely are due to inherent differences in the color *gamut* — range of colors that can be reproduced — that exist between monitors and photographic printers. If colors are widely off, of course, the shop that did the scans should be happy to try again. But understand that it may be your monitor — not the scanned image — that's the problem. In a lab, the scanner operator's monitor is calibrated to produce the most accurate color match to the original photo, whereas your home or office monitor probably isn't set up to such exacting standards. Again, talk with the scanner technician to discuss your concerns.

For more about color matching between printer and monitor, see Chapters 4 and 10.

Protecting Your Image Files

One of the biggest advantages of digital imaging is that you no longer have to worry that your photos won't stand the test of time. Unlike a photographic print or slide, a digital photo file doesn't degrade over the years. If a print that you make from a digital image fades, gets torn, or otherwise suffers damage, you can simply make another print from your digital image file.

Of course, this image longevity requires that you remember to save your digital files using an appropriate file-storage medium, such as an archival CD — and figure out some way to keep track of where you stored which pictures.

Chapter 1 covers the topics of archival storage media and introduces you to some photo-organizing software that you can use to manage your image files. The rest of this chapter explains everything you need to know to about the process of saving files and also shows you how to undo future damage that *you* may cause as a result of a bad retouching or restoration move.

Saving a digital image

A digital picture file is no different from any other data file on your computer. Until you save the image, any changes you make to the picture are only temporary. If you close the picture without saving, all your changes are lost. Additionally, if you scan a picture directly into your image-editing program and then close the picture without saving it, the entire scan gets trashed.

I'm guessing that you already know the basics of how to save a file, so I won't insult your intelligence by rehashing the process in depth here. Instead, the following sections give you some pointers about saving files in Photoshop Elements and provide a few details that are unique to working with digital photos.

Using the Save As command

In Photoshop Elements, as in most programs, you save the changes that you've made to a photo by choosing File⇨Save As. You can also use this command to save a picture that you've scanned directly into the program.

After you choose the Save As command, you see the Save As dialog box, where you can give the file a name, choose a file format, and specify the file-storage location. Figure 2-4 shows the dialog box as it appears on a Windows-based PC. Along with the standard Windows file-saving controls, the dialog box contains a few options specific to Elements. The Macintosh version of the dialog box looks slightly different but contains the same basic options.

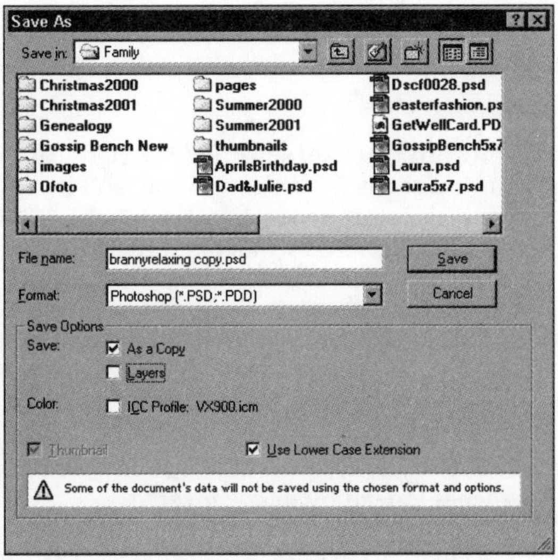

Figure 2-4:
In
Photoshop
Elements,
selecting
the As a
Copy
check box
preserves
your original
file and
creates a
new file for
your edited
photo.

If you want to preserve a copy of the image in its original, untouched state, be sure to give the edited file a name that's different from the one you gave the original. In Photoshop Elements, checking the As a Copy box in the Save As dialog box, as shown in Figure 2-4, automatically adds the word *copy* to the end of the original file name, saving you the trouble of renaming the file.

You see a warning at the bottom of the dialog box if you choose file-saving options that cause certain image features, such as layers, to be altered. For an introduction to layers, see Chapter 3. The next section provides guidance on which file formats to use if you want to retain layers.

As for the Color option found in the Elements dialog box, you can ignore it unless you turn on the program's color management features and want to retain the resulting color profile information with the image file. (The option is named ICC Profile or Embed Color Profile, depending on whether you're working on a Windows-based or Macintosh computer.) Unless you're sharing image files with others and have a serious need for color management, I suggest you leave all the related options turned off, which they are by default. Saving a color profile with an image destined for the Internet is especially inappropriate because the profile information adds to the size of the image file.

If you open a file, make some changes, and then want to save those changes as part of the currently open file — that is, you want to overwrite the open file — you can just press Ctrl+S (⌘+S on a Mac). The program saves your file without bothering you with a dialog box, using the same file name, format, and storage location as the last time you saved.

Selecting a file format

When you save a file, you have to select a file format. In Photoshop Elements, you make this choice via the Format drop-down list in the Save As dialog box, shown in Figure 2-4.

Whatever photo-editing software you use, selecting the right format is vital. Different formats treat your image file in different ways, and if you don't pick the right format, you can damage your image or make it impossible for other people to open. Here are the main photo formats and their uses:

- ✔ **Your software's native format:** A *native format* refers to a program's own special file format. In Photoshop Elements, the native format is PSD, as it is in Photoshop. Always use your software's native format to save your photos-in-progress because it enables the program to process your edits more quickly. In addition, the native format preserves special features, such as image layers, that other formats may not be able to handle. (See Chapter 3 to find out what I mean by *image layers*.)

- ✔ **TIFF:** TIFF is a universal format for print production, meaning that it's a good choice if you need to use a photo in a page-layout or word processing program that can't open files saved in your photo-editor's native format. TIFF also is the right format to use if you're scanning photos using a scanning utility that can't save in your photo-editor's format. Web browsers can't open TIFF images, so you can't use this format for online images.

Be aware, too, that TIFF file-saving options vary from program to program, and some of those options may prevent you from opening the file in other programs that normally accept TIFF files. When you save in the TIFF format in Elements, for example, you have access to the options shown in Figure 2-5. To ensure compatibility with other programs, I suggest that you leave all these options at their default settings. You can read more about the options in the Elements Help system or manual if you're curious about what they do.

✔ **JPEG:** Save images in this format only after you finish your editing work, and then only if you plan to distribute your photos electronically — for example, to post them on a Web page, share them via e-mail, or use them in a multimedia presentation. Almost every Web browser and e-mail program can open JPEG files. Many digital cameras also store original images in this format.

JPEG *compresses* image files to make the files smaller, which makes it an ideal format for online use and for storing lots of files on a digital-camera memory card. However, JPEG uses *lossy compression,* which means that it sacrifices image data to shrink file size. The result is a reduction in image quality. So you should always make a backup copy of the image in your software's native file format or TIFF before saving in the JPEG format.

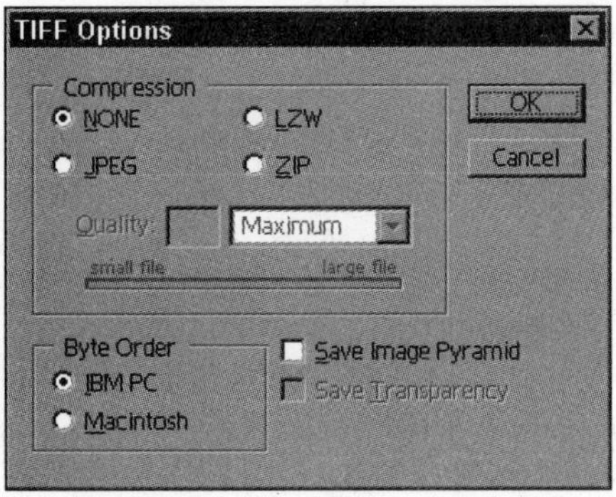

Figure 2-5:
To ensure compatibility with other programs, leave these options at their default settings when saving your picture in the TIFF format.

TIFF Options

Compression
◉ NONE   ○ LZW
○ JPEG   ○ ZIP

Quality: [ ] [Maximum ▾]
small file   large file

Byte Order   ☐ Save Image Pyramid
◉ IBM PC   ☐ Save Transparency
○ Macintosh

[OK]
[Cancel]

If you want the best image quality from your digital camera files, check your camera manual to find out whether you can adjust the amount of JPEG compression that's applied when you take a picture. Use a low amount of compression for important pictures. But understand that low compression means larger image files, which means you can fit fewer images in your camera's available memory.

✔ **GIF:** This format also is a Web-only format. With GIF, you can make part of your image transparent so that the Web-page background shows through. You also can create simple animations, such as a star that blinks on and off, by saving a series of GIF images in a single file. The bad news is that GIF images can have only 256 colors, which means pretty lousy photo quality.

Chapter 10 goes into more detail about preparing pictures for print and for on-screen use and also walks you through the process of saving files in the JPEG format.

Undoing mistakes

Sooner or later, everyone makes a bonehead move while editing photos. Fortunately, nearly every photo-editing program offers one or more ways to reverse bad decisions. The next three sections explore the safety nets found in Photoshop Elements. If you're using some other program, check your software's Help section to see which of these features may be available to you.

Using Undo and Redo

Use a real pen to draw a mustache on your company founder's conference-room portrait, and you're toast — may as well pack up your cubicle right now. But use your photo-editor's paintbrush to doodle on a digital photo, and you can undo the damage in seconds, without anyone being the wiser.

Whether you screw up an image intentionally or by accident, you can reverse an edit in Photoshop Elements as follows:

✔ **To undo your last change:** Choose Edit⇨Step Backward. Or, for faster results, press Ctrl+Z (⌘+Z on a Mac) or click the Step Backward button on the toolbar. You can see the button in Figure 2-6.

✔ **To undo additional changes:** Keep choosing Step Backward, pressing Ctrl+Z (⌘+Z on a Mac), or clicking that toolbar button.

✔ **To redo the edit you just "undid":** Choose Edit⇨Step Forward or press Ctrl+Y (⌘+Y on a Mac). Or click the Step Forward button, also shown in Figure 2-6. Now things are back to the way they were before you chose Step Backward.

✔ **To reverse more undo's:** Keep choosing that Step Forward command, pressing the shortcut keys, or clicking the toolbar button.

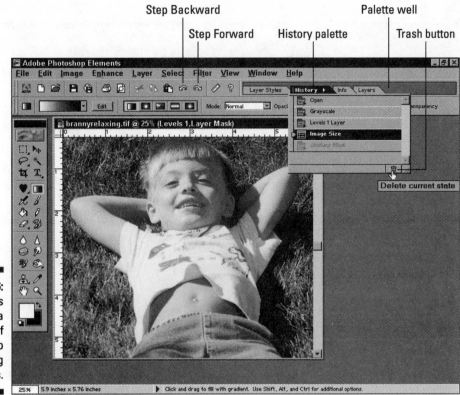

Figure 2-6:
Elements
gives you a
variety of
ways to
undo editing
blunders.

The shortcut keys I just mentioned are the defaults in Photoshop Elements. You can change the shortcut keys by choosing Edit⇨Preferences⇨General and making a different selection from the Step Back/Fwd drop-down list.

If you choose the Step Forward and Step Backward commands from the Edit menu, you may notice the Undo command, which lives at the top of the menu. You also can use that command to undo and redo edits. After you choose Undo, the command changes to Redo. In other words, the command toggles between Undo and Redo. I personally ignore this two-faced command and undo and redo using the Step Forward and Step Backward keyboard shortcuts. However, Undo/Redo can come in handy at times because it's capable of undoing/redoing more than one edit at a time.

After you use the Step Backward command several times in a row, take a look at the Undo command. Notice that it now is named Undo State Change. If you choose the command, you restore all the edits that you just reversed using the Step Backward command. Similarly, if you choose Redo State Change immediately after you use Step Forward several times in a row, you go back to the point before you first chose Step Forward.

Clearing out the palette well

By default, the palette well in Photoshop Elements contains eleven palettes. Although the well is a keen idea because it keeps the palettes handy, all the palette tabs get kind of crammed together, especially if you have a small monitor. With so many tabs resting shoulder to shoulder, clicking the right one to display the palette you want to see can be difficult. For that reason, you may want to remove palettes that you don't use often from the well. I removed all palettes except the Layers, Info, History, and Layer Styles palettes from my well (which is why you don't see them in the screen shots in this book).

To remove a palette, first drag it by its tab into the image-editing area. Now the palette is "undocked." Click the right-pointing arrow near the top-right corner of the palette to display a flyout menu. (In Elements 2.0, arrow rests on a button labeled *More*.) At the bottom of the menu, click Close Palette to Shortcuts Well (or, in 2.0, Dock to Palette Well), so that the checkmark next to the item disappears. Now click the Close button (the X button in the top-right corner of the palette). The palette no longer appears in the Shortcuts well.

You can still access a palette that isn't in the well. Just choose the palette name from the Window menu. If you want to put the palette back in the well, redisplay the palette menu and choose the Close Palette to Palette Well option again.

For an even more convenient — not to mention less confusing — method of undoing or redoing multiple edits, check out the next section, which explores an Elements tool known as the History palette.

Elements is a little different from many photo editing programs in that it enables you to save the image file and then go back and undo and redo changes that you made before you saved. But this flexibility remains only until you close the image file. After you close the image, you lose your chance to undo or redo the edits.

Going back in time via the History palette

Using the Photoshop Elements History palette, which you can see in Figure 2-6, you can wipe out or restore a series of edits at a time. (In Elements 2.0, the palette goes by the name Undo History.)

Many other programs offer a similar feature, so check your software's Help system to see whether you may also have this flexibility. If you're using Photoshop, explore the Help system to discover some additional History palette features that aren't available in the Elements version of the feature.

Initially, the palette appears docked in the palette well at the end of the Shortcuts bar, which lives near the top of the program window. (If you don't see the bar, choose Window⇨Show Shortcuts.) To unfurl the palette, as shown in Figure 2-6, click its tab in the well or choose Window⇨Show History in Elements 1.0 and Window⇨Undo History in Version 2.0. Your recent edits appear in the palette with the most recent change in the last position.

Adobe refers to each edit listed in the palette as a *state,* as in, "This is the state your photo was in at the time you made this change." (Now you know why the Undo/Redo command in the Edit menu sometimes reads Undo State Change or Redo State Change.)

The following list explains how to make use of the History palette functions:

✔ When you click any item in the list, you temporarily undo that change and any that follow. Those edits — states — appear dimmed in the palette, and your photo updates to show you how the picture will look if you permanently undo the changes. If you like what you see, click the Trash button at the bottom of the palette or just make your next editing move. All the dimmed states disappear from the palette.

✔ If you decide *not* to go forward with your undo, click any dimmed item in the palette to restore that edit and any that come before it.

✔ You also can use the Step Backward and Step Forward commands, explained in the preceding section, to dim and reveal states in the History palette.

✔ In addition, you can choose the Undo command from the Edit menu to restore edits that you wipe out via the History palette. Similarly, you can use Redo to undo edits that you restored. However, you must choose Undo or Redo immediately after you remove or restore the states in the History palette.

✔ By default, the History palette lists a maximum of 20 edits. You can tell the program to track as many as 100 changes, but raising the value increases the demands on your computer's memory. To raise or lower the number of states in the History palette, choose Edit⇨Preferences⇨ General to display the General dialog box and adjust the History States value.

✔ If you see a dialog box complaining that your computer is low on memory, you can free up some memory by choosing Edit⇨Purge⇨ Histories. This command removes all the states from the History palette. But use caution — you can't undo this action.

Returning to the last-saved version

At any time during a photo-editing session, you can chuck all your changes and restore the image to the way it looked when you last saved the image file. Just do either of the following:

✔ Close the image file, and when the program asks whether you want to save your changes, decline the offer. Then reopen the file.

✔ In Photoshop Elements, you can accomplish the same thing without closing and reopening the file. Just choose File⇨Revert.

If you change your mind about using that Revert command — having a little trouble with commitment, are we? — immediately choose Edit⇨Undo. Note that you can't undo the process of closing the file without saving it, so if you're uncertain at all about dumping your day's work, go with Revert instead.

Chapter 3

Prep Work

• •

In This Chapter

▶ Selecting the part of the picture you want to alter

▶ Using the basic selection tools

▶ Creating a soft framing effect

▶ Selecting areas based on color

▶ Painting precise selection outlines

▶ Using image layers to store selection outlines

▶ Adjusting existing selection outlines

▶ Saving and reusing selection outlines

• •

*W*hen you shoot a picture, whatever camera settings you choose apply to the entire image. You can't tell the camera to capture the darkest parts of the scene using a long exposure and record the lighter areas using a shorter exposure, for example.

By bringing the photo into your digital imaging studio, however, you can adjust any region of the picture independently of the rest of the image. You can make dark objects lighter and light objects darker. You can soften the crow's feet around someone's eyes while leaving the eye itself in sharp focus. You can even change the color of a teenager's shirt without also dyeing his or her hair — or the opposite, if the teen in question is in that rebellious, thinks-green-hair-is-cool stage.

To tell your photo-editing software what pixels to change and which ones to leave alone, you must create a *selection outline,* sometimes called a *marquee.* This chapter shows you the many techniques you can use to tackle this part of your retouching or restoration project.

I'll be candid and warn you right now that drawing selection outlines is probably the most boring thing you can do in a photo-editing program. But the process is key to getting professional results, so resist the urge to bypass this chapter and move on to something more exciting.

One reminder before you dive in: The specific instructions I give here, as in the rest of the book, feature Adobe Photoshop Elements. For the most part, the tools covered in this chapter work the same way in Photoshop. If you use some other software, your selection tools should operate similarly. So follow the basic guidelines and selection concepts presented here and check your program's Help system for any special options or instructions related to your selection tools. Also see Appendix A, which contains translation charts for Jasc Paint Shop Pro and Ulead PhotoImpact.

Using Basic Selection Tools

Almost every photo-editing program provides a set of basic selection tools, each of which is designed to handle specific selection jobs. You typically get the following tools:

- ✔ A Rectangular Marquee tool for drawing rectangular selection outlines
- ✔ An Elliptical Marquee tool for drawing round selection outlines
- ✔ One or more tools for drawing freehand selection outlines
- ✔ A tool for selecting areas based on color

The next few sections show you how to use the Rectangular and Elliptical Marquee tools; later sections discuss the other tools.

In Elements, you can activate selection tools by clicking their icons in the toolbox, which you display by pressing Tab or choosing Window➪Show Tools. A little triangle at the bottom of a tool icon indicates that two or more tools share the same slot in the toolbox. If you click the triangle, a menu showing all the tools flies out from the side of the toolbox; we in the computer biz refer to this kind of menu as a *flyout menu*. Click the icon for the tool you want to use. That tool then becomes visible in the toolbox, the flyout menu disappears, and the previously active tool becomes hidden.

In Elements 2.0, you don't need to bother with any of these tactics to switch from one tool on a flyout menu to another. When you select any tool on the flyout menu, the Options bar displays buttons corresponding to all the hidden tools. You can just click these buttons to change tools.

Selecting rectangular and elliptical areas

To select a rectangular area, first make sure that the New Selection button on the Options bar is selected, as shown in Figure 3-1. If it's not, click the button. Then activate the Rectangular Marquee by clicking its toolbox icon, labeled in Figure 3-1. To draw an elliptical outline, click the Elliptical Marquee icon, which shares the same slot in the toolbox.

If you're a keyboard shortcut kind of person, you can grab whichever of the two tools is currently visible in the toolbox by pressing M instead of clicking the icon. Pressing Shift+M toggles between the Rectangular and Elliptical Marquees. (This shortcut assumes the default program setting for toggling between tools. To change the setting, choose Edit⇨Preferences⇨General. The relevant option is called Use Shift Key for Tool Switch.)

When you activate either tool, the Options bar presents a few tool controls that you must set before drawing your selection outline. (If you don't see the Options bar, labeled in Figure 3-1, choose Window⇨Show Options.) You can feather the outline, choose from three outline styles, and, when you're using the Elliptical Marquee, apply anti-aliasing.

If that last sentence caused you to blink and say, "Huh?", check out the next three sections to find out what these options do.

After setting the tool controls, simply drag from one corner of the area you want to select to the other. In the figure, I dragged from the upper-left corner of the camera face to the lower-right corner.

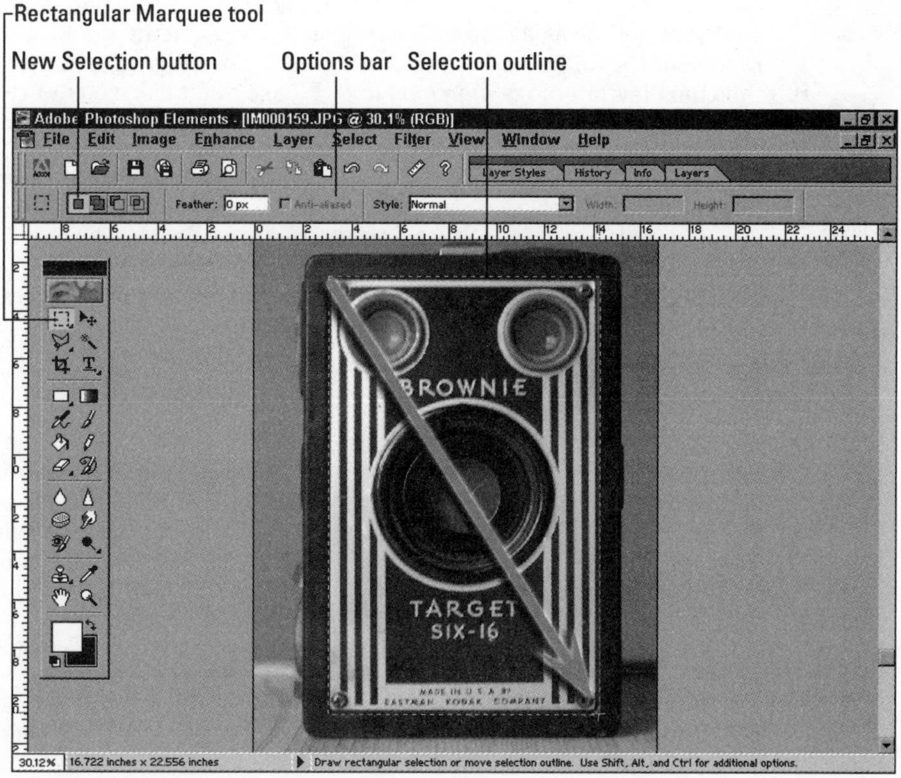

┌Rectangular Marquee tool

New Selection button   Options bar Selection outline

Figure 3-1:
Drag with
the
Rectangular
Marquee
tool to draw
a four-sided
selection
outline.

To draw a square selection outline, press Shift as you drag with the Rectangular Marquee. To draw a circular outline, Shift+drag with the Elliptical Marquee.

As you drag, a blinking, dashed line appears, indicating the boundaries of the selection outline, as shown in the figure. (You don't see the arrow — I added that for emphasis.) When you let up on the mouse button, the outline remains. Anything inside the outline is selected and will be affected by your next edit.

If you don't get your selection outline just right on the first try, see the upcoming section "Adjusting Selection Outlines" to find out how to fix things. Or, to trash your outline and start over, choose Select⇨Deselect, press Ctrl+D (⌘+D), or click anywhere in the image outside the selection outline. (If you drew your outline using the Fixed Size marquee style, explained next, clicking creates a new selection outline, however.)

Choosing a marquee style

As I mentioned in the introduction to this chapter, some people refer to a selection outline as a *marquee*, supposedly because the blinking dashes that represent the outline are reminiscent of a theatre marquee. Other people use the quaint terminology *marching ants*. Please don't ask me who came up with that one — some overworked graphics geek at a picnic, no doubt.

At any rate, before drawing a selection outline with the Rectangular or Elliptical Marquee tool, you need to choose a marquee style from the Style menu on the Options bar. (Refer to Figure 3-1.) Your choices are:

- ✔ **Normal** enables you to set the size and shape of the outline as you drag.

- ✔ **Constrained Aspect Ratio (renamed Fixed Aspect Ratio in Elements 2.0)** limits you to drawing a selection outline that has a specific width-to-height ratio, which you specify by entering values in the Width and Height boxes. (These boxes appear dimmed in Figure 3-1.)

- ✔ **Fixed Size** draws a selection outline with specific dimensions, such as 10 pixels tall by 40 pixels wide. Again, enter the dimensions in the Width and Height boxes on the Options bar before you draw your outline. If you choose this option, you can create your selection outline by simply clicking in the image window.

The second and third options can come in handy when you want to trim your photo to fit in a standard photo frame. For details, see Chapter 7.

Feathering (fading) a selection outline

In Elements, you can set the Rectangular and Elliptical Marquee tools to create a feathered selection outline. You also can feather outlines created with other selection tools, which I cover later in this chapter.

Feathering results in a gradual transition between selected and deselected pixels. When you then apply a color filter or some other change to the selected area, the effect fades toward the outer edges of the selection.

To get a better idea of what feathering does, take a look at Figures 3-2 and 3-3. The first figure shows a poorly composed picture of my grandfather and niece. My grandfather is no longer with us, and I wanted to preserve this moment for my niece. Because the area of interest is roughly circular, I decided to put the image into a circular "digital frame," which you can see in Figure 3-3. I created the example on the left using a non-feathered selection outline; the second image uses a feathered outline.

Figure 3-2: This photo captures a special moment, but is poorly composed.

This frame effect offers a great way to eliminate distracting background objects and create a better composition. And creating a frame is an easy process. The following steps show you how:

1. **Choose the Elliptical Marquee or Rectangular Marquee tool.**

   Pick a tool according to the shape of the frame you want to create.

Feather, 0   Feather, 20

Figure 3-3:
To create these frame effects, I used a Feather value of 0 (left) and 20 (right).

2. **On the Options bar, select Normal from the Style menu.**

   To display the Options bar, choose Window⇨Show Options. (Also make sure that the New Selection button is selected, as shown in Figure 3-1, earlier in this chapter.)

3. **Enter a feather value in the Feather box on the Options bar.**

   If you want your frame to have a crisp edge, like the one on the left side of Figure 3-3, set the Feather value to 0. If you want a soft, fuzzy frame, enter a higher value. I used a value of 20 to create the effect shown in the second image in the figure.

4. **Drag to draw a selection outline around the area you want to frame.**

   If you're feathering the outline, draw the outline a little larger than the area you want to preserve. As you can see from Figure 3-3, the feathered treatment eats away a little bit of the image around the edges.

5. **Choose Select⇨Inverse or press Ctrl+Shift+I (⌘+Shift+I).**

   The Inverse command reverses the selection outline, so that the area you initially selected becomes deselected, and vice versa.

   You can read more about the Inverse command in the section "Adjusting Selection Outlines," later in this chapter.

6. **Choose a frame color.**

   In the next step, you fill the selected area — which now is your unwanted background — with color to create the frame. To set the frame color, click the background color icon in the toolbox and select a color from the Color Picker.

   If you need help with this step, see Chapter 4, which explains the Color Picker and other color issues.

7. Press Delete.

The program fills the selected area with the background color.

In addition to providing a way to create a soft-edged frame, feathering can be useful when you're retouching an image. For some types of corrections, altered pixels blend more naturally with the surrounding area if you use a small Feather value when you select the area you want to edit. But in other cases, the slight blurring that results from feathering a selection can actually make your changes more apparent. If you can see a noticeable boundary between the corrected area and the neighboring pixels after you apply an edit, choose Edit⇨Undo or press Ctrl+Z (⌘+Z) to undo the change. Then redraw the selection outline, this time using a different Feather value.

If you draw the perfect selection outline but forget to set the Feather value beforehand, don't trash the outline. You can feather an existing outline by choosing Select⇨Feather. When the Feather Selection dialog box appears, enter a feather value in the Feather Radius box and then press Enter or click OK.

Anti-aliasing (softening) a selection outline

When you work with the Elliptical Marquee tool, the Options bar offers one additional option: the Anti-aliased check box. When you turn on this option, the program applies anti-aliasing to your selection outline.

Anti-aliasing smoothes the jagged edges that occur in curved or diagonal segments of a selection outline.

Figure 3-4 illustrates the results of anti-aliasing a selection outline. To create the left circle, I drew a selection outline with anti-aliasing turned off and then filled the selected area with black. See how raggedy the edges of the circle appear? Compare that result with the circle on the right, which I created with an anti-aliased selection outline. If you look closely, you can see that the pixels around the edge are slightly blurred, which makes the border of the circle appear smoother.

In most cases, you should turn on anti-aliasing, especially when you plan to use the selected pixels as part of a composite photo. When you copy a selection from one photo to another, anti-aliasing creates a better-looking transition between the copied pixels and the surrounding area.

To toggle anti-aliasing on and off, click the Anti-aliased check box. A check mark in the box means that the option is on.

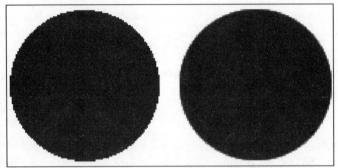

Figure 3-4:
The left circle, created without anti-aliasing, has jagged edges; the right example shows how anti-aliasing produces smoother boundaries.

You must select the check box before you draw your selection outline; you can't add anti-aliasing to an existing outline.

Creating Complex Selection Outlines

As capable as the Rectangular and Elliptical Marquee tools may be, they rarely play an important role in photo retouching and restoration work. Why? Because most objects and subjects in photographs aren't perfectly rectangular or elliptical. About the only time I ever pick up either the Rectangular or Elliptical Marquee is when cropping a picture to a specific frame size or creating a frame effect like the one shown in Figure 3-3.

Most selection tasks involve drawing outlines around irregular areas, which is why most photo-editing programs give you one or more tools for getting the job done. The next few sections introduce you to these tools and explain which tools work best for specific situations. Following that, I introduce you to a special technique that you can use to paint a selection outline using the Paintbrush tool, a method I think works even better than all the other selection tools combined.

Drawing a freehand selection outline

Photoshop Elements offers three tools for drawing freehand selection outlines: the Lasso, Polygonal Lasso, and Magnetic Lasso. Apparently whoever named these tools thought the process of roping off pixels was similar to rounding up stray cattle — uh, okay, sure. The name stuck, and so now all good photo-editing programs have a Lasso or two (although some programs have the good sense to refer to them as Freehand Selection tools).

Personally, I don't use any of the Lasso tools often, and then only to draw a very rough selection outline, which I then refine using one of the techniques discussed later in this chapter. (See "Adjusting Selection Outlines.") Creating a precise outline with these tools can be difficult, especially if you don't have a steady hand or are working with a mouse instead of a drawing tablet. Still, give the tools a try because you may have better results with them than I. And on occasion, they are perfect for the job.

The three Elements Lasso tools share a slot in the toolbox. (See the upcoming Figure 3-5.) You can activate whichever tool is visible in the toolbox by pressing L; press Shift+L to toggle between the tools. Again, these shortcuts assume the default tool-toggle setting on the General tab of the Preferences dialog box (Edit⇨Preferences⇨General). If keeping track of shortcut keys isn't your cup of tea, you can always click the triangle in the bottom right corner of the visible tool icon to display the flyout menu containing the hidden tools. Or, if you're using Elements 2.0, use the tool buttons on the Options bar to switch from one Lasso to another.

Using the Lasso and Polygonal Lasso

To create a selection outline with the Lasso, just drag around the area you want to select. As you drag, a selection outline trails your cursor, as shown in Figure 3-5. When you reach the point where you began, let up on the mouse button to close the outline. If you release the mouse button before you get to the start of the outline, the program closes the outline with a straight segment.

If the object you want to select contains mostly straight sides, use the Polygonal Lasso instead of the plain old Lasso. The Polygonal Lasso throws out straight segments of selection rope.

Click to set the start of the first segment in the outline, move the mouse to where you want that segment to end, and click again. Keep clicking to draw additional segments. When you get to the starting point of the outline and release the mouse button, the program closes the outline. You also can double-click at any point in the outline to automatically close the outline with a straight segment.

When you're working with either the Lasso or Polygonal Lasso, you can temporarily switch to the other tool by pressing and holding the Alt (Option) key. For example, if you're using the Lasso and want to draw a straight segment, press and hold down the Alt (Option) key. With the key down, let up on the mouse button. Then click to set the start of the straight segment and click again to end the segment. Keep clicking to create more segments. When you want to return to drawing regular freehand segments, release the Alt (Option) key.

Lasso

Figure 3-5:
Drag with
the Lasso
tool to draw
a freehand
selection
outline.

Similarly, you can use the Polygonal Lasso to draw a freehand segment by holding down the Alt (Option) key and dragging. When you let up on the key, the Polygonal Lasso reverts to its normal straight-segment function.

To sum up, the Lasso and Polygonal Lasso are two sides of the same coin — er, rope? So which tool you choose depends on whether your selection outline involves more straight segments or more irregular segments.

Selecting along color boundaries with the Magnetic Lasso

Turn to the Magnetic Lasso when the area you want to select is encircled by contrasting pixels. The Magnetic Lasso helps you isolate a subject by automatically placing the selection outline along the border between contrasting areas (see Figure 3-6).

This tool is one of those that's difficult to understand by simply reading about it. So open an image and follow these steps to get a feel for how the Magnetic Lasso works.

If you don't want to hunt through your own images, you can use the turtle image included on the CD included with this book. The image file is named Turtle.jpg and is located in the Sample Photos folder on the CD.

1. **Activate the Magnetic Lasso.**

   The toolbox icon for this tool looks like a little lasso with a magnet, recalling the days of the Old West, when cowboys reined in steel cows with big magnets.

   Make sure that the New Selection button on the Options bar is selected, as shown in the figure.

2. **Center the cursor over the border between the object you want to select and the background.**

   In Figure 3-6, for example, I centered the cursor along the edge of the turtle. (As explained in the sidebar "Switching tool cursors," I set the cursor style for the tool to Precise. The circle around the cross-hair represents the Width value, a Magnetic Lasso control that you can read about in the list that follows these steps.)

3. **Click to set the start of the outline.**

   A small square, which Adobe refers to as a *fastening point,* appears to mark the start of the outline. You can get a look at a fastening point in the figure.

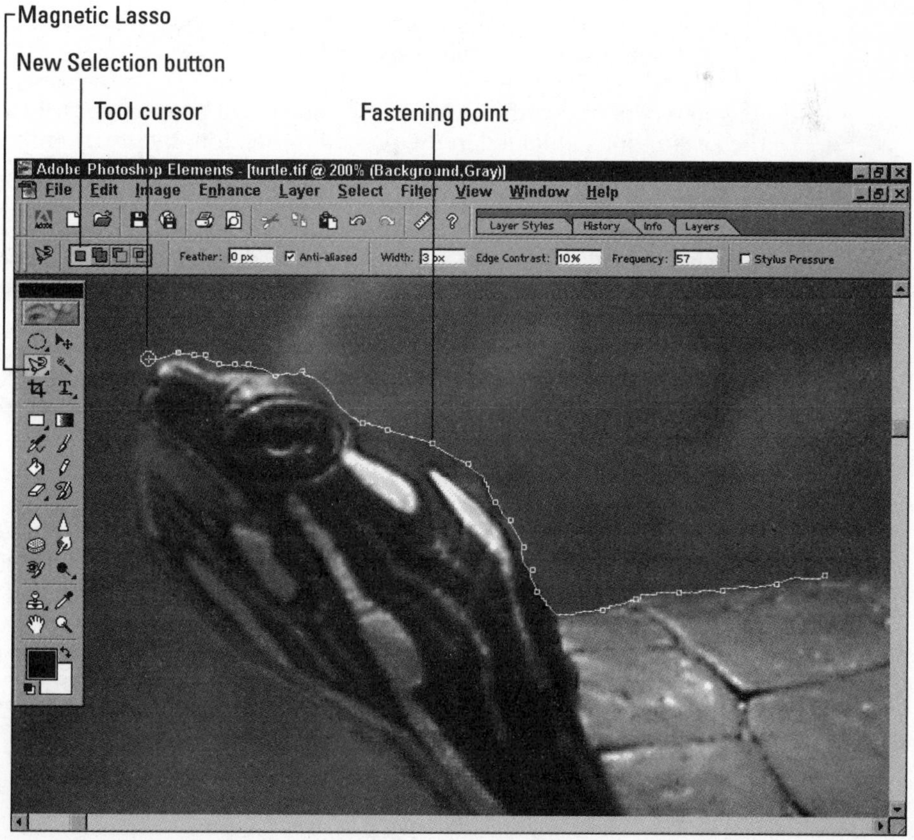

Figure 3-6: As you move the cursor, the Magnetic Lasso automatically draws a selection outline along the border between contrasting pixels.

4. Move or drag the mouse around the object, keeping the cursor centered over the edge of the area you want to select.

You can either move the mouse without any buttons pressed down or drag as you normally do when drawing with the Lasso. I prefer the drag method because it usually gives me better results, but try both ways to see which works best for you.

Either way, as the cursor passes over the image, the program looks for contrasting pixels and draws the selection outline between them, adding more fastening points every so often.

If the outline strays off course, move the cursor over the most recent fastening point and press Delete. The fastening point disappears, and you can redo the outline from that point forward. You can delete as many fastening points as necessary — just keep putting the cursor over the squares and pressing Delete.

Additionally, you can click to create your own fastening points if the program just can't seem to find the right position for a particular stretch of outline.

5. Finish the outline by clicking on the initial fastening point.

If you decide to abandon an outline-in-progress, press Esc to get rid of the segments you've already created.

As you're working with the Magnetic Lasso, you can temporarily switch to the Lasso tool, explained in the preceding section, by pressing the Alt (Option) key as you drag. When you let up on the Alt (Option) key, the Magnetic Lasso returns.

You also can adjust the performance of the Magnetic Lasso by using the controls on the Options bar, as follows. Set these options before you begin drawing your outline.

- **Feather and Anti-aliased:** These options work as described earlier in this chapter, in the sections "Feathering (fading) a selection outline" and "Anti-aliasing (softening) a selection outline."

- **Width:** This value, measured in pixels, determines how large an area the program considers when determining where to place the selection outline. If you use a low value, the program looks only at pixels very near the one that's under your cursor. You can enter any value from 1 to 40; start with a value of about 5 and experiment with raising and lowering the value a little. The appropriate value depends on your image. If you set your cursor style to Precise, the circle around the cursor reflects the Width value.

- **Edge Contrast:** This value tells the program how much contrast it should look for when placing the outline. If very little contrast exists between the object you want to select and the bordering pixels, use a low value. The maximum value is 100.

✔ **Frequency:** If you want the program to add fastening points at more frequent intervals, raise this value. Too many points may result in a jaggedy outline, however.

✔ **Stylus Pressure (Pen Pressure in Version 2.0):** This check box applies only if you're working with a pressure-sensitive drawing tablet. If you select the box, you can adjust the Width value on the fly by simply adjusting how hard you press down with the stylus. More pressure decreases the Width value. The circle around your cursor changes to reflect the adjustments, but the Width value displayed on the Options bar does not.

Switching tool cursors

In Photoshop Elements, the standard tool cursors resemble the icons you see in the toolbox. For example, the cursor for the Lasso looks like a lasso, as shown in Figure 3-5.

Although the icon-style cursors can help you remember which tool you're using, they sometimes obscure your view of the image. For precision editing, I recommend that you change the cursor style to one of the other two available options.

To switch cursor styles, choose Edit⇨ Preferences⇨Display and Cursors to display the panel of the General dialog box shown here.

Choose either the Precise or Brush Size option in the Painting Cursors section of the dialog box to set the cursor style for tools that have an adjustable brush size — including the Paintbrush, Pencil, and Eraser. If you select Precise, you get a simple cross-hair cursor; if you choose Brush Size, the cursor reflects the approximate size and shape of the current tool brush. I prefer the Brush Size option because it enables you to see exactly how large an area your edits will affect.

The Other Cursors options affect the non-brush tools, such as the Lasso tools. Select Precise to switch to a cross-hair cursor. Standard gives you the icon-style cursors.

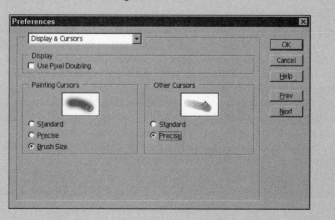

If you're thinking that the Magnetic Lasso is a little complicated, I agree whole-heartedly. I find that it works great as long as a significant change in contrast occurs all the way around the area that I want to select. But the tool is pretty hit-and-miss when only a moderate amount of contrast occurs between subject and background, as in the turtle image used in the example. You wind up doing a lot of work adding and deleting fastening points, and the payoff for your work is rarely a perfect selection outline anyway. As with the other Lasso tools, I use this one to make an approximate selection outline and then refine the outline using the methods described in "Adjusting Selection Outlines" and "Selecting Like the Pros," later in this chapter.

Selecting areas of similar color

Of all the basic selection tools, the one I'm about to introduce is the one I'm most likely to pick up when I'm not using the technique outlined later in "Selecting Like the Pros." This tool, known as the Magic Wand, selects areas based on color. Most photo-editing programs offer this tool, although it may go by another name, such as Color Selector or Color Wand.

When you click on your image with the Magic Wand, the program analyzes the pixel you click and then selects pixels of similar color. For example, if you have a red rose against a green background, you can click a red rose pixel to select all red areas in the flower.

You also can use the Magic Wand to select just the highlights or shadows in a photo, even when you're working with a grayscale image, as shown in Figure 3-7. In this photo, I wanted to lighten the exposure of the midtones and shadows while leaving the lightest parts alone. The easiest approach was to select the brightest areas first, which I did by clicking with the Magic Wand at the spot marked by the X in the figure. Then I used the Inverse command, which reverses a selection outline, so that everything *but* the highlights became selected.

Why not just use the Magic Wand to select the midtones and shadows from the get-go? Because those regions comprise a greater range of color and brightness values, making it more difficult to select the appropriate pixels with one click of the tool. You can Shift+click with the Magic Wand to add more and more pixels to the selection, but the more efficient approach in this photo was to go after the highlights first. All the highlights are very similar, and I was able to achieve the outline with one well-placed click. Then to inverse the selection outline, I just pressed the keyboard shortcut for the Inverse command, Ctrl+Shift+I (⌘+Shift+I).

For more about the Inverse command and adding to an existing selection outline, see the upcoming section "Adjusting Selection Outlines."

Magic Wand

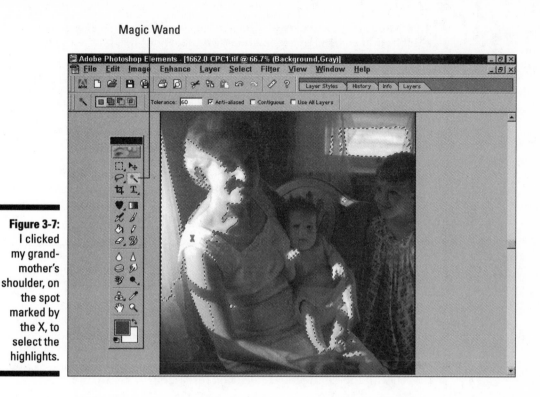

Figure 3-7:
I clicked
my grand-
mother's
shoulder, on
the spot
marked by
the X, to
select the
highlights.

Although the Magic Wand couldn't be simpler to use, you need to understand a few tool controls, all set via the Options bar, to get full advantage from it. As with the other selection tools discussed so far, you must set these controls before you create your selection outline.

If the Options bar isn't showing, choose Window➪Show Options. If you're not working with Photoshop Elements, check your software's Help system for details about your color-selection tool. If you have the equivalent of the Magic Wand, you no doubt also have access to similar controls.

✔ **Contiguous:** If you select this check box, the Magic Wand selects only pixels that are *contiguous* to the one you click. That is, for a pixel to be selected, a pixel of another color can't come between the pixel and the one you click.

To get a clearer idea of what that gibberish means, take a look at Color Plate 3-2. In the top left image, I selected the Contiguous check box and then clicked my grandmother's shoulder at the spot marked by the red X. The dashed line shows the extent of the resulting selection outline. Even though the window in the background contains pixels similar to the shoulder pixel I clicked, the window pixels aren't selected because differently colored pixels fall between them and the shoulder pixel.

In the top right image in Color Plate 3-2, I clicked at the very same spot, but this time with the Contiguous check box turned off. Now all pixels similar to the one I clicked become selected, regardless of their position in the image.

✔ **Tolerance:** This value determines how similar a pixel must be to the one you click in order to be selected. The higher the Tolerance value, the broader the range of colors that are selected — in other words, the tool is more tolerant of color differences. You can enter any value from 0 to 255, but 255 simply selects the entire image, which is hardly useful; you can select everything without using any tools by simply pressing Ctrl+A (⌘+A). Normally, I start with a Tolerance value between 5 and 40 and go from there.

Again, refer to Color Plate 3-2 to see how the Tolerance value affects the performance of the Magic Wand. In the two top images, I set the Tolerance value to 10; in the two lower images, I raised the value to 40, which selected a larger range of pixels.

Remember that your selection outline depends on both the Tolerance value and the Contiguous check box. You can see how the various control combinations created four different selection outlines in Color Plate 3-2. For this image, I found that the ideal combination was a Tolerance value of 60 with the Contiguous check box turned off, as shown in Figure 3-7.

✔ **Use All Layers:** If you're working on a multilayered photo, turn this option on to tell the Magic Wand to consider pixels in all layers of the image when creating the selection outline. Deselect the check box to tell the program to pay attention only to pixels on the active layer.

Regardless of whether you turn the option on or off, however, the completed selection outline *affects* only pixels on the active layer. The check box simply determines what pixels the program analyzes to draw the selection outline.

If you're not familiar with layers, see the upcoming section "Discovering layers" for an introduction.

✔ **Anti-aliased:** This check box, when selected, slightly blurs the selection outline to minimize jagged edges. For more about anti-aliasing and its counterpart, feathering, see "Feathering (fading) a selection outline" and "Anti-aliasing (softening) a selection outline," earlier in this chapter. When you use the Magic Wand, you can feather the outline only by using the Feather command after drawing the outline.

If ever a selection task called for anti-aliasing and feathering, by the way, it would be selecting highlights in a photo like the one in Figure 3-7. By softening and fading the selection outline, you ensure that the changes you make to the selected pixels blend in well with the surrounding, untouched areas. If you don't anti-alias and feather the outline, you wind up with noticeable, sharp-edged boundaries between edited and unedited pixels, destroying the soft quality of the lighting in the image.

Selecting like the Pros

Adobe Photoshop offers a high-end selection feature called Quick Mask, which enables you to use the painting tools to easily create even the most complex selection outline. Instead of dragging a lasso or other marquee tool to lay down an intricate selection outline — a task that's almost certain to cause you to pound your desk in frustration — you paint over the pixels you want to select. If you make a mistake, you just erase the paint. You can work with a hard-edged brush to create an outline with precise edges, or you can use a soft, fuzzy brush to create a feathery outline. You can work with a large brush to select big areas and then switch to a tiny brush to select nooks and crannies. This method of creating selection outlines is so much easier and more precise than using any of the selection tools discussed earlier in this chapter that I use it almost exclusively when working on photographs.

Unfortunately, Photoshop Elements does not offer the Quick Mask feature. Version 2.0 does offer a new Selection Brush tool, which mimics the basic functionality of the Quick Mask selecting. (See the upcoming sidebar "Exploring the Elements 2.0 Selection Brush.") The tool's not bad, but it's less powerful and flexible than the Photoshop Quick Mask feature. You can't really blame Adobe — after all, the company can't be expected to provide the same sophisticated tools in its $99 program as it provides in its $600 offering.

The good news is that by using a few tricks outlined in upcoming sections, you can enjoy most of the benefits of the Quick Mask selection feature no matter whether you're using Elements 1.0, 2.0, or some other photo editor that doesn't offer the equivalent of Quick Mask. Before I show you the secret, though, I need to introduce you to *layers,* which are crucial to the technique. The next section tells all.

Discovering layers

The secret to my faux Quick Mask technique lies in a feature known as *layers*. To understand layers, think of those sheets of acetate used to create transparencies for an overhead projector. A layer is like a single sheet of acetate. A scanned image or photo from a digital camera starts life with just one layer, but you can add as many new layers as you need in your image-editing program (assuming that your software offers this feature). By putting different elements of a photo on different layers, you open up new editing options.

For example, suppose that you want a picture of your dog and cat together. The two animals can't be in the same room together without brawling, which means that getting them to pose all nice and friendly-like for a joint portrait is out of the question. So you take a picture of each animal separately and then open both photos in your image editor. After selecting the cat, you copy the selected pixels into the dog photo, putting the cat image on a new layer. Wherever the cat layer is empty, the pixels on the dog layer show through. But where the cat pixels exist, the dog pixels are obscured. The composite image shows peace among the species, courtesy of digital imaging.

To help you get a better grasp on the concept of layers, I created a multilayered example featuring the two images shown in Figure 3-8. Because I had neither cat nor dog handy, I opted to combine a turtle and giraffe, whose pictures I snapped at the zoo.

First, I created the selection outline that you see in the turtle image in Figure 3-8. Next, I chose the Copy command, which copies selected pixels to a virtual holding tank known as the Clipboard. Finally, I switched to the giraffe image and chose the Paste command, which deposits the contents of the Clipboard into the active image.

The Copy and Paste commands reside on the Edit menu. But don't waste time slogging through menus to choose the commands. Instead, memorize these keyboard shortcuts: For Copy, press Ctrl+C (⌘+C); for Paste, press Ctrl+V (⌘+V).

Figure 3-8: I used a mask layer to select the part of the turtle image that I wanted to copy into the giraffe photo.

Figure 3-9 shows the composite image, along with the Layers palette, which lists layers according to the position they occupy in the image. The palette also provides thumbnail views showing the contents of each layer.

In the thumbnails, transparent areas of a layer appear as a checkerboard pattern. (You can specify how you want transparent areas to appear by choosing Edit⇨Preferences⇨Transparency.)

Because the turtle layer is above the giraffe layer, the turtle pixels totally hide any giraffe pixels beneath. But where the turtle layer is empty — in this case, everywhere but the lower-right corner of the layer — the giraffe pixels are fully visible.

Although layers make for great compositional fun, they also play an important part in many retouching and restoration tasks. Later chapters show you how to take advantage of layers to get easier, more professional results when doing a variety of image corrections, and Chapter 9 provides more detail about building composite images using Copy, Paste, and other commands. For now, you have the fundamentals you need to use layers as a powerful selection tool, which I show you how to do in the following sections.

Figure 3-9:
After copying the turtle selection, I pasted the copied pixels into the giraffe photo, creating an unlikely confab between two species.

Painting a mask

Before the days of desktop publishing, graphic artists used sheets of a thin, red material, known by its trade name, *Rubylith,* to keep darkroom and reproduction processes from affecting a particular area of a photograph. Areas covered by the Rubylith were said to be *masked.* If that explanation doesn't help, you can remember what a mask does by thinking of how you use household masking tape when painting a room, taping off areas that you want to protect from paint.

In the first step of the selection technique I'm about to explain, you create what I refer to as a *mask layer,* which simply means that you create a mask on a separate layer from the rest of the image. But in this case, you create a reverse mask — that is, you create a mask that covers the areas you *do* want to edit. Of course, after you create the mask, you can always use the Inverse command to swap the selection outline, so that areas outside the mask become selected.

Okay, enough build-up already. The following steps reveal the secret to this selection process.

If you want to work along with the steps — and I strongly suggest that you do — either open one of your own photos or grab the turtle image provided on the CD that accompanies this book. (The file is named Turtle.jpg and is located in the Sample Photos folder on the CD.) If you previously selected the turtle when exploring the Magnetic Lasso earlier in this chapter, and the selection outline still exists, get rid of the outline by choosing Select⇨ Deselect or using the command's keyboard shortcut, Ctrl+D (⌘+D).

As with other procedures detailed in this book, the steps here feature Photoshop Elements 1.0 and 2.0. If you are using another photo editor, use your software's manual in conjunction with these steps to figure out what specific commands and controls you need to use.

1. **Display the Layers palette.**

   Normally, the Layers palette appears docked in the palette well at the top of the Elements window. Because you need to access the Layers palette frequently as you create your selection outline, I suggest that you drag the palette (by its tab) out of the well and into the image window, as shown in Figure 3-10. The palette then remains open and readily accessible. If the palette isn't visible in the palette well, choose Window⇨Show Layers.

2. **Click the New Layer button at the bottom of the Layers palette to create a new layer.**

   I labeled in the button in Figure 3-10. Clicking the button creates a new, empty layer. The layer automatically becomes selected, or active. (The active layer appears highlighted in the Layers palette.)

3. **Name the layer.**

   In Elements 1.0, double-click the layer name to open the Layer Properties dialog box, where you can enter a name for the layer. In Elements 2.0, you can double-click the layer thumbnail to open the dialog box or double-the layer name itself and just type the new name right in the Layers palette. Click somewhere off the layer name to make the name change official.

Give the layer a name that will remind you of the purpose of the layer. I used the inventive name *Mask Layer* in Figure 3-10.

4. **Set the layer opacity to 50 percent.**

You can set the opacity by double-clicking the Opacity box in the Layers palette, typing 50, and pressing Enter. Or click the arrow at the end of the box to display a slider, drag the slider to set the value, and then click anywhere off the slider to close it.

Lowering the opacity enables you to see your image through the paint that you apply to create your mask. You can adjust the Opacity value as needed if you have difficulty seeing through the mask.

5. **In the Layers palette, select Normal from the Blending Mode menu, labeled in Figure 3-10.**

Layer blending modes enable you to mix pixels on one layer with pixels of another layer in different ways. For this job, select Normal. Also make sure that the two Lock check boxes that appear underneath the menu are deselected.

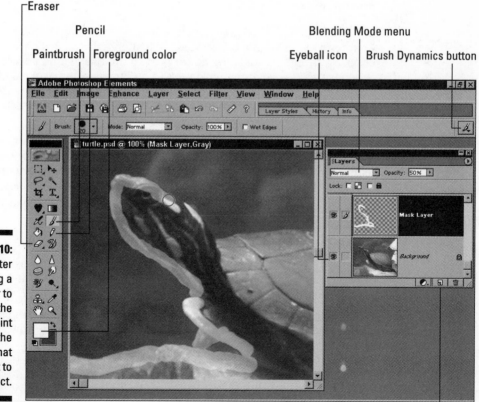

Figure 3-10: After creating a new layer to hold the mask, paint over the pixels that you want to select.

New Layer button

For more about layer blending modes and their uses, see Chapter 6.

6. **Activate the Paintbrush by clicking its toolbox icon.**

   I labeled the tool icon in Figure 3-10. Note that this tool is located in a different spot in the Elements 2.0 toolbox and goes by the name Brush tool instead of Paintbrush.

   After you activate the tool, the Options bar changes to offer the controls shown in the figure. Again, the figure reflects the Version 1.0 options; Version 2.0 is slightly different but offers the same basic controls.

7. **Set the tool options.**

   On the Options bar, choose Normal from the Mode menu and set the Opacity value to 100 percent. For the Elements 1.0 Paintbrush, deselect the Wet Edges check box.

   If you're working with a drawing tablet, you may want to investigate the controls available by clicking the Brush Dynamics button on the Options bar in Elements 1.0 and the Airbrush and More Options buttons in Elements 2.0. Chapter 6 explains more about some of these controls, which enable you to vary your paint stroke simply by adjusting your pressure on the pen stylus.

8. **Choose a brush tip.**

   Chapter 6 explains this process, so I'll just give the basics here. To choose a brush tip, click the arrow next to the Brush icon to display the Brushes palette, as shown in Figure 3-11. (The palette has a slightly different design in Elements 2.0.) Each icon in the palette represents a different size and shape of brush. Click the icon to select the brush tip.

   If you want your selection outline to have precise edges, choose a hard brush. To create a selection with feathered edges, choose a softer brush. The softer the brush, the more feathering you get. If you prefer, you can feather your selection outline after the fact using the Feather command, explained in the upcoming section "Adjusting Selection Outlines."

   See "Feathering (fading) a selection outline," earlier in this chapter, to see examples of the effects you can create with feathering.

9. **Set the foreground color to white.**

   You can do this quickly by pressing D and then X. The D key restores the default foreground and background colors, which are black and white, respectively. Pressing X swaps the two colors.

   If the colors in your image make white difficult to see, you can use any other color you want. See Chapter 4 for information about how to select colors other than black and white.

10. **Paint over the area you want to select.**

    I start by painting along the outside edges of the area I want to select, using a small brush, as I'm doing in Figure 3-10. Then I switch to a larger brush and fill in the middle.

Figure 3-11:
Choose a
hard-edged
brush for a
clean-
edged
selection
outline;
work with a
soft brush
for a
feathered
outline.

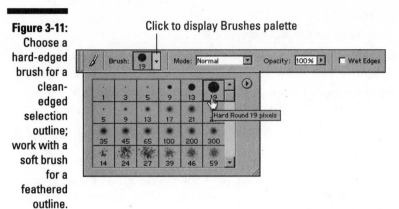

Click to display Brushes palette

As you paint, your paint strokes appear on the mask layer, as indicated in the Layers palette. If you make a mistake, use the undo features covered in Chapter 2 to fix things. You also can use the Eraser tool, labeled in Figure 3-10, to erase errant paint strokes. Because you're working on a layer, the tool erases to transparency. (When you work on the bottom layer, the tool paints in the background color.)

You can change the brush size and other brush features for the Eraser tool just as you can for the Paintbrush tool.

11. **When the mask is finished, Ctrl+click (⌘+click) the mask layer name in the Layers palette.**

    This key-click combo selects all non-transparent areas of a layer — in this case, all the pixels in your mask. Your new selection outline appears in the image window.

12. **Hide the mask layer by clicking the eyeball icon in the left column of the Layers palette.**

    Your selection outline remains, but the mask is no longer visible. As long as the layer is hidden, the mask doesn't show when you print your image, either.

13. **Click the layer that contains the pixels you want to edit.**

    A selection outline always affects the active layer, no matter what layer was active when you created the outline. So all you need to do to transfer the outline that you created in Step 11 to the layer you want to edit is click the layer name.

Although 13 steps may sound like a lot of work, keep in mind that most of these steps simply break down the tool and layer options you should select before painting the mask, which takes just seconds. In truth, the technique boils down to just four steps:

1. **Create a new layer.**

2. **Paint your mask on the new layer.**

3. **Ctrl+click (⌘+click) the mask layer name in the Layers palette to create the selection outline.**

4. **Hide the mask layer and click the layer you want to edit. Your selection outline now affects pixels on that layer.**

Most people find that painting a mask is much easier than creating a selection outline with any of the marquee tools, and I'm guessing that you will, too. But the mask layer technique has another, equally important benefit: You can resurrect your selection outline at any time — even after closing and reopening your image file. The upcoming sections "Reusing a mask" and "Preserving a mask" explain how.

Be sure to also check out "Turning an existing outline into a mask layer," which explains how you can enjoy the benefits of mask layers even when you use one of the standard selection tools to create your selection outline. The last two sections in this chapter discuss other ways that you may be able to save and reuse a selection outline.

Reusing a mask

After painting a mask, you can recreate the resulting selection outline at any time simply by Ctrl+clicking (⌘+clicking) the mask layer in the Layers palette, as shown in Figure 3-12. You don't need to click the layer eyeball in the Layers palette to make the layer visible for this technique to work.

Notice that when you place your cursor over a layer name and press the Ctrl (⌘) key, a little dotted outline appears near your cursor to indicate that a selection outline is in the offing.

After you click, remember to then click the name of the layer you want to edit to transfer the selection outline to that layer.

Preserving a mask

If you want to be able to reuse your mask layer in a future editing session, you must save the image in a file format that supports layers. In Elements, choose the PSD format, which is the program's native format.

In Elements, also be sure to turn on the Layers check box in the Save As dialog box, as shown in Figure 3-13.

Figure 3-12:
To
regenerate
the
selection
outline,
Ctrl+click
(⌘+click)
the mask
layer in the
Layers
palette.

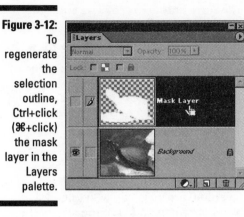

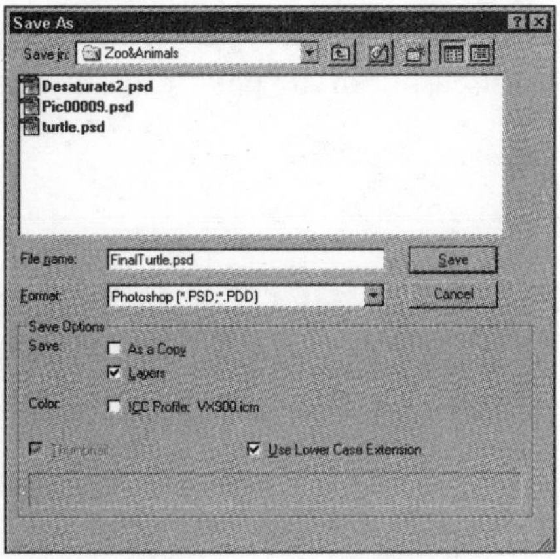

Figure 3-13:
To save a
mask layer
as part of
the image
file, select
PSD as the
file format
and select
the Layers
check box.

Turning an existing outline into a mask layer

If you prefer to use one of the standard selection tools — Rectangular Marquee, Color Wand, and so on — to create your selection outline, you can still enjoy the advantages that a mask layer offers. After creating your outline, take these steps:

1. **Create a new layer by clicking the New Layer button in the Layers palette.**

   Name the layer to indicate that it holds the mask, as explained in the section "Painting a mask." As before, select Normal from the Blending Mode menu in the Layers palette, set the layer Opacity value to 50 percent, and deselect the Lock check boxes.

2. **Set the foreground color to white (or whatever color you want the mask to be).**

3. **Press Alt+Backspace (Option+Backspace) to fill the outline with white.**

   You now have a painted mask on your new layer. If you want to refine the mask, you can use the Eraser and Paintbrush as you would when painting a mask from scratch. You must first deactivate the existing selection outline, however. Press Ctrl+D (⌘+D) or choose Select⇨Deselect to do so.

Deleting a mask layer

If you are finished using your mask layer and are sure you won't need the selection outline again, delete the layer. Every layer adds to the size of the image file, which means more strain for your computer.

To delete a mask layer, just click its name in the Layers palette and then click the Trash button in the lower-right corner of the palette. Or drag the layer name to the Trash button.

Exploring the Elements 2.0 Selection Brush tool

Photoshop Elements 2.0 offers a new selection tool, called the Selection Brush, that enables you to create a selection outline by dragging over your image, just as you do when painting a mask using the mask layer technique explored elsewhere in this chapter. Because the Selection Brush tool is pretty program specific, I don't want to spend a great deal of space in this book explaining it. But if you're using Elements 2.0, I do want to bring the Selection Brush to your attention because you may find it a good alternative to the mask layer technique.

When you pick up this tool, labeled in the figure shown here, you can work in two different modes, which you select from the Mode menu on the Options bar.

In Mask mode, dragging over the image lays down a protective mask. Anything covered by the mask won't be affected by your edits. By default, a red translucent color indicates the extent of the mask as you drag with the tool. You can change the mask color and opacity by using the Options bar controls. In addition, you can adjust the tool brush by using the other controls on the Options bar. If you drag over pixels that you didn't mean to cover with the mask, you can remove the mask from those areas by pressing Alt (Option) as you drag over them with the Selection Brush.

When you choose another tool or apply an editing command, the mask overlay disappears, and the program automatically creates a selection outline that selects everything *but* the areas under the mask. Alternatively, you can hide the mask and display the selection outline by choosing Selection from the Mode pop-up menu on the Options bar while the Selection Brush is active.

Again, remember that the outline selects everything but the areas you masked. You can use the Select⇨Inverse command if you want to reverse the outline so that areas that previously were masked become selected.

If you prefer, you can ignore the Mask mode and draw your outline directly by using the Selection Brush in Selection mode. Now dragging across the image selects the pixels underneath your cursor. Alt (Option)+drag to remove areas from the selection outline. To add to the selection outline, just drag — with this tool, you don't press Shift as you do with standard selection tools.

Be sure to read the section "Saving and Loading Selection Outlines" for information about retaining a selection outline for later use.

You also can remove a mask layer by doing either of the following:

✔ Hide the layer and then choose Layer⇨Flatten. Again, you show and hide a layer by clicking the corresponding eyeball icon in the Layers palette. When you choose the Flatten command, which merges all your layers into one, the program asks for your permission to discard hidden layers. Answer in the affirmative to trash the layer. Note that any other hidden layers also get destroyed, and the remaining visible layers are merged, which means you can no longer edit pixels on individual layers separately from the rest of the image.

✔ Hide the layer and then save the image file with the Layers check box turned off in the Save As dialog box (see Figure 3-13). Or save to a format that doesn't offer that check box. Hiding the layer before you save is crucial; otherwise, the painted mask layer merges with the other image layers, leaving you with a big blob of paint in your photo. Again, saving this way merges all visible layers into one, so it's a good option only when you're completely done editing your photo.

Adjusting Selection Outlines

When you complete a selection outline in Elements, be careful not to click or drag in the image *outside* the outline with any of the selection tools. Assuming that the New Selection icon on the Options bar is active, as it is by default, your click or drag eliminates the existing selection outline and, with some tools, begins a new outline.

That doesn't mean that you need to get your outline just right on the first try, however. In addition to painting and erasing on a mask layer to refine a selection outline, you can reposition, expand, reduce, and otherwise tweak the outline in Elements as follows:

- **Relocate a selection outline:** First, check the Options bar and make sure that the New Selection button, labeled in Figure 3-14, is active. Then drag inside the outline with any of the selection tools.

  You also can use the arrow keys to nudge an outline into place. After activating a selection tool, press an arrow key to move the outline one pixel in the direction of the arrow. For example, to shift the outline three pixels to the left, press the left-arrow key three times. Press the Shift key along with an arrow key to move the outline 10 pixels in the direction of the arrow.

- **Add to a selection outline:** You can select additional areas in your image by pressing the Shift key as you use any of the selection tools. For example, if you use the Magic Wand to select all the blue areas in an image, you can Shift+click on a green pixel to select the green areas, too.

  As an alternative to pressing the Shift key, you can switch the selection tool into the addition mode by clicking the Add button on the Options bar, labeled in Figure 3-14.

- **Subtract from a selection outline:** To reduce a selection outline, set your selection tool to the subtractive mode by clicking the Subtract button on the Options bar or by pressing and holding the Alt (Option) key. Now use the selection tool to rope off whatever areas you want to remove from the selection outline. For example, in Figure 3-14, I first drew a rectangular selection around the camera face. Then I picked up the Elliptical Marquee tool, set the tool mode to Subtract, and dragged around the lens to deselect that area.

  The camera photo is provided in the Sample Photos folder of the CD; the image file name is Camera.jpg.

- **Intersect a selection outline:** Although I find this option so convoluted that I don't ever use it, I'm going to tell you about it because I know you probably are wondering about the purpose of the Intersect button shown in Figure 3-14. Say that you draw a circular selection outline. Then you set the tool to Intersect and draw a second circular outline that partially overlaps the first one. The result is selection outline that occupies just the area where the two outlines overlap. If you can find a good use for this option — heck, if you even can remember that you *have* this option — bully for you.

✔ **Expand and contract a selection outline:** To expand a selection outline by a precise number of pixels in all directions, choose Select⇨Modify⇨ Expand. Enter a pixel value and click OK. Similarly, you can choose Select⇨Modify⇨Contract to reduce a selection by a specified number of pixels all the way around.

Alternatively, you can use the Grow and Similar commands, also on the Select⇨Modify submenu, to expand the selection outline to include pixels similar in color to those already selected.

Grow is like using the Magic Wand with the Contiguous option turned on; only pixels adjacent to selected pixels qualify for inclusion in the new outline. Similar selects pixels throughout the image, like the Magic Wand when the Contiguous check box is turned off. Both Grow and Similar operate according to the Tolerance value currently set for the Magic Wand.

New Selection button

Add

Subtract

Intersect

Figure 3-14: You can use Options bar controls to set a selection tool to add or subtract pixels from an existing selection outline.

For more about the Magic Wand, see the earlier section "Selecting areas of similar color."

✔ **Smooth a selection outline:** The Select⇨Modify⇨Smooth command rounds off any sharp edges in a selection outline. After choosing the command, you can specify the amount of smoothing by entering a Smooth value in the resulting dialog box. The higher the value, the more rounded the edges of your selection outline become.

✔ **Reverse a selection outline:** With some photos, you may find that it's easier to select the area that you don't want to edit than to select the pixels you do want to change. You can then *inverse* — technospeak for *reverse* — the selection outline so that everything that previously was selected becomes deselected and vice versa.

For an example of a selection task that lends itself to this technique, look again at Figure 3-14. Suppose that you wanted to select the entire camera. You could create a mask layer and carefully paint around the inside of the camera, being careful to capture the smooth, rounded corners and the knobs that stick out slightly from each side. But because the background of the image contrasts with the camera, an easier option presents itself. Just click the background with the Magic Wand a few times, with the Contiguous option enabled, to select the background. Then inverse the selection to select the camera.

Keep in mind that when you're refining a selection outline, you don't have to stick with the same tool you used to create the initial outline. In fact, most selection tasks call for the use of two or more different tools. After you get some practice with selecting, you'll begin to get a feel for what tools to use to handle each part of a complex selection challenge.

Selecting Everything

On occasion, you may want to make wholesale changes to an image — or, more likely, to everything on a particular image layer. In either case, you usually don't have to mess with any selection tools.

In Elements, when no selection outline exists, your edits automatically apply to everything on the active image layer. To select the layer you want to edit, click the layer name in the Layers palette. If the image contains only one layer, your changes affect the entire image.

However, in order to use some commands, including the Copy command, you must first draw a selection outline that encompasses the entire image. You also must create a selection outline in order to use commands on the Transform menu on a single-layered image.

To create the selection outline quickly, press Ctrl+A (⌘+A). You also can choose Select➪Select All, but that's a lot of bother, so just go ahead and memorize the keyboard shortcut. Almost every photo-editing program uses that same shortcut for selecting the entire image.

Chapter 7 shows you how to use some of the commands on the Transform submenu.

Removing Selection Outlines

To quickly get rid of a selection outline in Elements, you have two options:

✔ Click outside the outline with the Lasso, Rectangular Marquee, or Elliptical Marquee. In order for this technique to work, the New Selection button on the Options bar must be active.

✔ Press Ctrl+D (⌘+D) or choose Select➪Deselect. Again, store the keyboard shortcut in your long-term memory — you'll make use of it often.

Saving and Loading Selection Outlines

Some photo editors, including Photoshop Elements 2.0, enable you to save a selection outline as part of the image file. You can use this option however you create the selection outline; you don't have to use the mask layer technique that I discuss earlier in this chapter.

After creating your selection outline, take these steps to make it part of the image file in Elements 2.0:

1. **Choose Select➪Save Selection.**

   You then see the dialog box shown in Figure 3-15.

2. **Select New from the Selection menu in the dialog box.**

3. **Enter a name for the outline in the Name box.**

   Use a name that will remind you what the outline selects, such as "Bobby's face" or "Dark sky areas."

4. **Click OK to close the dialog box.**

The next time you save a selection outline in the same photo, you can choose to create a new outline by following these same steps. Or you can modify or replace an outline that you previously saved by selecting its name in Step 2. In that case, you get four Operation options. Choose replace to overwrite the existing outline with the new one. The other three Operation options — Add,

Subtract, and Intersect — work the same as outlined in the earlier section, "Adjusting Selection Outlines."

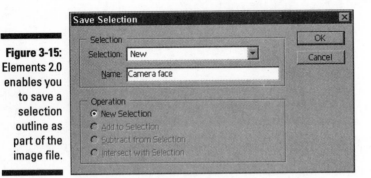

Figure 3-15: Elements 2.0 enables you to save a selection outline as part of the image file.

To reuse a selection that you saved with a photo, choose Select⇨Load Selection. You see a dialog box that looks similar to the Save Selection dialog box. Choose the outline you want to use from the Selection pop-up menu. If you want, you can invert the selection outline by selecting the Invert check box that appears beneath the Selection pop-up menu in this dialog box. When you click OK, the dialog box closes and your selection outline appears in the image window.

If you draw a selection outline before opening the Load Selection dialog box, you can use the Operation options in the dialog box to add, subtract, or intersect the saved outline with the one you just drew.

In order to retain saved selection outlines between editing sessions, you must save the file in the Elements native file format, PSD. See Chapter 2 for information about saving files.

Restoring Selection Outlines

Don't panic if you accidentally wipe out a selection outline and you didn't create the outline via the mask layer technique or didn't save the outline using the Save Selection feature described in the preceding section. The Reselect command, found on the Select menu in Elements, restores your most recent selection outline. You can choose the command quickly by pressing Ctrl+Shift+D (⌘+Shift+D). However, when you close your image, whether you save the image file or not, you lose the chance to restore the outline.

As another option, you may be able to use your photo editor's Undo or Step Backward commands to go back to the point in time where you just created the selection outline. The drawback to this method is that you also undo any edits you made since you drew that outline.

Part II
Makeover Magic

The 5th Wave   By Rich Tennant

©RICHTENNANT

"Well, well! Guess who just lost 9 pixels?"

In this part . . .

Think of this part of the book as one of those makeover episodes that you see on TV talk shows, only with your pictures as the subject of the transformation.

Just as beauty experts use makeup and hair-styling tricks to turn someone from ho-hum to glamorous, you can use the techniques presented in Chapters 4 through 8 to bring out the best in your photographs while at the same time disguising the flaws.

Chapter 4

Correcting Colors

• •

In This Chapter

▶ Understanding how computers create color

▶ Setting foreground and background paint colors

▶ Checking color values using the Info palette

▶ Using layers to make color corrections without changing the original image

▶ Correcting color balance with the Variations and Levels commands

▶ Strengthening weak colors

▶ Turning a color photo into a grayscale image — and vice versa

• •

If you're a person of a certain age — mine — you may remember *Winky Dink and You,* a television cartoon that aired during the 1960s. Winky Dink was great not so much because of characters or plot, but because the production team behind the black-and-white program sold a kit that enabled their young viewers to colorize the show. You attached this special sheet of plastic to your television screen and then used "magic" crayons to color Winky Dink and pals.

I recently learned that we kids were instructed to draw tools and other devices that would help Winky Dink get out of whatever jam he was in during an episode. I don't recall this educational aspect of the show — I just thought it would be fun to turn black-and-white pictures into color images. Sadly, I never got the official Winky Dink screen, and I discovered that using my mother's plastic kitchen wrap was an unacceptable substitute, not to mention unpopular with my mother. (At least I was smart enough not to color directly on the TV screen, like some kids did.)

To all my fellow Winky Dink fans, whether or not you were one of the lucky kids who got the coloring kit, this chapter is especially for you. In it, you can discover more ways to manipulate color than Winky Dink ever imagined. Instead of a plastic overlay and magic crayons, you can use your photo software's color tools to add, remove, and shift colors wherever and however your creative eye sees fit. And with these color tools, you can print your handiwork as well as enjoy it on-screen.

Winky Dink would be so proud.

Winky Dink would also want you to check out Chapters 8 and 9, which feature additional color excitement.

Seeing Color in a New Way

As a grade-school student, you probably learned how to mix red, yellow, and blue paints — sometimes known as *primary colors* — to make other colors. Red plus yellow makes orange; yellow plus blue makes green; red plus blue makes purple; and so on.

When you work with digital color, you need to throw all those color-combination rules out the window — or, at least, put them on the window ledge, away from your immediate field of vision. Digital devices make color by mixing red, green, and blue light, which requires a different way of thinking about combining colors.

Color gurus use the term *color model* or *color space* to refer to a method of mixing a set of primary colors to create a spectrum of other colors. For example, the color model based on red, green, and blue light is called the RGB color model. The other commonly known color model, CMYK, uses as its primary colors cyan, magenta, yellow, and black, the traditional ink colors used in commercial offset printing and in most consumer inkjet printers.

The next few sections give you the basics of RGB color theory. You don't need to memorize this stuff, but understanding the fundamentals will help you take better advantage of the color tools available in your photo software.

Exploring RGB color

As I mentioned a few paragraphs ago, digital devices such as computer monitors, digital cameras, scanners, televisions, and digital projectors all create colors by mixing red, green, and blue light. And every color in a digital image can be described by the brightness of its red, green, and blue components.

In the digital imaging world, brightness values are measured on a scale from 0 to 255 (for 256 total steps), with 0 being the complete absence of light and 255 being the maximum brightness. By combining the red, green, and blue brightness values in different proportions, you can create more than 16.7 million colors. (256 x 256 x 256 = 16,777,216.) For example, the formulas for black and white are:

- 0 red + 0 green + 0 blue = black
- 255 red + 255 green + 255 blue = white

Those two are pretty obvious. And if you're really on the ball, you can probably guess that equal parts red, green, and blue in any amount produces a shade of gray. But predicting brightness values for the other millions of colors isn't as easy — at least, not until you get familiar with thinking about color as a product of light.

For example, take a look at Color Plate 4-1. In the photo, I centered my cursor over each of the four feather areas marked by the white boxes. Next to the photo, you see the Photoshop Elements Info palette, which you can set up to display the RGB brightness values for the image area under your cursor. From top to bottom, the Info palettes in Color Plate 4-1 show the RGB values for the sampled red, blue, yellow, and green areas.

To find out how to customize your Info palette display, see the upcoming section "Monitoring Colors in the Info Palette."

You could reasonably expect that the red feathers around the neck would have a pretty high red value, although you may not expect any green or blue to be present. Ditto for the blue feathers — a high blue brightness value makes sense. But most people wouldn't guess that the yellowish feathers represent high red and green values, with zero blue. In paint mixing, red and green make brown, right? Not so when you use light as your color generator.

Similarly, you may be surprised to see that the green feathers actually contain lots of blue and red light, when at first glance they appear to be a pure green. In reality, full intensity green, with zero red and blue, is almost a neon green.

Fortunately, today's photo editing programs don't require you to calculate RGB formulas to select colors; instead, you can blend colors using visual displays like the one in the dialog box shown on the left in Color Plate 4-2. But getting familiar with RGB color-mixing is helpful when you're correcting color-balance problems because you have some idea what colors you need to add or subtract to arrive at the right hues.

The section "Setting the Foreground and Background Colors," later in this chapter, explains how to mix a custom paint color.

Digging deeper into color models

RGB, the color model of light, and CMYK, the color model of ink, are just two of several color models used in digital imaging and publishing. Another commonly used color model is HSB, which defines colors based on hue, saturation, and brightness, which is closest to how we humans perceive color. The color filters in many photo-editing programs, including some filters discussed later in this chapter, are based on the HSB model. A fourth color model, Lab, defines colors based on lightness and position within two color ranges (green to red and blue to yellow).

To see how these four color models compare, see Color Plate 4-2. The left side of the color plate shows the Adobe Photoshop Color Picker, where you select your paint tools' foreground and background colors. The Photoshop Color Picker displays the RGB, HSB, Lab, and CMYK values for the selected color — orange — in the color plate. The Color Picker also shows the numeric code assigned to the color in the HTML programming language, which is used to create Web pages. (The Photoshop Elements Color Picker looks exactly like the one in Color Plate 4-2 except that it lacks the Lab and CMYK options.)

Again, understanding the math behind any of the color models isn't important to the average digital imaging enthusiast. In fact, unless you're doing high-end color corrections and working in Adobe Photoshop, you can ignore Lab altogether. Lab is a professional's color model; most image-editing programs, including Elements, can't open Lab images. Even in Photoshop, you can't use some editing tools on Lab images.

What you *should* take away from this little side trip into color theory is the following tidbit: Each color model encompasses a precise color spectrum, or *gamut* (say it *gam-mutt*). And as it turns out, RGB and HSB produce a wider spectrum than CMYK, the printing color model.

The most vivid RGB and HSB colors just can't be reproduced by putting ink on paper, which is why what you get from your printer may not exactly match what you see on-screen. When your printer encounters a color that it can't print, it substitutes the closest printable color, and the result is a printed image that usually looks duller than its on-screen counterpart.

Colors that a printer can't reproduce are said to be *out of gamut,* by the way.

The Photoshop Color Picker alerts you when a color is outside the CMYK gamut, as shown in Color Plate 4-2. That little warning triangle to the left of the Cancel button is the out-of-gamut alert. If you're using Elements or some other photo editor that doesn't offer a gamut warning feature, just keep in mind that the most brilliant hues in your paint box may lose some intensity when printed.

Chapter 10 offers some additional insights on color printing, including tips for getting the closest possible match between the colors you see on-screen and the ones that your printer produces.

Looking at color channels

When you mix different shades of paint to create a custom color for a home redecorating project, the individual colors merge into one new shade. If you screw up the color, you can't separate the colors out and start over.

Bits of color

Techie types sometimes describe digital color palettes in terms of *bits* or *bit depth.* A bit is a single unit of computer data and can represent two values. The more bits you have, the higher the bit depth, and the more colors you can create:

✔ 1-bit images can contain only two colors, black and white.

✔ 8-bit images can contain 256 colors.

✔ 16-bit images can contain 32,000 colors.

✔ 24-bit images can contain roughly 16.7 million colors.

For more about bit depth as it relates to scanners, see Chapter 2.

By contrast, the primary colors in an RGB image always retain their independence. The brightness data for the red, green, and blue components reside in separate parts of the image file, in virtual paint cans known as *channels*. To display the color for any one pixel, the computer dips into each channel to check the brightness data, but the three values remain separated in the image file.

When you display or print a single color channel, you get a grayscale image, as shown in Color Plate 4-3. If you're new to digital imaging, you may have been expecting a red picture from the red channel, a green image from the green channel, and a blue scene from the blue channel. But remember, each channel holds only brightness values, using that scale of 0 (no light) to 255 (maximum light) that I introduced earlier in this chapter. The actual composite color of each pixel isn't manufactured until your computer's brain adds up the brightness values from all three channels.

In Photoshop and other high-end photo editors, you can view and manipulate independent color channels, which can come in handy for some advanced imaging techniques. In Elements, although you can't display or print the red, green, and blue channels individually, you can tweak color balance by adjusting the brightness levels in a single channel. The upcoming section "Balancing colors channel by channel" explains this technique.

Setting the Foreground and Background Colors

During the fascinating journey into color theory that I led you on in the preceding sections, I brought up the topic of mixing digital paint colors several times. Although you don't need to blend custom colors to do any of the corrections discussed in the rest of this chapter, I want to cover the subject now while all that color science is still fresh in your mind. (If you started reading here, you may want to skim through those earlier sections so that you can better understand what's going on when I sling around terms like RGB and HSB.)

In most photo-editing programs, you can stroke paint on a photo using a variety of tools. For retouching purposes, you may want to turn to these tools for such tasks as removing red-eye and bringing color back into washed-out skin, as illustrated in Chapter 8. The paint tools also come in handy for creating some special effects, such as "hand-tinting" a grayscale photo, a topic covered in Chapter 9. You select the paint color by setting the *foreground color* or *background color*, depending on which tool you want to use. Some tools apply the foreground color, while others apply the background color. In Photoshop Elements, the breakdown is as follows:

✔ In Elements 1.0, the Paintbrush, Pencil, Airbrush, Shape (Line, Rectangle, and so on), and Paint Bucket apply the foreground color. The left toolbox in Figure 4-1 offers a map to these tools.

✔ In Elements 2.0, the Paintbrush tool goes by the shortened name of Brush tool and is positioned to the left of the Pencil instead of above it as in Elements 1.0. The Airbrush is no longer provided as a separate tool in the toolbox but instead is available as an option when working with the Brush tool. The Version 2.0 toolbox appears in the right side of Figure 4-1.

✔ In both versions of the program, the Eraser applies the background color, but only when you're erasing on the bottom layer of an image. (By default, the bottom layer is named *Background*.) Otherwise, the Eraser wipes pixels clean, making them transparent.

The color swatches at the bottom of the toolbox reflect the current foreground and background colors, as shown in Figure 4-1. Black is the default foreground color; white is the default background color. To change either color, you can use the Eyedropper tool, Color Picker dialog box, or Swatches palette. The next three sections show you how.

Press D to return to the default foreground and background colors; press X to swap the foreground and background colors. Or click the default and swap icons in the toolbox (see Figure 4-1).

Matching a color in your photo

With the Eyedropper tool, labeled in Figure 4-1, you can "lift" a color from your photo to use as the foreground or background color. To activate the Eyedropper, click its toolbox icon or press the I key. With the Eyedropper in hand, you can set the foreground and background colors as follows:

Checking monitor color settings

Before you begin working on the color aspects of your photo, be sure that your computer's video card and monitor are set up to properly display them. With most systems, you can choose to display 8-bit color (256 colors), 16-bit color (32,000 colors), or 24-bit color (approximately 16.7 million colors). You may see the latter two settings referred to as *high color* and *true color*, respectively.

Obviously, you need to see all the colors in your image, which means that you need 24-bit color. Check your computer manual to find out how to check and change your monitor settings — the process varies depending on your operating system, monitor, and video card.

Note that the more colors you ask the system to display, the more you tax the computer's resources. If you experience problems, you may need to upgrade your video card, system memory (RAM), or both. Also try setting the monitor display to a lower screen resolution — for example, if you're using a screen resolution of 1280 x 1024, lower it to 800 x 600.

For more details about screen resolution, see Chapter 2.

✔ To set the foreground color, click in the image window on the color you want to use.

✔ To set the background color, Alt+click (Option+click) instead.

When you select the Eyedropper, the Options bar contains a single control: the Sample Size menu. The three options found on this menu enable you to adjust the Eyedropper's take on the color that you click, as follows:

✔ When set to Point Sample, the Eyedropper looks only at the pixel you click to determine the color. Use this option to perfectly match the pixel that you click.

✔ When set to 3 x 3 Average, the tool looks at a 3 x 3-pixel area centered on the pixel that you click and then averages the colors of those 9 pixels.

✔ The 5 x 5 Average option works the same as the 3 x 3 Average option but considers the color values of a larger grid of pixels.

When you're working with the Paintbrush (Brush in Version 2.0), Pencil, Airbrush, or one of the Shape tools, you can temporarily access the Eyedropper and establish a new foreground color by pressing the Alt (Option) key and clicking in the image. When you release the Alt (Option) key, your paint tool becomes active again.

If you think you may need to use the same color again, add a swatch for the color to the Swatches palette. For details, see "Storing colors in the Swatches palette," later in this chapter.

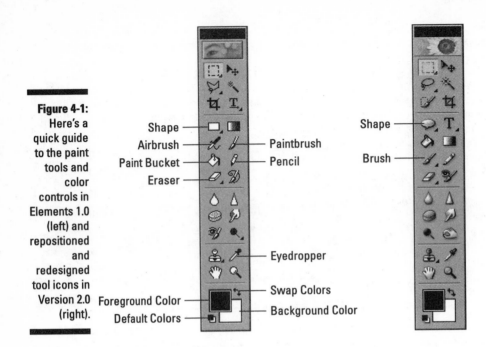

Figure 4-1:
Here's a
quick guide
to the paint
tools and
color
controls in
Elements 1.0
(left) and
repositioned
and
redesigned
tool icons in
Version 2.0
(right).

Shape

Airbrush ——— Paintbrush

Paint Bucket ——— Pencil

Eraser

Shape

Brush

Eyedropper

Swap Colors

Foreground Color

Background Color

Default Colors

Mixing colors in the Color Picker

Mixing a custom paint color in Elements requires a trip to the Color Picker dialog box, shown in Figure 4-2. To open the dialog box, click the foreground or background color swatch in the toolbox, depending on which color you want to set.

If you see the standard Windows or Macintosh operating system color picker instead of the one shown in the figure, choose Edit⇨Preferences⇨General to display the Preferences dialog box. Then select Adobe from the Color Picker pop-up menu in the dialog box. Elements enables you to choose between its own color picker and the system version; I recommend that you go with the Adobe version.

If you know the HSB or RGB values for the color you want to use, enter those values in the appropriate boxes and press Enter. Otherwise, you can select a paint color by clicking or dragging in the color slider and color field, both labeled in Figure 4-2.

You can customize the slider and color field by clicking one of the options to the right of the slider. (You can click on the letter or the adjacent circular button, known in computer lingo as a *radio button*.) The slider represents the color component that corresponds to the selected option, and the color field represents the other two components. For example, in Figure 4-2, the H option is selected, so the color slider represents the Hue value, and the color field represents the Saturation and Brightness values. (Most people find this setup the most intuitive.)

When you work with the HSB model, it helps to understand that the Hue values are based on a *color wheel,* a graph that plots out colors on a 360-degree circle. You can see the color wheel on the right side of Color Plate 4-2. As shown in the color plate, Red takes the 0-degree position (or 360 degrees, if you prefer). Green lives at 120 degrees, and blue resides at 240 degrees. Yellow lies directly opposite blue, at 60 degrees; magenta lies opposite green, at 300 degrees; and cyan lies opposite red, at 180 degrees. By raising the H value, you move the color clockwise around the color wheel; lowering the value shifts the color counterclockwise.

Regardless of how you set up the Color Picker's slider and color field, the top color swatch (labeled *New color* in Figure 4-2) shows the custom color you've made. The bottom swatch (labeled *Current color*) displays the color that was in effect when you opened the dialog box. When you get the new color just right, click OK or press Enter to close the dialog box.

What's a "Web-safe" color?

One of the biggest challenges that a Web designer faces is the lack of control over how a particular color appears on a viewer's monitor. As explained in the sidebar "Checking monitor color settings," most computer systems enable the user to switch between several color settings, each of which results in a different number of viewable colors. If you view a Web page on a system operating at the lowest color setting — typically 256 colors — and the page contains colors outside that spectrum, the Web browser mixes two available colors to try to create the extra colors. This process is known as *dithering,* and it usually leads to splotchy-looking images.

Complicating the situation, the base set of colors in the 256-shade palette is different on a Windows-based computer than on a Macintosh system. So the same Web page may look altogether different on a PC than on a Mac!

In an attempt to gain a little color consistency, the Web community established a *Web-safe palette.* The palette is a collection of 216 colors that are common to all major system palettes and therefore should look the same no matter what setup is used to view the Web page. When you're creating text and simple graphics for a Web page, staying within the Web-safe palette is a good idea.

When you're working with photographs, however, a 216-color limit is rarely practical; you simply need more shades than that to produce an acceptable image. Even reducing a photo to 256 colors leads to blotchiness, as you can see in the lower-right example in Color Plate 10-1. So most Web designers stick with full-color images and simply hope that the majority of people who visit the site do so with their monitors set to display high color (32,000 colors) or true color (16.7 million colors).

New color

Color field   Current color   Web safe alert

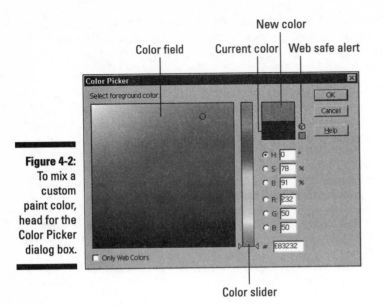

Figure 4-2:
To mix a
custom
paint color,
head for the
Color Picker
dialog box.

Color slider

If you plan on using your picture on a Web page, you may want to select the Only Web Colors check box at the bottom of the Color Picker. The color field and slider change to limit you to colors in the 256-color Web-safe palette. When you don't have the check box enabled, an alert box appears if you define a color outside the Web-safe palette, as shown in Figure 4-2. If you're unfamiliar with this issue, see the sidebar "What's a Web-safe color?"

Storing colors in the Swatches palette

The Swatches palette gives you quick access to a basic array of colors. Figure 4-3 shows the Elements 1.0 Swatches palette; the Version 2.0 palette has a slightly different design but offers the same essential controls.

To display the palette, click the palette tab in the palette well or choose Window⇨Show Swatches in Version 1.0; choose (Window⇨Color Swatches in Version 2.0. You can then set the foreground and background colors as follows:

✔ Click a swatch to make that color the foreground color. Any tool can be active when you do this. As soon as you move your cursor into the palette, the Eyedropper tool cursor temporarily appears.

✔ In Elements 1.0, Alt+click (Option+click) a swatch to set the background color. In 2.0, you must instead Ctrl+click (⌘+click).

TIP

Although choosing colors this way involves fewer steps than using the Color Picker, the Swatches palette doesn't give you access to a very broad selection of colors. The real benefit of the palette is that you can store custom-blended colors in it so that you don't have to go through the process of mixing them again the next time you need them.

For example, suppose that in preparation for doing a little facial touch-up work, you blend a paint color that perfectly matches your subject's skin. After doing the skin repairs, you move on to something else. But later, you discover that you need to do more work to the skin. If you stored the touch-up color in the Swatches palette, you can just click its swatch to restore it as the foreground color.

The following steps show you the easiest way to add a swatch for the current foreground color:

1. **Move your cursor over an empty spot in the swatches area.**

   Your cursor changes into a little paint bucket, as shown in Figure 4-3.

2. **Click to create the swatch.**

   You also can click the New Swatch button at the bottom of the palette to add a swatch. Either way, a dialog box appears, giving you the chance to name the color. When you later pause your cursor over the swatch, the program displays the name you entered. (The label appears only if you select the Show Tool Tips option on the General panel of the Preferences dialog box. To display the panel, choose Edit⇨Preferences⇨General.)

Figure 4-3:
Click an empty area in the Swatches palette to add a swatch for the current foreground color.

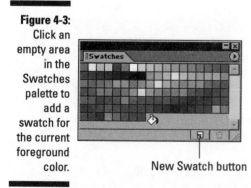

New Swatch button

If you want to add a swatch for the current background color, you must first swap the foreground and background colors. (Press X to do it quickly.) After you add the swatch, swap the colors again to return to the original foreground/background color setup.

To delete unneeded swatches, you use the opposite clicking maneuver that you use to select the background color. In Elements 1.0, Ctrl+click (⌘+click) the swatch; in Elements 2.0, Alt+click (Option+click) the swatch. A little scissors cursor appears to show you that you're about to cut out the swatch.

If you create swatches that you want to be able to reuse in future editing sessions, you may want to create and save a custom swatch library by using the Elements Preset Manager. The software's manual explains how to create and manage swatch libraries.

Note that the program ships with several swatch libraries; the default library is named, coincidentally, Default. You can load different libraries by choosing them from the palette menu in Version 1.0 (click the triangle at the top of the palette) and from the Select a Swatch pop-up menu at the top of the palette in Version 2.0.

If you add a custom swatch and then load a different library, you lose your custom swatch unless you save it as part of a swatch library. Again, refer to the software's manual to find out how to save a custom swatch.

Monitoring Colors in the Info Palette

The Info palette, shown in Figure 4-4, gives you a convenient way to check the RGB and HSB values of a color in your image. To display the Info palette, choose Window⇨Show Info or click the palette's tab in the palette well. Pause your cursor over a color in the image window to display the values for the color in the palette.

When you make an adjustment inside a color or exposure-adjustment dialog box and move your cursor into the image window (with the dialog box still open), you see two numbers for each value, as shown in Figure 4-4. The left number shows the original value, and the right number shows the value that you get if you apply the adjustment at the current settings. In the figure, my cursor is located at the spot labeled *Sampled color*. The "after" values in the Info palette reflect the fact that I've raised the Hue value 25 degrees in the Hue/Saturation dialog box, spinning the color clockwise around the color wheel.

If you need a refresher course in the color wheel setup, flip back to "Mixing colors in the Color Picker," earlier in this chapter. Chapter 9 offers more information about shifting colors by altering the Hue value in the Hue/Saturation dialog box.

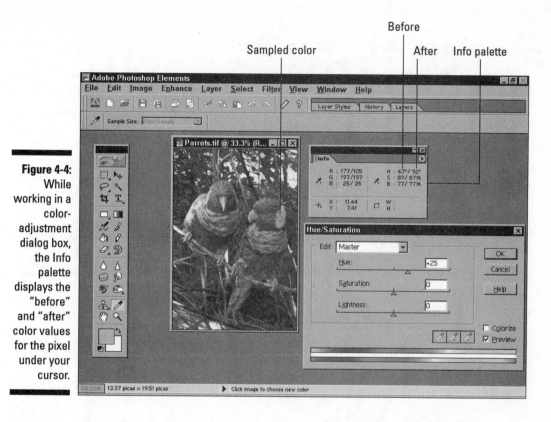

Sampled color   Before   After   Info palette

Figure 4-4:
While
working in a
color-
adjustment
dialog box,
the Info
palette
displays the
"before"
and "after"
color values
for the pixel
under your
cursor.

I use the Info palette most often to monitor the effects of color and exposure corrections, especially when I'm working on two related photos. For example, if I have two pictures of the same person and I want the skin tones to be approximately the same in both pictures, I open both images and compare the Info palette values for a few different facial areas. Although my eye is sometimes fooled by what I see on the monitor, I can rely on the Info palette to tell me the real story.

As shown in Figure 4-4, you can display values for two different color models in the Info palette. To specify the color models, click the arrow at the top of the palette (found on the More button in Elements 2.0) and choose Palette Options from the resulting palette menu. You then see the Palette Options dialog box, shown in Figure 4-5. Select the color models from the two Mode menus. (Note that the Actual Color option delivers the same results as choosing the image's current color mode. In most cases, that will be RGB if you're working with a color image in Elements.)

The lower-left box in the Info palette displays the X and Y coordinates for your cursor, and the lower-right box shows the dimensions of the current selection outline, if one is active. You can set the unit of measure for these two readouts by selecting an option from the Ruler Units menu in the Palette Options dialog box.

Help! This dialog box/palette/toolbox is in the way!

As you work on a photo, your view of the image may be obscured by an open dialog box, palette, or toolbox. You can move the offending element out of the way by dragging it by the bar that runs across its top. (We geeks refer to this area as a *title bar,* even though you may not see an actual title in the bar.) Alternatively, relocate the image window itself, again by dragging its title bar.

Unfortunately, in most cases you can't move a toolbox, palette, or image window while a dialog box is open. So if moving the dialog box itself doesn't reveal the image area you need to see, you have to close the dialog box, rearrange things as necessary, and then head back to the dialog box. (Click Cancel to close a dialog box without making any changes to the image.)

For a quick way to hide all open palettes, the toolbox, and the Options bar in Photoshop Elements, press Tab. Press Tab again to bring everything back into view. But again, this trick doesn't work when a dialog box is open.

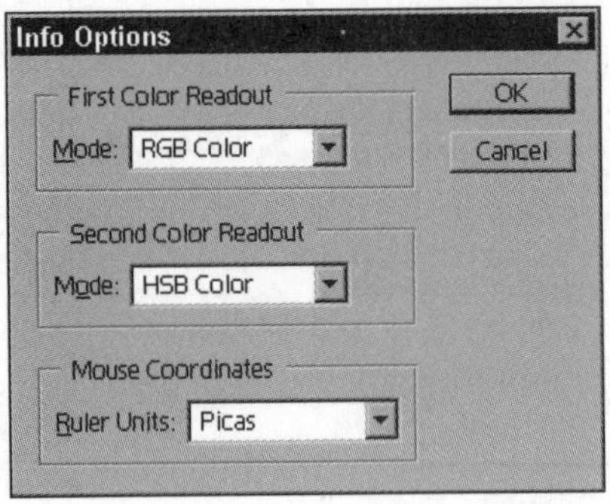

Figure 4-5:
Customize
the Info
palette
display
here.

Info Options

First Color Readout
Mode: RGB Color

Second Color Readout
Mode: HSB Color

Mouse Coordinates
Ruler Units: Picas

OK
Cancel

Safely Editing Colors Using Layers

Adjusting colors is one of the trickiest jobs a photo retoucher can do, not because the actual techniques and commands are difficult to use, but because so many factors can influence how colors appear on-screen. A change in ambient light or in the angle at which you're viewing the screen can cause colors that looked dead-on five minutes ago to suddenly look horrible. Fatigued eyes may perceive colors differently than a refreshed set of peepers. And colors that look incredible on your computer monitor may come out of the printer looking totally wrong.

I share these discouraging words so that when you encounter your own color conundrums — and you will — you can at least take heart in knowing that you're in good company. At the same time you're snarling "That face looked *perfect* when I saved this image yesterday, and now it looks *orange* and prints *red!*", well, I'm likely singing a similar refrain, as are countless photo-editing brethren around the world.

In addition to this psychological pat on the back, I can offer a practical tip that will make your color-correction work easier and less stressful. Just make your changes on a separate layer from the rest of the image.

Chapter 3 introduces the concept of layers, but here's a brief recap: Layers are like clear sheets of acetate stacked one atop another. You can put different image elements on different layers and then edit one layer without affecting anything on the other layers.

When it comes to color corrections, you can make use of layers in two ways, which the next sections explain.

Using adjustment layers

An *adjustment layer*, a feature available in Photoshop Elements and Photoshop, does just what it implies: enables you to make color adjustments on a layer that's separate from the rest of the image. Clear as mud, right?

Well, think of it like this: An adjustment layer works like a filter on a camera lens. Just as you can use filters to add warmth, contrast, and other color effects to a shot, you can apply an adjustment layer to fiddle with the colors, brightness, and contrast in your image. This approach offers a number of benefits:

- Just as with a lens filter, you can remove an adjustment layer at any time if you decide you don't like the effect. Your original image remains unaltered.

- You can vary the impact of the correction by varying the layer blending mode or opacity of the adjustment layer, as explained in "Adjusting an adjustment layer," later in this chapter.

- You can correct multiple image layers at once. If you apply a correction without an adjustment layer, your change affects only the current image layer. But an adjustment layer affects all layers underneath it. You can even affect only selected pixels throughout a stack of layers by creating a selection outline before creating the adjustment layer.

- After you apply an adjustment layer, you can use the Eraser tool to rub away parts of the layer, thereby removing the correction from areas underneath the erased regions. In addition, you can paint on the adjustment layer to extend the correction to previously unaltered pixels.

- You can copy an adjustment layer from one image to another by simply dragging the layer from the Layers palette into the second image window. This trick can be a big time-saver when you have a batch of images that all suffer from the same problem.

In Photoshop Elements, you can apply several color- and exposure-correction commands via an adjustment layer, with the most useful being Levels and Hue/Saturation. Later sections in this chapter explain those two commands; the next two sections explain how to create and edit adjustment layers in general.

If you want to sound like a digital imaging professional, use the word *filter* when referring to a program command that applies a color, exposure, or focus correction. Commands that create special effects also get this label.

If you're using a photo editor that does not offer the equivalent of adjustment layers, see the upcoming section "Editing on a duplicate layer" to find out how you can enjoy some of the same flexibility that adjustment layers provide. That section also explains how to safely apply color corrections that can't be applied via an adjustment layer in Elements.

Adding an adjustment layer

To add an adjustment layer in Photoshop Elements, take these steps:

1. **In the Layers palette, click the name of the topmost layer you want to correct.**

   If you don't want a particular layer to receive the correction, drag it to the top of the Layers palette and click the layer underneath to set the position of the adjustment layer.

   You also can confine the effects of an adjustment layer to a set of layers by creating a *layer group.* That topic's beyond the scope of this book, but if you're interested, you can find details in the Elements manual and Help system.

2. **Select the area you want to alter.**

   If you want to change only specific areas of the image, use the selection techniques described in Chapter 3 to create a selection outline. If you don't select anything, all pixels on all layers under the adjustment layer are affected.

   Keep in mind that after you create an adjustment layer, you can use the techniques explained in the upcoming section "Adjusting an adjustment layer" to expand the adjustment into previously unselected areas. Similarly, you can remove the adjustment from previously selected regions.

3. **Choose Layer⇨New Adjustment Layer and choose the filter you want to apply.**

   You see a dialog box named New Layer. Accept the default settings and press Enter or click OK to close the New Layer dialog box. (You can change the dialog box options later if you want.) Your adjustment layer appears in the Layers palette, as shown in Figure 4-6, and the related filter dialog box opens.

For a quicker route to an adjustment layer, click the New Adjustment Layer button, labeled in Figure 4-6, and choose the filter name from the resulting pop-up menu. When you go this route, you bypass the New Layer dialog box.

4. **Apply the filter settings and click OK or press Enter.**

If you're not happy with the results of the filter, you can adjust the effect by using the techniques outlined in the next section.

Figure 4-6:
Adjustment
layers
protect your
image from
being
permanently
altered by a
color
correction.

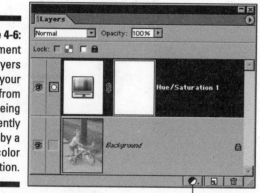

New Adjustment Layer button

Adjusting an adjustment layer

After you create an adjustment layer, you can really explore the power of this method of applying correction filters. You can tweak the filter's impact in several ways:

↙ To reopen the filter dialog box and change the filter settings, double-click the dialog box thumbnail in the Layers palette. I labeled the thumbnail in Figure 4-7.

You can also reduce the strength of the filter by lowering the Opacity value at the top of the Layers palette. Be sure to first make the adjustment layer active by clicking its name in the Layers palette. The layer name becomes highlighted, as shown in Figure 4-7.

↙ Also experiment with different blending modes, which control how pixels in one layer mix with those in the underlying layers. With the adjustment layer active, choose an option from the Blending Mode menu at the top of the Layers palette. The most helpful modes for image correction are Multiply, Screen, and Overlay.

Eraser

Blending Mode menu

Dialog Box thumbnail

Mask thumbnail

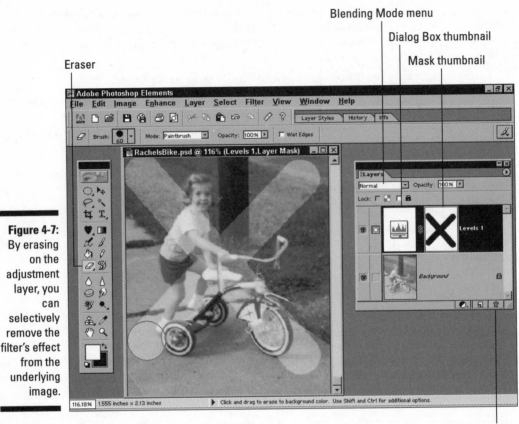

Figure 4-7:
By erasing
on the
adjustment
layer, you
can
selectively
remove the
filter's effect
from the
underlying
image.

Trash button

If you want to keep the effect for some areas but lose it for others, you don't need to draw a new selection outline and reapply the filter. Instead, you can simply edit the adjustment layer's *mask*.

As first explained in Chapter 3, a mask is like a protective coating that prevents an alteration from affecting the image. When you create an adjustment layer, the program automatically creates a *mask* that determines which areas on underlying layers receive the filter effect. The initial mask corresponds to the selection outline that you drew prior to creating the adjustment layer. If you didn't create a selection outline, the entire layer is automatically selected, and nothing is masked.

In the Layers palette, the mask is represented in the mask thumbnail, labeled in Figure 4-7. White areas indicate pixels that are unmasked and thus currently affected by the filter. Black areas represent pixels that are masked and not affected by the filter.

To edit the mask — and thereby reduce or expand the area affected by the filter — all you do is paint on the adjustment layer with white or black. White paint removes a mask; black paint applies a mask.

First, click the adjustment layer name in the Layers palette. Now set the foreground color to white and the background color to black, as shown in Figure 4-7. (The program does this automatically for you the first time you click an adjustment layer, but if you swapped the two colors during a prior adjustment-layer editing session, you may need to reset the colors. You can do so quickly by pressing D.)

With white as the foreground color and black as the background color, you can edit the mask as follows:

✔ To unmask an area so that it receives the filter, switch to the Paintbrush (Brush in Elements 2.0) and drag over the area in the image window. The mask thumbnail updates as you paint, with areas corresponding to your paint strokes turning white.

✔ To mask an area and prevent it from being altered by the filter, drag over it in the image window with the Eraser tool, labeled in Figure 4-7. On an adjustment layer, the Eraser applies the background color, which is currently black. In Figure 4-7, I erased a big X through the middle of the photo, which added a mask to those areas. Wherever I added the mask, the exposure correction applied via the Levels adjustment layer has no effect, as you can see in the image window.

Remember to set the tool opacity to 100 percent (using the Opacity control on the Options bar) if you want to completely mask or unmask an area; at a lower opacity, the tool only partially adds or removes the mask. For example, if you add a mask with the Eraser set to 50 percent opacity, the filter is applied at 50 percent strength, just as if you set the opacity of the adjustment layer to 50 percent in the Layers palette.

Although the program sets up the foreground and background colors to assist you with using the Eraser and Paintbrush to edit a mask, you can achieve the same results by using any tool or command that applies white or black paint. If you want to mask a square area of the image, for example, you can draw a square selection outline and then using the Fill command to fill the square with black. You can even use the Gradient tool to fill the adjustment layer with a white-to-black gradient, which results in a mask that starts at full opacity and then gradually fades out.

For information on the Fill command and the Gradient tool, see Chapter 9. To find out how to adjust tool opacity and other tool characteristics, check out Chapter 6.

After you modify the mask, click any other image layer to return to the foreground and background colors that were active before you clicked the mask layer.

If you totally screw up an adjustment layer and just want to trash the thing and start over, drag the layer to the Trash button in the Layers palette.

Saving and merging adjustment layers

Although I've provided you with only the sketchiest of lessons in adjustment layers, I hope that you can at least begin to see the advantages they offer. The more you experiment, the more ways you'll discover to make use of the feature.

Remember that if you want to retain independent image layers and adjustment layers in Elements and Photoshop, you must save the image file in the PSD format, with the Layers check box in the Save As dialog box turned on. For more about saving layers, see Chapter 3.

When you're completely finished with your image corrections, you may want to merge all layers into one to reduce the image file size. To do so, choose Layer⇨Flatten Image.

Editing on a duplicate layer

Not all color corrections can be made with adjustment layers, unfortunately. For example, you can't apply the Variations filter, used to balance colors, as an adjustment layer. (See the upcoming section "Tweaking color with Variations" for details about that filter.) And of course, not all photo editing programs offer adjustment layers in the first place.

That doesn't mean you can't enjoy most of the same flexibility and convenience that adjustment layers offer, however. The trick is to duplicate the layer you want to edit and apply your changes just to that duplicate layer. You can use this technique in any program that offers layers.

In Photoshop and Elements, follow these steps to work with a layer safety net:

1. **In the Layers palette, drag the layer you want to edit to the New Layer button, as shown in Figure 4-8.**

   Dragging a layer to the button duplicates the layer and places the duplicate immediately above the original, as shown in the figure.

2. **With the duplicate layer active, apply your edits.**

   As long you set the layer blending mode to Normal and the Opacity value to 100 percent, as shown in the right palette in Figure 4-8, your edited layer completely obscures the original. Now you can experiment with freedom. If you don't like an effect or series of changes, just trash the duplicate layer and start over.

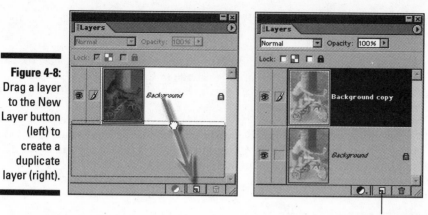

Figure 4-8:
Drag a layer
to the New
Layer button
(left) to
create a
duplicate
layer (right).

New Layer button

Additionally, you can play with the duplicate layer's blending mode and opacity settings to mix the edited layer with the original to achieve different effects.

3. When you're finished with your image, choose Layer⇨Flatten Image.

All your layers get merged into one, reducing the image file size.

The only reason *not* to use this technique is if your computer complains that it's running low on system resources. (In Photoshop and Photoshop Elements, the complaint mentions a lack of space in the scratch disk.) Additional layers mean more strain on your computer, and if you're working with a very large image file or puny computer system, you may not be able to take advantage of the safety and convenience that layers provide. In that case, just be sure to work on a copy of your original image file.

If system resources allow, you can even segregate different steps of your retouching or restoration to individual layers. For example, if you need to color balance and sharpen an image, duplicate the original image layer and apply the color changes on the duplicate layer. Then duplicate the color-corrected layer and sharpen focus on that second duplicated layer.

I always do my sharpening on a duplicate layer because sharpening is one of those corrections that can look great when you first see it and then bug the heck out of you later on. Keeping the correction on its own layer enables me to undo the sharpening (by trashing the layer) at any time, long after I've saved the image to disk. I can also reduce the amount of sharpening just by lowering the opacity of the sharpened layer. (Chapter 5 explains sharpening in detail.)

Fixing Color Balance Problems

When an image has an unhealthy amount of one or more colors, it's said to have a *color balance* problem. The original image in Color Plate 4-4 is a perfect example of out-of-whack colors. Over time, deterioration of this 1950s print caused a serious overdose of red.

In modern photographs, color balance problems typically occur when the camera can't deal with tricky lighting conditions. If you take a picture in an office building, for example, fluorescent lights may cause a sickly green tint. I've also gotten prints back from the photo lab and discovered that the skin tones are way off, thanks to automatic color "correction" that most labs do when processing consumer films.

Whatever the cause, you can use the techniques outlined in the next two sections to address color casts. The first section introduces you to the Variations filter, a color-correction filter found in Photoshop Elements and many other photo editing programs. The second section shows you how to use another common filter, Levels, to fix color casts by playing with the red, green, and blue color channels.

Tweaking color with Variations

For most people, the Variations filter provides the most intuitive way to correct colors. You can balance colors by clicking thumbnail previews in a filter dialog box like the one shown in Figure 4-9 and Color Plate 4-4. I refer to these thumbnails as *color-shift thumbnails* for lack of a more inspired name. Both the figure and the color plate show the dialog box as it appears in Photoshop Elements 1.0; the dialog box sports a new design in Elements 2.0 but contains the same basic controls.

The Variations filter works according to the 360-degree color wheel shown in Color Plate 4-2 and described earlier in this chapter in the section "Mixing colors in the Color Picker." When you click one of the color-shift thumbnails, you add more of that color and subtract its opposite. For example, if you click the More Blue thumbnail, you add blue and subtract yellow.

In Photoshop Elements, you apply the Variations filter as outlined in the following steps. You can adjust image shadows, highlights, and *midtones* (areas of medium brightness) independently, all with one trip to the dialog box. The feature works the same way in most other image-editing programs, although it may go by another name.

As always, remember that you can limit the effect of your changes to a certain area of the image by creating a selection outline before applying the Variations filter. Applying the filter to a duplicate of the layer that you want to change is also a good safety measure, as explained in the earlier section "Editing on a duplicate layer."

1. **Open the Variations dialog box.**

   In Elements 1.0, choose Enhance⇨Variations to do so. In Version 2.0, choose Enhance⇨Adjust Color⇨Color Variations.

   At the top of the dialog box, you're provided with two previews. The left preview shows your original image, and the right preview displays the cumulative effects of all changes you apply within the dialog box. In Elements 1.0, these previews are labeled Original and Current Pick; in Elements 2.0, the previews have the more intuitive labels Before and After.

   In Elements 1.0, the Current Pick thumbnail also appears in the lower portion of the dialog box, surrounded by the color-shift thumbnails.

2. **Click the Shadows, Midtones, or Highlights option to specify which color component you want to adjust.**

3. **Adjust the Color Intensity control.**

   The control, labeled in Figure 4-9, determines how much your image changes each time you click one of the color-shift thumbnails. To make major shifts with each click, drag the slider to the right (toward Coarse in Elements 1.0). To lessen the change, move the slider to the left (toward Fine in 1.0).

   Keep in mind that you can click the color shift thumbnails as many times as necessary to arrive at the right color balance.

4. **Click a color-shift thumbnail to add more of that color and remove the opposite color.**

   The previews and thumbnails update to show you the results of your change. If you went too far, click the thumbnail opposite the one you just clicked, adjusting the Color Intensity amount if necessary.

   The Version 2.0 dialog box offers Undo and Redo buttons so that you can more easily reverse one or more thumbnail clicks. Just keep clicking the buttons until you get back to where you want to be. To remove all changes that you've made without leaving the dialog box, click the Reset Image button.

   In Elements 1.0, you can reset the image to its original state by pressing Alt (Option) and clicking the Cancel button. When you press Alt (Option), the Cancel button changes to the Reset button. (This same trick works in 2.0, too.)

Color Intensity slider

Color shift thumbnail

Figure 4-9:
Click a
color-shift
thumbnail to
add that
color and
subtract its
opposite.

The Show Clipping check box that appears in the Version 1.0 dialog box
provides a visual indication of colors that have shifted to pure black or
pure white, a phenomena known as clipping. When the check box is
selected, clipped pixels appear as bright neon spots in the thumbnails. If
you want to eliminate the clipping, click the thumbnail opposite the one
where the neon spots appear.

 5. **Repeat Steps 2 through 4 to correct the rest of the image.**

 6. **Click OK or press Enter to close the dialog box.**

The one drawback to the Variations filter is that you can't see its effect in the
image window until you close the dialog box — you just have to go by the
dialog previews. Adobe enlarged the previews in Elements 2.0, which is a step
in the right direction. Still, when you're working with large images, getting the
color correction just right can be difficult because the previews aren't big

enough to enable you to check details in the image. I can offer two solutions to this problem:

- ✔ Before opening the dialog box, use the Rectangular Marquee to select a small area of your image. Select a critical area — for example, if you're working on a portrait, select the subject's face. The previews in the Variations dialog box display only the area inside the selection outline, giving you a closer view of things. After you get the color balance of the selection just right, click OK to apply the changes and close the dialog box. Then press Ctrl+Shift+I (⌘+Shift+I) to inverse the selection outline, so that you select all the areas you didn't select before, and choose the Variations command again. The dialog box retains the settings you applied when you last applied the filter. So just click OK to make the same color corrections to the rest of the image.

- ✔ Set aside the Variations filter and adjust color balance using a Levels adjustment layer, as explained in the next section.

You also can adjust image saturation and exposure in the Variations dialog box. However, the preview issue just discussed makes the Variations dialog box a less than ideal place for these changes. Instead, adjust saturation using the methods outlined later in this chapter, in the section "Restoring Faded Colors." And to manipulate exposure, use the techniques outlined in the next chapter.

Balancing colors channel by channel

The second method for fixing color casts in Photoshop Elements takes advantage of the Levels filter. This technique requires a little more brain function than Variations, but offers the advantage of a live preview in the image window. In addition, you can apply this correction via an adjustment layer, something you can't do with Variations.

To find out more about adjustment layers, refer to the section "Using adjustment layers," earlier in this chapter.

Before I give you the step-by-step instructions, I want to introduce you to the core component of the Levels dialog box, shown in Figure 4-10. The middle of the dialog box displays a *histogram,* which is a chart that shows the distribution of the brightness values of all pixels in your image.

The horizontal axis of the chart indicates the brightness values, ranging from 0 (black) on the left to 255 (white) on the right. The vertical axis measures the number of pixels that fall at a particular brightness level. A tall spike means that many pixels in the image have the same brightness value. In Figure 4-10, the histogram reveals an image where all the brightness values are clumped toward the middle, with a lack of pixels at the very darkest and very brightest ends of the spectrum — in other words, an image that's lacking in contrast.

Figure 4-10:
Drag the
sliders
underneath
the
histogram
to adjust
image
shadows,
midtones,
and
highlights.

Shadows   Highlights

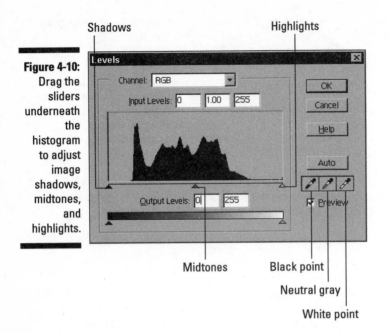

Midtones   Black point

Neutral gray

White point

Initially, the Levels dialog box shows the histogram for the composite RGB image — that is, the brightness values of the red, green, and blue color channels combined. When you adjust the composite brightness values, you change the overall image exposure and contrast, a process I explain in the next chapter. But the filter also lets you manipulate individual channels, which means that you can use Levels to color-balance your picture. In addition, in the composite mode, you can adjust colors by establishing a new black point, white point, and neutral gray.

If all this sounds like gibberish to you, don't panic — everything will become clear as you work your way through the upcoming steps. For a full-color reference to what's happening, refer to Color Plate 4-5. When I shot this picture of a friend and her granddaughter, I had just purchased a hot new camera and couldn't wait to show it off. Too bad that in my excitement over the new equipment, I forgot that the roll of film I picked up off my desk was one that had been with me on a recent trip to southern Louisiana, where the temperature had been somewhere in the mid-100s and the humidity even higher. When I picked up the prints from the film lab, I discovered that all the heat had seriously damaged the film, leaving me with a set of dark pink images. Color my face red — literally.

Fortunately, I was able to rescue the picture, although my professional pride is still stinging. To try out the technique I used, open up your own maladjusted photo and proceed as follows:

1. **In the Layers palette, click the name of the topmost of the layers you want to adjust.**

   Remember, this technique involves an adjustment layer, and an adjustment layer affects all layers underneath it.

2. **If you want to adjust a particular area of the image, create a selection outline as explained in Chapter 3.**

   If you select nothing, everything on the active layer and below will be affected. If you create a selection outline, you still alter the active layer and all underlying layers, but only within the boundaries of the selection outline.

3. **Choose Layer⇨New Adjustment Layer⇨Levels.**

   You see the New Layer dialog box, where you can give the layer a name. I suggest that you name the layer *Color Balance* to remind yourself of the purpose of the adjustment layer. Leave the other dialog box options as is for now.

   After you close the New Layer dialog box, you see the Levels dialog box.

4. **Inside the dialog box, select RGB from the Channel drop-down list.**

5. **Use the dialog box eyedroppers to set the black, white, and neutral gray points.**

   First, click the black eyedropper, labeled *Black point* in Figure 4-10, and then click a spot in your photo that should be pure black. The program automatically shifts your image colors so that the pixel you clicked indeed becomes black. Follow up this change by clicking an area that should be white with the white eyedropper, labeled *White point* in the figure. Finally, click the middle eyedropper, labeled *Neutral gray* in the figure, and click an area that should be gray.

   To see your changes in the image window, select the Preview check box at the bottom of the Levels dialog box.

   If you're lucky, this step fixes your color balance problem, in which case you can click OK or press Enter to close the Levels dialog box. If the image doesn't look right yet, you can undo your changes by pressing Alt (Option) and clicking the Cancel button inside the dialog box. (The button changes to the Reset button when you press Alt or Option.) After resetting the image to its original colors, try again with the eyedroppers.

   It's not a good idea to keeping clicking again and again without undoing an unwanted color shift because each click alters the original color values, and you can wind up destroying some image detail as you go.

   If you don't get satisfactory results after one or two tries, move on to the next step to do some manual, channel-by-channel adjusting. In Color Plate 4-5, clicking with the three eyedroppers at the spots marked by the white boxes in the original image made a significant improvement. You can see the result in the second image. Notice the change to the composite histogram — the brightness values are now spread out all along the brightness scale. (I explain the other histograms momentarily.) But a slight green cast remained, so more work was needed.

6. **In the Channel drop-down list, select the channel that corresponds to the color component you want to refine.**

   For example, in the second image in Color Plate 4-5, I had a smidgeon too much green, so I selected Green from the Channel drop-down list. (In some cases, you may need to work with all three channels, so don't worry too much about which channel you adjust first.)

7. **Drag the Shadows, Midtones, and Highlights sliders at the bottom of the histogram to adjust the amount of the selected channel's color.**

   The sliders are labeled in Figure 4-10. Drag the sliders to the right to reduce the amount of the selected channel's color and add its opposite. If you want to add more of the selected channel's color, drag the sliders to the left.

   You may need to adjust only one of the sliders to get the image where it needs to be. For example, to remove the green cast from my image in Color Plate 4-5, I dragged the white point slider a short distance to the right, which subtracted just a bit of green and added a hint of magenta.

   Again, the famous color wheel is in play here — check out Color Plate 4-2 and the earlier section "Mixing colors in the Color Picker" for a review.

8. **Select the other channels to adjust them as necessary.**

9. **Click OK or press Enter to close the dialog box.**

After making your corrections, you can use the techniques outlined earlier in this chapter, in the section "Adjusting an adjustment layer," to refine your image further.

Restoring Faded Colors

Over time, the effects of light and chemicals in the environment can cause the colors in a photo to fade. Bringing the colors back to life is a fairly easy task, but the best approach may not be what you expect.

Most people gravitate toward their photo editor's Saturation filter to boost color strength. If a photo is only slightly faded, the Saturation filter may work just fine. But for a severely faded image, like the original in Color Plate 4-6, the Saturation filter alone probably won't do the trick. The top right image shows the photo after I increased color saturation by applying the Saturation filter. Colors are undoubtedly stronger, but the little girl's skin has taken on an unnatural orange glow. (That's my little sister as a young 'un, and I can attest to the fact that she definitely did not have orange skin.)

In the lower-left example, I used a professional's secret trick for intensifying colors: duplicating the image and then blending the original and duplicate using the Multiply layer blending mode. The Multiply mode multiplies the brightness values on one layer with those on the underlying layer, and the result is instant color strengthening without the color shifts that you sometimes get from the Saturation filter.

Although the multiplied image looks much better than the original, it's still a little dull. As with most images you'll edit, the answer lies in a combination of corrections. After multiplying the original and duplicate, I used the Levels filter to brighten the exposure, and then used the Saturation filter to boost saturation just a little. The bottom right image in the color plate shows the result of all these changes.

As a final step in restoring this photo, I would apply some sharpening and maybe get rid of that distracting telephone pole in the background. Chapter 5 discusses sharpening, and Chapter 6 shows you how to cover up unwanted background objects.

The next sections show you how to restore faded colors using Multiply and Saturation, and also introduce you to the Sponge tool, which you can use to "paint" saturation on and off.

Before leaving Color Plate 4-6 behind, though, I want to point out that I applied all of my changes using adjustment layers. If your photo editor offers adjustment layers, be sure to take advantage of them to give yourself additional editing flexibility and protect your original image. Flip to the section "Using adjustment layers," earlier in this chapter, for the full story on adjustment layers.

Multiplying pixels to boost colors

Using the Multiply layer blending mode to strengthen faded colors is one of the easiest color correction techniques I know. Almost every photo-editing program that offers layers also offers the Multiply blending mode.

In Photoshop Elements, take these steps to try this technique:

1. **Open the Layers palette by clicking its tab in the palette well or choosing Window⇨Show Layers.**

2. **Duplicate the layer that contains the colors you want to adjust.**

   The easiest way to do this is to drag the layer to the New Layer button at the bottom of the Layers palette. (Refer back to Figure 4-8 if you need help).

3. **In the Layers palette, select Multiply from the Blending Mode menu at the top of the palette.**

   Instant intensity! If the effect is too strong, lower the Opacity value in the Layers palette. (Keep reading for other ways to adjust the effect.)

Sometimes, you may need to duplicate the original layer more than once to strengthen colors enough. You may also need to strengthen some areas of the picture and not others.

As an example, check out Color Plate 4-7. The picture's badly faded and also has taken on a yellowish cast. To fix the image, I first created a duplicate image layer and blended it with the original using the Multiply mode, resulting in the middle left image in the color plate. The right half of the picture — the dog half — looks pretty good, but the little boy's half is still pretty faded. So I dragged the Multiply layer to the New Layer button to create a second Multiply layer, which resulted in the middle right image.

With that second multiplied layer, the boy looked just about right, but the truck area behind him and the dog became very dark, and there was almost no separation between the two. No problem — I just picked up the Eraser tool and erased the dark truck areas on the second multiplied layer, as shown in Figure 4-11. I also swiped away a little bit of one of the dog's legs, which also had gotten too dark. The areas represented by the checkerboard in the figure are the erased, transparent areas. The lower left image in Color Plate 4-7 shows the result of my erasing.

Note that the image window Figure 4-11 shows only the second multiplied layer; I hid the other two layers so that you can easily see what areas I erased. To hide all but one layer in Elements, go to the Layers palette and Alt+click (Option+click) on the eyeball icon for the layer you want to see, as shown in Figure 4-11. Alt+click (Option+click) the eyeball again to reveal all the hidden layers.

As an alternative to erasing areas that become too dark, you can select the portion of the image that you want to strengthen before you duplicate the layer. This way, you duplicate and multiply only the selected pixels. Follow these steps in Elements:

1. **In the Layers palette, click the name of the layer that contains the area you want to adjust.**

2. **Select the area you want to strengthen.**

   See Chapter 3 if you need a refresher course on selection techniques.

3. **Press Ctrl+J (⌘+J) or choose Layer⇨New⇨Layer via Copy.**

   The program copies the selected pixels and places them on a new layer immediately above the original layer.

4. **In the Layers palette, set the blending mode to Multiply to multiply the copied pixels with the underlying originals.**

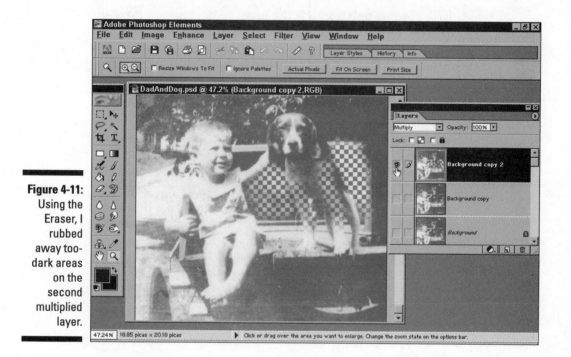

Figure 4-11:
Using the Eraser, I rubbed away too-dark areas on the second multiplied layer.

Either of these approaches would have worked for the photo in Color Plate 4-6. I usually opt for the first method, multiplying everything and erase areas that get too dark, but that's just a personal preference.

As with the photo in Color Plate 4-6, the image in Color Plate 4-7 required some additional work after I strengthened the colors with the Multiply mode. First, I got rid of that yellow cast by using the Hue/Saturation filter, which you can use to suck the color out of an image while still leaving the image in the RGB mode. (See the upcoming section "Going from Color to Gray" for more about this technique.) Next, I adjusted the exposure using Levels and then removed the black gunk that appears just below my father's ear by using the cloning technique discussed in Chapter 6.

Applying the Saturation filter

For a small color bump, the Saturation filter, found in most every photo editor, usually does the trick. With the Photoshop Elements version of this filter, you can increase or decrease saturation of all colors or selectively adjust the reds, greens, blues, yellows, cyans, and magentas.

I recommend that you apply the filter via an adjustment layer, for reasons discussed earlier in this chapter. To do so, take these steps:

1. **In the Layers palette, click the name of the topmost layer that you want to adjust.**

   Remember that an adjustment layer affects all underlying layers, so if you don't want to modify a particular layer, you have to place the adjustment layer underneath that layer.

2. **Select the area you want to edit.**

   See Chapter 3 if you need help with the selecting process. If you want the filter to alter all pixels on the affected layers, you don't need to create a selection outline; your click in Step 1 already did the trick.

3. **Choose Layer➪New Adjustment Layer➪Hue/Saturation.**

   Alternatively, click the New Adjustment Layer button at the bottom of the Layers palette and choose Hue/Saturation from the pop-up menu. (Refer back to Figure 4-6 if you're not sure which icon to click.)

   If you choose the command from the Layer menu, the New Layer dialog box opens, and you can give the adjustment layer a name. When you click OK or press Enter, the Hue/Saturation dialog box appears, as shown in Figure 4-12. If you add the adjustment layer by clicking the palette button, the program skips the New Layer dialog box and takes you directly to the Hue/Saturation dialog box.

4. **In the dialog box, choose the color you want to adjust from the Edit drop-down list.**

   If you select Master, you affect all colors in the image. To tweak just a single color, select it from the drop-down list.

5. **Drag the Saturation slider to the right to increase saturation; drag left to decrease saturation.**

   Alternatively, you can enter a numeric value in the box at the right end of the slider.

   Select the Preview check box at the bottom of the dialog box to preview your changes in the image window.

6. **Press Enter or click OK to close the dialog box.**

Because you applied the filter via an adjustment layer, you can reopen the dialog box and change the filter settings at any time. You also can use all the other techniques discussed in the section "Adjusting an adjustment layer," earlier in this chapter, to alter the impact of the filter.

Note that if f you select a color from the Edit drop-down list in Step 4, you don't alter just that color in its purest form. Instead, you adjust a range of hues along a certain arc of the color wheel. (See Color Plate 4-2 for a look at the color wheel.) The saturation change is applied at full strength to a

30-degree range of colors and then fades to nothing over an additional 30 degrees on either side. The values above the color bars at the bottom of the Hue/Saturation dialog box indicate these ranges, as shown in Figure 4-13.

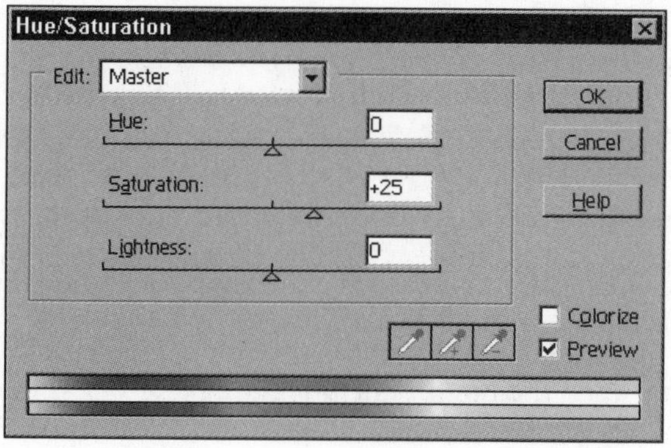

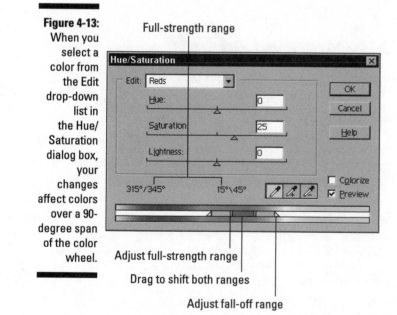

Figure 4-12: Raise the Saturation value to strengthen colors.

Figure 4-13: When you select a color from the Edit drop-down list in the Hue/ Saturation dialog box, your changes affect colors over a 90-degree span of the color wheel.

Full-strength range

315°/345°   15°\45°

Adjust full-strength range

Drag to shift both ranges

Adjust fall-off range

Suppose that you select Reds from the drop-down list, as shown in the figure. Colors located between 345 degrees and 15 degrees get the full saturation adjustment, as indicated by the two inner values above the color bars.

The effect then fades out over 30 additional degrees in both directions, taking you to 45 degrees (moving clockwise) and 315 degrees (moving counterclockwise). As a result, colors reaching from near magenta to near yellow get some degree of adjustment.

If you want to get really tricky with your saturation adjustments, you can vary the range of colors that are affected at full strength and also the range over which the effect fades out. Use the controls labeled in Figure 4-13 as follows:

✔ To adjust the fall-off range, drag one of the outer triangles..

✔ To adjust the full-strength range, drag one of the inner bars.

I don't really recommend that you mess with these options, though, because you can cause *color banding* (noticeable breaks in what should be a smooth transition of colors in your image). A safer and more useful trick is to drag the dark gray area between the inner bars along the color bar. (I labeled this area *Drag to shift both ranges* in Figure 4-13.). By doing so, you can shift both ranges to another spot on the color wheel without affecting the size of the full-strength and fall-off ranges.

Sponging saturation on and off

In addition to a Saturation filter, your photo editor may offer a tool that enables you to adjust color intensity by dragging over the pixels you want to change. In Elements, this tool is called the Sponge tool. To try out the tool, click its toolbox icon, labeled in Figure 4-14, or press the Q key.

When the Sponge tool is active, the Options bar offers several tool controls. Figure 4-14 shows these controls as they appear in Elements 1.0; in Version 2.0, a few things are different but you get the same basic options. The controls work as follows:

✔ Choose a brush size and shape from the Brushes palette. (Chapter 6 provides more details about selecting brushes.) You also can adjust the brush size in Elements 2.0 by using the Size control next to the palette. In both programs, you also can press the left and right bracket keys to enlarge and reduce the brush.

✔ Select Saturate from the Mode drop-down list to increase saturation; select Desaturate to fade colors.

✔ To vary the impact of the tool, adjust the Pressure value in Elements 1.0. This option is named Flow in Version 2.0.

✔ You also can use the Brush Dynamics options in Elements 1.0 to adjust brush size and Pressure value on the fly. In Elements 2.0, click the Airbrush button to toggle the tool between regular and airbrush mode. See Chapter 6 for a complete discussion of these options.

Sponge tool   Brush Dynamics

Figure 4-14:
Dab at your
image with
the Sponge
tool set to
Saturate to
boost colors
under your
cursor.

To apply the tool, just click or drag on the pixels that you want to adjust. If you
set the tool to airbrush mode in Elements 2.0, you can hold down the mouse
button to apply more and more saturation (or remove more and more color).
The tool continues to adjust the image as long as you hold down the mouse
button, until you reach 100 percent saturation or completely desaturate the
image.

Notice that in Figure 4-14, I'm working on a duplicate of the original image
layer. Remember to always make this kind of change on a duplicate layer,
both to protect your original image and to give yourself some added editing
flexibility. If you go too far with the Sponge tool, for example, you can lower
the Opacity value of the duplicated layer to bring back some of the original
color. Refer to the earlier section "Safely Editing Colors Using Layers" for
more insights into this technique.

Going from Color to Gray

For certain photo projects, you may want to convert a full-color image to a
grayscale image. You may want to publish the picture in a black-and-white
newsletter, for example. Or you may just prefer the grayscale version of a picture for aesthetic reasons. Whatever your reasons, you can do the color conversion in just about any photo editor.

You can go about this conversion in two ways:

✔ Convert the photo to the *grayscale color mode,* which allows just 256 colors — black, white, and shades of gray — and a single color channel. The resulting image is what I refer to as a *true grayscale* image.

Because it contains so few colors, a true grayscale image has a much smaller file size than a full-color image, which may contain more than 16.7 million colors. For this reason, converting a photo to the grayscale mode is a great option for pictures that you want to use on the Web, where small file sizes are critical.

See the first part of this chapter for an explanation of color modes.

✔ Leave the picture in the RGB color mode but simply desaturate all the image pixels. This option doesn't have the file-shrinking advantages of going to a true grayscale mode, but it does enable you to add colors besides black, white, and gray to your image to create special color effects, such as the hand-tinted effect shown in Color Plate 9-1. In addition, when you convert a picture to a true grayscale image, the red, green, and blue color channels become merged into a single channel. So you no longer can manipulate the channels independently of each other as you can if you simply desaturate the image.

Some entry-level photo editors don't offer the first option. So if you need a true grayscale image, you need to have a friend with a more capable program do the conversion for you.

To convert an RGB image to the grayscale color mode in Photoshop Elements, take these steps:

1. **Save a backup copy of your full-color image.**

   After you convert the photo to grayscale and save the new image, you can't get your original colors back. So be sure to save a copy of the image before you make the shift to gray. (Before saving, you can use Undo and Step Backward to bring your colors back, of course.)

2. **Choose Image⇨Mode⇨Grayscale.**

   If your image contains layers, the program asks you whether you want to merge all layers into one. Click Flatten if that's your preference; click Don't Flatten to keep your layers separate.

3. **When the program asks you for permission to discard color information, click OK or press Enter.**

If you think you may want to apply color effects to your image later, or you're just not sure that you really want to change the image permanently to grayscale, don't use the Mode⇨Grayscale command. Instead, use either of the following techniques to simply change all colors to shades of gray:

✔ Add a Hue/Saturation adjustment layer, as discussed earlier in this chapter, and drag the Saturation slider in the Hue/Saturation dialog box all the way to the left, until the Saturation value is –100. This is the best option because you can restore your original image colors at any time by simply trashing the adjustment layer. In addition, you can use this option to desaturate just some colors in the image, as I did in Color Plate 9-4.

✔ Choose Enhance⇨Color⇨Remove Color in Elements 1.0; choose Enhance⇨Adjust Color⇨Remove Color in Elements 2.0. This command does the same thing as lowering the Saturation value to –100. Make a backup copy of your image first, however, because you lose the option of getting your original colors back after you save the image file or exceed the number of edits that the program can undo.

Exploring Other Color Changes

This chapter touches on only some of the many ways you can alter the colors in your photograph. Future chapters show you additional techniques, including the following:

✔ **Painting in lost color information:** In addition to adding color to a grayscale image to create special effects, you can use paint tools to retouch blown highlights and restore areas where all color information has been lost. Chapter 8 shows you how to do this kind of retouching on portraits.

✔ **Painting over red eyes and other flaws:** Most photo-editing programs offer a red-eye reduction filter — and I haven't worked with one of 'em yet that's worth a plugged nickel, whatever that is. Painting over the red eyes using a process outlined in Chapter 8 works much better. You can also touch up other flaws by merely painting over them, just as you dab on paint to hide scuff marks on a hallway wall. Chapter 6 explores this technique.

✔ **Shifting the color of objects in a photo:** Don't like the color of the background in your latest portrait? No problem. You can change it in a variety of ways, including using the Hue filter, which hangs out with the Saturation filter introduced in this chapter. You also can use a variety of other techniques to spin colors in your image around the color wheel. Chapter 9 provides some examples of these kinds of alterations.

Chapter 5

Manipulating Focus and Exposure

• •

• •

Almost every camera sold today, whether it captures digital or film images, offers automatic focus and exposure. These two features are designed to enable even beginners to shoot sharp, perfectly exposed photographs without having to deal with tricky technical issues like focal length, aperture, and shutter speed. Problem is, few amateur photographers understand how to take advantage of autofocus and autoexposure, so keep they churning out pictures that are blurry, too dark, or too light.

If you haven't been getting good results from your autofocus/autoexposure camera, chances are that you haven't been framing and shooting your pictures in a way that enables the camera mechanisms to function properly. First off, you have to frame your subject so that it's within the zone analyzed by those mechanisms. Your camera manual should map out this zone — usually, the viewfinder also displays tiny lines that indicate the framing area. In addition, you have to use a two-step approach to pressing the shutter button. Pressing the button halfway down kicks the autoexposure and autofocus tools into gear. When the camera's done with its preliminary work, it should alert you by beeping or displaying a light near the viewfinder. That's your signal to press the shutter button the rest of the way down.

You may be surprised that I would provide this information, given that people would no longer have as much need for a book on photo retouching if they discovered the trick to autofocus and autoexposure. Well, much as I'd like to be thought of as a giving soul, I'm not too worried that sharing this tip will put me out of a job. For one thing, proper framing and shutter-pressing technique doesn't guarantee perfect focus and exposure for every picture; camera sensors can be fooled by complex subjects and lighting conditions.

Second, I'm guessing that you have plenty of old pictures to keep you at your retouching and restoration work for a long time. And third, lots of people don't bother to read these chapter introductions anyway. (See what you've been missing?)

Whatever the reasons behind the focus or exposure problem you're trying to correct, this chapter provides you with some tools for setting things right. It explains how to sharpen focus, blur portions of an image to create the effect of shallow depth-of-field, brighten or darken an image, boost contrast, and more.

Sharpening Focus

Sharpening filters, found in every photo-editing program, can make slightly soft photos appear to be in sharper focus. Don't expect miracles from sharpening filters — even the most sophisticated ones can't rescue a totally blurry or even moderately blurry image, despite what you may have seen done on your favorite TV crime drama.

When you apply a sharpening filter, the photo editor doesn't really change the focus of the image. What it does is increase contrast along the edges of the image, which fools the eye into thinking that the picture is in sharper focus.

By *edges,* I don't mean the boundaries of the photo. In digital imaging-speak, the term *edge* refers to an area where a color change occurs.

To create the heightened contrast, sharpening filters add dark and light halos along the boundary where two colors meet. Pixels on the lighter side of the border become lighter; pixels on the darker side become darker.

For a clearer notion of what sharpening filters do, take a gander at Figure 5-1. The left side of the figure shows you the sand dollar photo in its original state. In the right side of the photo, I applied a significant amount of sharpening. Look at the area at the top of the picture, where the sand dollar meets the sand. In the sharpened side of the picture, you can see a dark halo on the sand side of that border and a light halo on the sand dollar side. If you look closely, you can see the same light/dark halos along every color boundary.

Although a modicum of sharpening can do wonders, too much sharpening can result in a grainy image and unnatural halos along the edges. The sharpened sand dollar in Figure 5-1 borders on being too sharp — I purposely overdid things a little so that you can more easily see the sharpening halos.

For more examples of good and bad applications of a sharpening filter, turn to Color Plate 5-1. I shot the original image with a high-end digital camera, so it was already in pretty decent shape. But never one to leave well enough alone, I applied a touch of sharpening in the upper-right version of the image to bring out the details of the flower petals. I adjusted the sharpening effect a little in the lower-left image. (The next section explains the sharpening filter settings that I used for these two images.) Both pictures look fine — which sharpening amount is better is a matter of artistic taste.

In the lower-right image, though, I cranked up the sharpening machine much too far. Portions of the image appear grainy, as if someone sprinkled them with sand. And around the edges of the flower, the excessive sharpening creates weird, glowing color halos. Notice too, that even with all that sharpening, the background areas don't appear to be any more in focus than in the original. As I said earlier, even excessive sharpening can't bring very soft areas into sharp focus.

Now that you understand what sharpening can and can't do, the next two sections show you how to apply the effect.

Original   Sharpened

Figure 5-1:
Sharpening filters add light and dark halos along color boundaries to create the illusion of sharper focus.

Always make sharpening the very last step in your retouching or restoration project. Changes in image size and resolution and certain other editing processes affect the amount of sharpening that's needed. If you sharpen before making those changes, you may find yourself with an oversharpened image that you can't rescue. The only change *not* to make before you sharpen is to apply a solid border around a picture, as I did for all the images in this book. If you add a border and then sharpen, the sharpening destroys the clean edges of the border.

Also, always do your sharpening on a duplicate layer rather than on the original image. That way, you can remove the sharpening by simply deleting the sharpened layer. In addition, you can lower the layer's opacity to reduce the sharpening effect or erase parts of the layer to remove the effect from some parts of the image.

For more information about the best order to follow when correcting your photos, flip back to Chapter 1. For details about editing on duplicate layers, see Chapter 4.

Applying sharpening filters

If you're working with a very basic photo editor, your sharpening toolkit may be limited to one simple sharpening filter. The filter either applies a set amount of sharpening or, in some cases, enables you to drag a slider or manipulate some other control to increase the amount of sharpening.

Intermediate and high-end programs give you more sharpening flexibility. In Photoshop Elements, for example, you have a choice of four sharpening filters, plus a tool that you can use to sharpen a part of the image by dragging over it. (The next section explores this tool.)

Truth be told, however, only one of the sharpening filters, Unsharp Mask, deserves your attention. The other three — Sharpen, Sharpen More, and Sharpen Edges — are one-shot, automatic filters that don't give you any control over how the sharpening is applied. For that reason, I'm not even going to bother with them. Unsharp Mask, by contrast, offers three sharpening controls. Most programs in the same class as Elements and above offer this filter, although it may go by a different name.

The upcoming steps walk you through the process of applying the Unsharp Mask filter. But first, I want to explain the trio of sharpening options available in the Elements rendition of Unsharp Mask: Amount, Radius, and Threshold. (If you want a look at the filter dialog box, peek ahead at Figure 5-4.) If you're not using Elements, remember that these controls sometimes go by other names; check your software's manual for details about its version of Unsharp Mask.

✔ **Amount:** This one's easy; it controls the amount of sharpening. Raise the value to apply more sharpening. Nothing to see here, move along.

✔ **Radius:** Ah, here's where things get interesting. With this option, you can control the width of the sharpening halos — that is, how far the area of increased contrast extends from either side of an edge. A higher value spreads the effect over a wider distance. In Figure 5-2, for example, I sharpened the left and right thirds of the image. In both cases, I set the Amount value to 200 and Threshold value to 0. But I used a Radius value of 1.0 on the left side and 10.0 on the right side. Compare the width of the sharpening halos in the two sides to see how the Radius value alters the sharpening effect.

Typically, a Radius value from .5 to 1.0 works well for on-screen images, while a value in the 1.5 to 2.0 range is appropriate for printed images.

✔ **Threshold:** With this option, you can specify whether you want sharpening throughout your image or just along significant edges. (Again, remember that *edges* in this sense refers to areas of contrast.) If you set the Threshold value to 0, you get sharpening along all edges. By raising the value, you sharpen just areas where a large shift in color occurs. The higher the Threshold value, the bigger the shift that's required before sharpening is applied.

Practically speaking, though, keeping the Threshold value under 15 usually produces the best results. Any higher than that, and you either don't get much sharpening at all or wind up with unnatural transitions between sharpened and unsharpened areas. Start out with the value at 0, and then bump it up slightly if you get too much sharpening in areas that should be smooth, such as the sky or the skin on a baby's face. You can see the difference between two Threshold value settings in Figure 5-3. In both examples, I set the Amount value to 300 and the Radius value to 2.0. At the higher Threshold value, low-contrast areas of the sand dollar don't receive any sharpening.

Radius, 1.0   Original   Radius, 10.0

Figure 5-2: Raise the Radius value to create bigger sharpening halos.

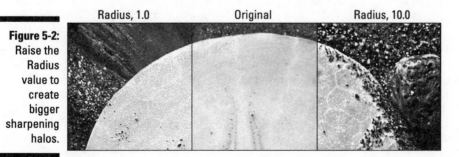

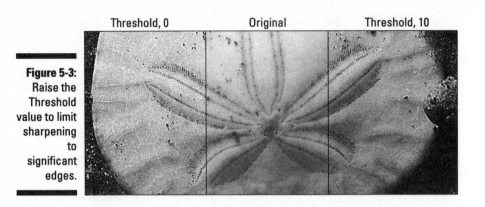

Threshold, 0   Original   Threshold, 10

Figure 5-3:
Raise the
Threshold
value to limit
sharpening
to
significant
edges.

Every image requires a different set of Amount, Threshold, and Radius values. And you can create similar effects by using different combinations of the three values, as illustrated by the upper-right and lower-left examples in Color Plate 5-1.

To try out the Unsharp Mask filter in Photoshop Elements, follow these steps:

1. **Open the Layers palette by clicking its tab in the palette well or choosing Window➪Show Layers.**

2. **Select the area that you want to sharpen.**

   See Chapter 3 if you need help using the selection tools. If you want to sharpen an entire layer, you don't need to create a selection outline. You can just click the name of the layer that you want to sharpen in the Layers palette. (If your image has just one layer, click that layer to sharpen the entire image.)

3. **Put the selected pixels on a new layer.**

   You should always sharpen on a separate layer so that you don't permanently alter the image. If you drew a selection outline in Step 2, you can send the selected pixels to a new layer by pressing Ctrl+J (⌘+J) or choosing Layer➪New➪Layer via Copy. If you want to sharpen an entire layer, you can use the same command or just drag the layer to the New Layer button at the bottom of the Layers palette.

4. **Choose Filter➪Sharpen➪Unsharp Mask.**

   The Unsharp Mask dialog box appears, as shown in Figure 5-4.

5. **Adjust the Amount, Radius, and Threshold values as needed.**

   Turn on the Preview check box in the dialog box so that you can see the results of your adjustments in the image window.

   You can also monitor the effect in the thumbnail preview inside the dialog box. Click the plus sign under the thumbnail to zoom in for a closer look; click the minus sign to zoom out. Drag inside the thumbnail to scroll the display to another area of the image. Or just click in the image window on the area that you want to inspect; the program displays the area you click in the dialog box preview.

By displaying the image at a large size in the image window and keeping the dialog box preview zoomed in, as shown in Figure 5-4, you can inspect the filter's impact on details and on the overall image at the same time.

   6. Click OK or press Enter to apply the filter and close the dialog box.

After you sharpen, check to make sure that the sharpening you applied is the right amount for the picture's final output. In other words, print the image or view it on-screen at the size it will be displayed. If you need to sharpen more, just repeat Steps 4 through 6. If you sharpened too much, you can use the Undo features discussed in Chapter 2 or just trash the sharpening layer by dragging it to the Trash button at the bottom of the Layers palette.

Alternatively, you can soften the sharpening effect by reducing the sharpened layer's opacity (by using the Opacity control in the Layers palette). You also can nip at the layer with the Eraser tool, rubbing out areas that you decide look better without any sharpening. The unsharpened pixels from the underlying original layer show through the erased areas. (See Chapter 6 for details about working with the Eraser.)

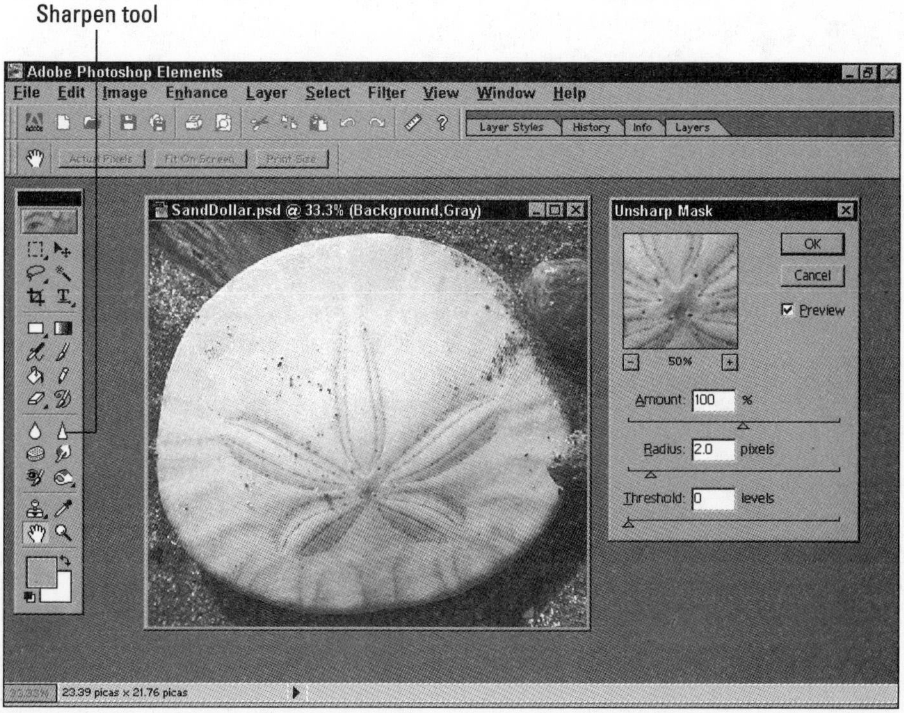

Sharpen tool

Figure 5-4:
The
Unsharp
Mask filter
offers
advanced
options that
deliver
better
results than
automatic
sharpening
filters.

For an alternative approach to sharpening, check out the demo version of nik Sharpener! Pro Complete included on the CD at the back of this book. This program enables you to apply automatic sharpening with a specific output device in mind. The program is a Photoshop *plug-in,* which means that you can run it while working inside any program that accepts Photoshop plug-ins, including Elements and many other photo editors. After you install the program, it appears as an option on the Filter menu in Photoshop and Elements.

Brushing on focus with the Sharpen tool

Although you can apply the Unsharp Mask filter to specific image areas by creating a selection outline, if you want to sharpen just a few pixels here and there, you may find the Sharpen tool more convenient. With this tool, labeled in Figure 5-4, you simply click on or drag over the areas you want to sharpen.

Many programs offer a Sharpen tool. In Elements, you can vary the impact of the tool by using the following Options bar controls:

- ✔ To adjust the brush size, shape, and behavior, use the Brushes palette and other Options bar controls as explained in Chapter 6.

- ✔ To control the amount of sharpening that's applied with each click or drag, adjust the Pressure value in Elements 1.0 and the Strength value in Elements 2.0. If you raise the value, the tool produces a greater degree of sharpening.

- ✔ To sharpen pixels on all layers, select the Use All Layers box. Otherwise, the tool affects only the active layer.

- ✔ To change how the sharpened pixels blend with the original pixels, select a Mode option. These options work the same as those available from the Mode menu in the Layers palette. For most jobs, you should keep this option set at Normal. But try the Luminosity mode if you notice unwanted color shifts when you apply the tool.

I don't use the Sharpen tool very much because I find it a little difficult to control. I prefer to create a selection outline and then apply the Unsharp Mask filter. However, when you're retouching portraits, the Sharpen tool can come in handy for adding a little extra pop to the eyes. Just position the cursor over the eyeball and click once or twice to give the eyes extra definition.

Remember, always apply the Sharpen tool on a duplicate layer so that you can easily remove or adjust the effect later if needed. See Chapter 4 for a refresher course in editing on duplicate layers.

Softening Focus

Blur filters perform the opposite function of sharpening filters. They create the appearance of softer focus by reducing contrast along image edges.

You can use blur filters to change the *depth of field* of a photograph, as I did in Figure 5-5. (Color Plate 5-2 shows the color versions of this image.) Depth of field refers to the range of sharp focus in a picture. On cameras with a zoom lens, zooming in and out changes the depth of field. (Note that on digital cameras, this applies only when you're using a true, optical zoom lens, not the digital zoom feature.) With high-end cameras, you also can adjust the aperture setting to manipulate depth of field. If your camera doesn't offer these options, or you just didn't take advantage of them when you shot the picture, you can alter depth of field after the fact by careful application of a blur filter.

Figure 5-5:
Blurring
everything
but the
main
subject
helps
minimize
distracting
background
elements.

In addition to creating a shift in focus, blur filters offer a way to improve photos that have a jagged or rough look due to oversharpening or too much JPEG compression. (JPEG compression reduces file size by tossing out some data when you save the image, as explained in Chapter 10.) Blurring also helps soften facial lines and image flaws such as dust and scratches.

The next section introduces you to a variety of blur filters found in Photoshop Elements and many other photo-editing programs. Following that, you can read about the Blur tool, which you can use to touch up smaller areas of your image.

Choosing a blurring filter

Photoshop Elements offers a choice of blur filters, all of which are found on the Filter⇨Blur submenu. Each filter applies the blur effect a little differently.

- ✔ **Blur and Blur More** are one-shot, automatic filters that apply a set amount of blurring to all selected areas. Because they don't offer any way to adjust the blur, I suggest that you bypass these filters and use the more capable Gaussian Blur filter.

- ✔ **Gaussian Blur** enables you to specify how much blurring you want to apply. This filter is just the ticket for blurring the background, as I did in Figure 5-5 and Color Plate 5-2. You can read more about Gaussian Blur in the next section.

- ✔ **Motion Blur and Radial Blur** are special-effects blurring filters. Motion Blur creates a sense of movement by blurring the image in a linear direction; Radial Blur blurs pixels in a circular direction, creating that spinning-out-of-control effect you've seen in movies. Neither filter is particularly helpful from a retouching or restoration standpoint, but if you want to have some fun, they're easy enough to use. Just fiddle with the filter dialog box options until you get an effect you like. Check the program Help system if you need guidance.

- ✔ **Smart Blur** enables you to soften areas of low contrast while leaving strong edges — areas of high contrast — alone. The upcoming section "Blurring without destroying edges" shows you how this filter works.

Whichever filter you choose, remember the number-one rule of photo editing: Always make your changes on a duplicate layer so that the original image pixels remain untouched. See Chapter 4 for more information about how to take advantage of this editing safety net.

Also, save a backup copy of your original image before you merge your duplicate (blurred) and original layers. You can't remove a blur effect by using sharpening filters, contrary to what you may expect. Of course, you can use the Undo command, Revert command, and History palette to restore the image in some cases, but saving a backup is a good safeguard strategy anyway.

See Chapter 2 for details about saving files and about Undo, Revert, and the History palette.

Shortening depth of field with Gaussian Blur

The original image in Figure 5-5 and Color Plate 5-2 has a large depth of field; the altered photo has a short depth of field. Shortening the depth of field is a good way to make a distracting background less prominent, as this photo shows. And the Gaussian Blur filter is the perfect tool for creating the effect. Most intermediate and advanced photo editors offer this filter.

In case you're curious, the filter is so named because the blurring effect is based on a Guassian curve, a specific type of curve that was defined by a mathematician by the name of Gauss. (Sorry you asked, eh?)

Take these steps to pay tribute to Mr. Gauss and blur your image in Elements:

1. **Save a backup copy of your image.**

2. **Select the area that you want to blur.**

   See Chapter 3 for help with creating a selection outline. If you want to blur an entire image layer, you don't need to draw a selection outline; just click the layer's name in the Layers palette.

   In most cases, you're better off not feathering the selection outline. Doing so tends to leave a noticeable transition between blurred and non-blurred areas.

3. **Choose Layer⇨New⇨Layer via Copy or press Ctrl+J (⌘+J).**

   This step copies the selected area (or layer) to a new layer.

4. **Choose Filter⇨Blur⇨Gaussian Blur to display the dialog box shown in Figure 5-6.**

Figure 5-6: The Gaussian Blur filter enables you to adjust the amount of blurring.

5. **Adjust the Radius value to control the amount of blurring.**

   Select the Preview check box in the dialog box so that you can monitor the filter's effect in the image window. The thumbnail preview in the dialog box works as described in the steps provided in the section "Applying sharpening filters," earlier in this chapter.

6. **Press Enter or click OK to apply the effect and close the dialog box.**

   Because you applied the filter to a separate image layer, you can alter the impact of the filter by changing the layer opacity. Just adjust the Opacity value in the Layers palette.

Blurring without destroying edges

With the Gaussian Blur filter, you can control the amount of blurring, but the only way to specify exactly what area you want to blur is to create a selection outline. With the Smart Blur filter, you can limit the blur to areas that don't contain significant edges — that is, you can blur just low-contrast regions and leave high-contrast areas untouched. To put it another way, the filter looks for strong color boundaries and then blurs pixels within those boundaries but not along the boundaries themselves.

The left image in Figure 5-7 shows an example of a situation in which Smart Blur can provide a solution. This photograph has been subjected to too much JPEG compression, a file-saving option that I explain in Chapter 10. Overcompression can cause smooth areas to look jagged or result in random, unnatural specks of color known as *artifacts*. In Figure 5-7, the problem is most evident in the sky.

To apply the Smart Blur filter, follow the same steps — and precautions — outlined in the preceding section, but choose Smart Blur from the Filter⇨Blur submenu in Step 4. You then see the Smart Blur dialog box, shown in Figure 5-8.

Although the dialog box controls look intimidating at first, you really need to worry about only the top two options, Radius and Threshold. But just for good measure, here's what all four options do:

- **Radius** controls the distance of the blur, similar to the Radius option in the Unsharp Mask filter. A higher value results in a more pronounced blur effect.

- **Threshold** tells the program how much contrast must exist between two areas for the area to be considered an edge. As you increase the Threshold value, more and more pixels receive the blur.

- **Quality** affects the way that the program processes the image preview and the filter application. A higher setting produces smoother results, but requires more time for the program to produce. While you're playing with the settings in the dialog box, you can set the option to Low to get quicker previews, but before you actually apply the filter, always set the option to High.

✔ **Mode** is an odd duck. For standard image blurring, use the Normal setting. Edge Only and Overlay Edge create special effects. With Edge Only, you get a black-and-white, line-drawing image. With Overlay Edge, you get a bizarre blurred and brightening effect that I can't even begin to describe.

Although some people love the Smart Blur filter, I rarely use it. The main reason is that this filter, unlike Gaussian Blur, doesn't offer a live preview in the image window. You have to rely on the thumbnail preview inside the dialog box, which doesn't really give you a clear idea of how your image will look. So you may end up applying the filter, undoing the effect, and applying the filter again and again before you get an effect you like.

Frankly, I just don't find the results worth all the trouble. In the right image in Figure 5-7, for example, although the artifacts are lessened, the image has taken an odd, watercolor-ish look, especially in the cloud area. In fact, some people use Smart Blur precisely for the purpose of *creating* a watercolor effect, which may be the best use of the filter. For precise blurring without drawing a selection outline, I prefer to use the Blur tool, described next.

Figure 5-7: When your image exhibits compression artifacts (left), the Smart Blur filter can help (right).

Figure 5-8: With Smart Blur, you can soften areas of low contrast without affecting strong edges.

Painting on soft focus with the Blur tool

To apply a blur exactly where you want it — without fussing with a selection outline or applying and reapplying the Smart Blur filter — pick up the Blur tool. If your photo editor offers a Sharpen tool, you probably also have a Blur tool.

Figure 5-9 labels the Photoshop Elements Blur tool. As in most programs, you use the Elements Blur tool by simply dragging over or clicking on the area you want to blur. In Elements, pressing and holding down the mouse button adds more and more blurring to the pixels under your cursor.

When you activate the Elements Blur tool, the Options bar offers the same controls as when you work with the Sharpen tool. I explain all these controls in the section "Brushing on focus with the Sharpen tool" earlier in this chapter, so I won't bother to repeat them here. However, in addition to the Normal and Luminosity tool blending mode options described earlier, two other modes, Darken and Lighten, can work wonders when you're using the Blur tool.

In Normal mode, the program adjusts pixels on each side of an edge to soften contrast. But when you select Darken from the Mode menu, the tool darkens the light side of the edge without altering the dark side. In Lighten mode, the opposite occurs.

If your photo editor offers the Darken and Lighten blending modes for its Blur tool, the tool becomes a good option for removing dust spots and other small flaws in an image. I used the tool to remove the black spots that mar the lower portion of the original image in Figure 5-5 and Color Plate 5-2. You can see the results of my dust-busting in the right image in Figure 5-5 and Color Plate 5-2.

Blur tool   Tool cursor

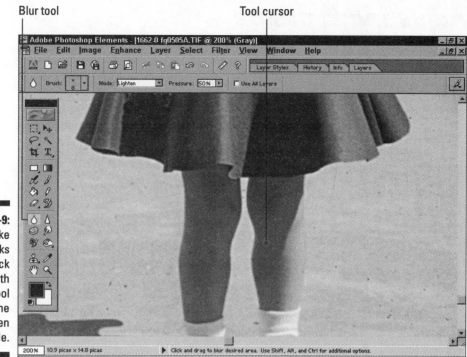

Figure 5-9:
To make dark specks vanish, click them with the Blur tool set to the Lighten mode.

✔ To remove dark flecks, set the tool mode to Lighten (by selecting it from the Mode menu on the Options bar) as shown in Figure 5-9. Then position the tool cursor over the blemish and press and hold down the mouse cursor until the spot fades away.

✔ If you have light specks on a dark background, do the same thing, but with the tool set to Darken mode.

Either way, be sure to choose a small brush — about the size of the specks — to do this work so that you don't create a noticeable blur.

You also can use the Clone tool and Dust and Scratches filter to cover up dust specks; see Chapter 6 for details.

In addition to removing dust specks, the Blur tool can act as a wrinkle cream when you're retouching faces. Chapter 8 shows you how to use the tool to "reduce the appearance of fine lines and wrinkles," as they say in the beauty magazines.

Adjusting Exposure

Chapter 4 introduces you to the Levels filter and shows you how you can use it to adjust colors in an image. But the Chapter 4 discussion tells only one side of the Levels story. You also can turn to Levels to correct exposure problems.

The Levels filter is just one of a handful of exposure tools that may be available in your photo software. The rest of this chapter explains the best of the most common exposure tools.

I *don't* cover automatic exposure correction tools, which promise to solve all of your exposure problems with one mouse click. Feel free to explore these tools if your software offers them, but don't be surprised if they either don't do the job, turn your image weird colors, or both.

Using the Brightness/Contrast filter (not)

Figure 5-10 shows the Photoshop Elements Brightness/Contrast filter, an exposure control offered in many programs. Most novices turn first to this filter to make exposure adjustments, and logically so. Unfortunately, despite its name, this filter isn't the best way to tackle exposure or contrast corrections.

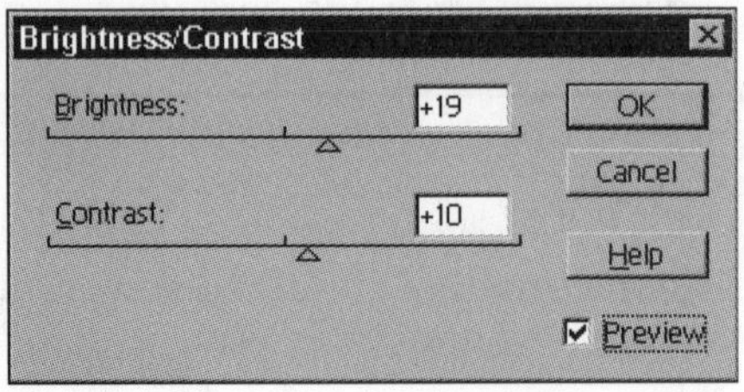

Figure 5-10:
Although easy to use, the Brightness/ Contrast filter isn't the best answer to exposure or contrast problems.

Brightness/Contrast	
Brightness: +19	OK
	Cancel
Contrast: +10	Help
	☑ Preview

When you raise the Brightness value, you make all pixels in your image lighter, and when you lower the value, all pixels get darker. What's wrong with that? Well, in most photos, *all* pixels don't need lightening or darkening.

For example, in the left image in Figure 5-11, the shadows are just where they need to be. Only the midtones and highlights are too dark. When I lightened the image using the Brightness filter to get the highlights and midtones where they need to be, the shadows also became lighter, as shown in Figure 5-11. The result is a washed-out look.

Figure 5-11: Raising the Brightness value brought the midtones and highlights into the proper range, but also lightened shadows, giving the image a faded look.

The next natural assumption is that you can use the Contrast filter to improve images like the right example in Figure 5-11. But when you under-stand what the Contrast filter does, you can see that this isn't so. When you raise the Contrast value, the program darkens all pixels that are darker than the medium brightness value, following the 0–255 brightness scale that I introduce in Chapter 4. All pixels that are lighter than the medium brightness value get lighter. So pixels toward the light end of the scale can shift all the way to white, and pixels toward the dark end can move all the way to black. As a result, you may increase contrast, but at the expense of details in the shadows and highlights.

As an example, inspect the left side of Figure 5-12, which shows how the washed-out image on the right side of Figure 5-11 appears after raising the Contrast value enough to bring the shadows closer to their original level. The formerly light gray areas of the face, shirt, and hat are now white or nearly white, resulting in the loss of subtle details in those areas. Now look at the same image in the right side of the figure, which I corrected using the Levels filter, explained in the next section. With Levels, you can adjust shadows, midtones, and highlights independently. Compare the range of shadows, highlights, and details maintained in this image with the left image, and you will understand why I long ago abandoned Brightness/Contrast — and why you should avoid it from the get-go.

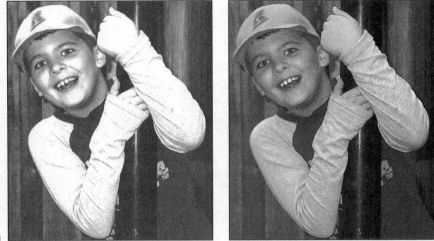

Figure 5-12: The cumulative effects of the Brightness/ Contrast filter (left) don't measure up to the results available via the Levels filter (right).

Tweaking exposure and contrast with Levels

As the preceding section makes clear, for proper exposure and contrast correction, you need to be able to adjust image shadows, highlights, and midtones independently, which is just what the Levels filter offers. Check your software manual to find out if you have access to this valuable filter (it may go by a different name).

In Elements, you can apply the Levels filter via an adjustment layer, which I recommend that you do. The following steps show you how. (Because I cover the topics of selecting pixels and working with adjustment layers in Chapters 3 and 4, I won't explain them again here.)

1. **In the Layers palette, click the topmost of the layers that you want to adjust.**

   Remember that an adjustment layer affects all layers underneath it.

2. **Create a selection outline if you want to adjust only a portion of the layer(s).**

3. **Click the New Adjustment Layer button at the bottom of the Layers palette and choose Levels from the pop-up menu.**

   The Levels dialog box appears, as shown in Figure 5-13. In the center of the dialog box, you see a *histogram,* which is a chart that maps out the distribution of all brightness values in the image, using the 0 to 255 brightness scale. (See Chapter 4 if that scale doesn't ring a bell.) The horizontal axis represents the brightness values, with 0 (black) at the left end and 255 (white) at the right end. The vertical axis indicates the distribution of pixels across that brightness scale.

Shadow slider   Highlight slider

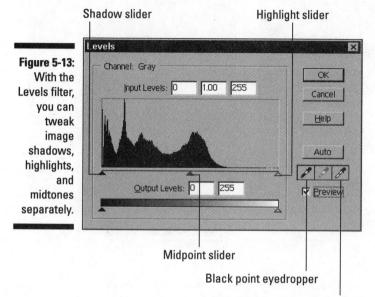

Figure 5-13:
With the
Levels filter,
you can
tweak
image
shadows,
highlights,
and
midtones
separately.

Midpoint slider

Black point eyedropper

White point eyedropper

For example, in Figure 5-13, the histogram indicates that the image has lots of dark pixels, a moderate amount of pixels in the middle brightness range, and almost no light or white pixels. This is the histogram that appeared when I first opened the levels dialog box to correct the too-dark image on the left side of Color Plate 5-3, (shown in grayscale in the upcoming Figure 5-14).

You use the three sliders underneath the histogram to manipulate your image. I labeled these *Shadow slider, Midpoint slider,* and *Highlight slider* in Figure 5-13. (Note that if you use a program other than Elements, the Midpoint slider may go by the name *Gamma* or *Gray Point.*)

4. Drag the Highlight slider to the left to make the brightest areas of the image lighter.

If the histogram shows a lack of pixels at the highlight end, as in Figure 5-13, drag the slider to the leftmost point where the histogram indicates a presence of image pixels, as I did in the right image in Figure 5-14 and Color Plate 5-3.

When you drag the Highlight slider, the Midpoint slider moves in tandem, which also lightens the midtones in the image. You can adjust the midtones later if needed (see Step 6).

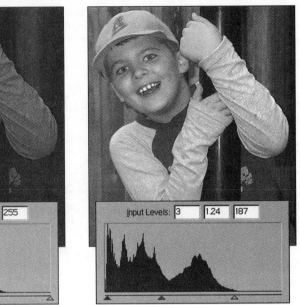

Figure 5-14:
I dragged
the Midpoint
and
Highlight
sliders to
the left to
brighten
midtones
and
highlights.

5. Drag the Shadow slider to the right to make shadows darker.

This slider performs the opposite function of the Highlights slider.

If the histogram indicates a complete lack of pixels at the dark end, as in Figure 5-15, drag the slider to the leftmost point where the histogram indicates a pixel population. This movement makes the darkest pixels black.

In Color Plate 5-3 and Figure 5-14, I decided to nudge the Shadow slider just slightly to the right even though the histogram shows that there are some pixels at the far left end. The histogram indicates that there aren't many pure black pixels, and bumping up the slider slightly deepened the darkest shadows to make them black as well. As a rule, you don't want to move both the Highlight and Shadow slider because you wind up reducing contrast. But let your eyes be the final judge. In the case of this image, I liked the added shadow boost that I got from moving the Shadow slider a couple of notches. Note, however, that I moved the slider only slightly to avoid a real downshift in contrast.

As with the Highlight slider, moving the Shadow slider also shifts the Midpoint slider, but this time, the midtones get darker. The next step shows you how to adjust the midtones if needed.

6. Drag the Midpoint slider to adjust midtones (areas of medium brightness).

Drag the slider to the left to lighten the midtones; drag to the right to darken the midtones. For example, I dragged the slider left to lighten the midtones in the example shown in Color Plate 5-3 and Figure 5-14.

Figure 5-15:
With this image, I adjusted shadows while preserving the midtones and highlights.

In Figure 5-15, I also lightened the midtones to reverse the darkening that occurred when I dragged the shadow slider rightward in Step 5. This photo shows a close-up shot of an antique transferware bowl, and the original midtones were already where I wanted them. Darkening just the shadows, while keeping the highlights and midtones at their original levels, made the details of the pattern more prominent.

7. Press Enter or click OK to close the dialog box.

Before you close the dialog box, you can restore the original image brightness values by pressing the Alt (Option) key as you click the Reset button. The Cancel button turns into the Reset button when you press Alt (Option).

If the Levels dialog box offered only the histogram and sliders, it would be a fine tool. But wait — there's more! If you order now, you also get a few additional features, which you can use as follows:

✔ **Input Levels boxes:** The three Input Levels boxes above the histogram reflect the shadow, midpoint, and highlight values at the slider positions. The original values are always 0 for black and 255 for white.

The midpoint value, though, isn't measured on the 0 to 255 brightness scale. Rather, this value represents the brightness value of neutral gray. Known as the *gamma value* in technical circles, this value always starts out at 1.0 in the Levels dialog box. You can raise the value as high as 9.99 and lower it to .10. Raising the value darkens midtones; lowering it lightens them.

If you know the Levels adjustments you want to make, you can enter the values into the Input Levels boxes instead of dragging the corresponding sliders. This option comes in handy if you want to apply the same adjustment to multiple images. Jot down the values you use in the first image, and then just enter the same values as you open the dialog box for the subsequent images.

Even easier, you can copy a Levels adjustment layer from one image to another to use the same settings again. Just open both images, adjust the first image, and then drag the adjustment layer into the second photo's image window.

✔ **Output Levels sliders and boxes:** These options, located underneath the histogram, enable you to limit the maximum brightness and darkness values. For example, by lowering the brightness value from 255 to, say, 250, you shift any pixels with values higher than 250 down to 250. Similarly, by raising the darkness value from 0 to 10, you can prevent any pixels from having a brightness value lower than 10.

As you can probably guess, neither adjustment is a good idea because you simply wind up decreasing contrast. If you have blown-out highlights, try fixing the problem using the Burn tool or the Multiply blending mode, discussed later in this chapter. Similarly, try the Dodge tool and Screen mode, also explained later, to bring some light back into your shadows.

✔ **Eyedroppers:** The black point and white point eyedroppers, labeled in Figure 5-13, enable you to click pixels in your image to establish a new black point and a new white point. If you click in the image with the middle eyedropper, the color you click becomes neutral gray, and all other colors shift up or down the scale accordingly. (When you're working on a grayscale image, this third eyedropper becomes unavailable.)

As illustrated in Color Plate 4-5, the eyedroppers are useful mainly for color correction. Because clicking with the eyedroppers usually brings about a color change, don't do so if all you want to do is adjust exposure.

✔ **Auto Levels:** Ignore this button. It takes all the pixels in your image and spreads them out across the entire brightness range. In some cases, you get major color shifts. In others, not much happens. On rare occasions, you may see exactly the results you were hoping for, but you can save time and guess work by simply dragging the histogram sliders. (Come on, you're not *that* lazy, are you?) By the way, clicking this button does the same thing as choosing the Auto Levels command on the Enhance menu in Elements.

Blending layers to lighten and darken

If you happened upon the Chapter 4 section that discusses ways to strengthen faded colors — or Color Plates 4-6 and 4-7, which illustrate the same — you already know that you can use the Multiply layer blending mode to darken and intensify image colors.

Just in case you haven't been to Chapter 4 and don't care to travel there now, here's a quick recap. Layer blending modes enable you to change the way in which pixels on one image layer mix with the pixels on the underlying layer. Some blending modes create special effects, but others, including the afore-mentioned Multiply and the about-to-be-mentioned Screen, prove useful for exposure correction. In Elements, you set the blending mode via the Blending Mode menu at the top of the Layers palette.

To use blending modes to tweak exposure, first duplicate the layer that you want to adjust. Then set the blending mode for the duplicate layer according to whether you want to darken or lighten the image, as follows:

✔ **To darken the image, select Multiply as the blending mode.** This mode multiplies the brightness values of pixels on the original layer with the brightness values of pixels on the duplicate layer. The result is always a darker, more intense color; however, black and white pixels don't change.

✔ **To lighten the image, select Screen as the blending mode.** Screen accomplishes the opposite of Multiply. I won't even get into the math involved in this one — it has to do with multiplying the inverse of the brightness values on the two layers. Just remember that when you blend two layers with Screen, you brighten the image. As with Multiply, black and white pixels are unaffected.

The examples in Chapter 4 and Color Plates 4-6 and 4-7 adequately show you the power of Multiply, so I won't illustrate that mode again here. To see the Screen mode in action, see Figure 5-16. I used the Screen method to lighten the same dark image used in the preceding sections in this chapter. For this image, I had to duplicate the original image layer twice, setting the blending mode for both of the duplicate layers to Screen.

You're probably thinking that the result I achieved in Figure 5-16 looks an awful lot like what I did earlier in this chapter with the much acclaimed Levels filter. But there's an important difference between working with Levels and with the Multiply and Screen layer blending modes. With Multiply and Screen, you can't alter midtones, highlights, and shadows independently as you can with Levels.

A close, side-by-side comparison of the two corrected images reveals the impact of this limitation. The left image in Figure 5-17 shows the Screen version of the correction, and the right image shows the Levels version. Pay special attention to the lower portion of the black pole. When I corrected the image using Levels, I moved the midpoint sliders to the left (refer to Figure 5-14). This lightened the middle-gray areas of the pole. With the screened image, those areas don't get nearly as light. Sure, I could have kept duplicating and screening additional layers to make the pole more closely match the one in the Levels version, but that would also have brightened up the rest of the image, taking the lighter grays too far. The hands, shirt, and cheeks are already showing a loss of detail due to the lightening. You don't lose the same amount of detail as when you use Brightness/Contrast, but you do give up something.

Figure 5-16: To correct exposure this time, I duplicated the original image layer twice and set the layer blending mode for both of the duplicate layers to Screen.

All that said, Screen and Multiply are pretty darned effective and certainly quick and easy to use. For everyday, quick-and-dirty photo projects, I usually start with one or the other to do exposure correction. If I don't get the results I'm after, I just delete the duplicate layer and head for the Levels dialog box. Or, in some cases, I apply a Levels adjustment layer after multiplying or screening to perfect the image.

Brushing on lightness and darkness

In traditional photo darkrooms, technicians use processes known as *dodging* and *burning* to selectively brighten or darken portions of a photo. Many photo-editing programs, including Elements, adopted those names for tools that enable you to "paint" exposure changes on your image by dragging over or clicking on the area you want to adjust.

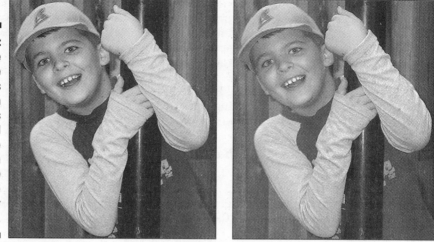

Figure 5-17:
You can see subtle differences between images lightened using the Screen mode (left) and the Levels filter (right).

✔ **To lighten pixels, use the Dodge tool.** The Dodge tool comes in especially handy for facial retouching. You can use it to brighten teeth, as shown in Color Plate 8-4, and for lightening the whites of the eyes.

✔ **To darken pixels, use the Burn tool.** For example, in Figure 5-18, I dragged the tool over the sign letters to make them easier to read.

Figure 5-18:
To darken the letters on the sign, I dragged over them with the Burn tool.

In Elements 1.0, the Dodge and Burn tools share a flyout menu in the toolbox, as shown in Figure 5-19. To grab the hidden tool, click the triangle on the visible icon to display the flyout menu and then click the tool that you want to use. In Version 2.0, the Dodge and Burn tool no longer live together; each now has a permanent slot in the toolbox.

For details on the Dodge and Burn tools, see the next section. Following that, check out the section "Burning color images" for a special technique that you may find useful when you want to darken highlights in a color photo.

Applying the Dodge and Burn tools

When you activate either tool in Elements, the Options bar offers the standard brush controls. Figure 5-19 labels these controls as they appear in Elements 1.0; Version 2.0 offers slightly different options. If you're unfamiliar with these features, refer to Chapter 6.

In addition, the Options bar offers two more controls, Range and Exposure, which are specific to the Dodge and Burn tools. bar. These controls work as follows:

Figure 5-19:
With the Dodge and Burn tools, you can paint exposure changes onto shadows, midtones, and highlights independently.

✔ **Range:** This option controls whether the tool tweaks shadows, midtones, or highlights. The Range options are, curiously enough, named Highlights, Shadows, or Midtones. Hey, sometimes software designers *can* speak the same language as the rest of us!

✔ **Exposure:** Raise or lower this setting to adjust how much impact the tool makes with each pass over the image. I suggest that you start out at the default setting, 50 percent, or lower. Each time you apply the Dodge or Burn tool to the same area, the pixels become increasingly lighter or darker, depending on which tool you're using.

Applying either tool is easy — just click or drag over the area you want to alter. For safety and flexibility, though, always do your dodging and burning on a duplicate of the layer you want to edit, as discussed in Chapter 4.

Burning color images

When you're working with grayscale images, the Dodge and Burn tools work as you'd expect. But on color images, one aspect of the Burn tool may throw you off. When used on very strong highlights, burning sometimes simply makes the area gray. If you're trying to darken a gray object, that's fine. But if the original color of the overexposed object wasn't gray, that's not so fine.

As an example, flip to Color Plate 5-4. I shot this picture of an Italian window on a bright, sunny day. Because my camera's autoexposure mechanism figured the exposure based on the center of the scene, the stucco areas of the building wall are overexposed. To improve the situation, I dabbed here and there with the Burn tool set first to Midtones and then to Shadows. In addition to burning the overexposed areas, I burned some areas of the ornate interior to increase contrast. The upper-right image in the color plate shows the result of this retouching work.

So far, so good. But look at the lower-left image. When I swiped over the remaining overexposed areas with the Burn tool set to Highlights, the highlights turned gray — definitely not what I was after.

You may be able to use the Burn tool in combination with some layer-blending-mode trickery to get the results you want, however. The technique involves the Overlay blending mode, which is available in most programs that offer layers and blending modes.

The following steps spell out this technique. I'm not going to get into the technical explanation of why it works — sorry, but I've already taken enough extra-strength aspirin today. Just give the technique a try.

1. **In the Layers palette, click the name of the layer that contains the area you want to edit.**

2. **Click the New Layer button at the bottom of the Layers palette to create a new, empty layer.**

(I labeled the button in the upcoming Figure 5-21.) You may want to give the layer a name that reminds you of the layer's purpose — *Burn Highlights Layer,* for example. In Elements 1.0, double-click the layer name in the Layers palette to open the Layer Properties dialog box and rename the layer. In Elements 2.0, you can open the dialog box by double-clicking the layer thumbnail. Or just double-click the layer name and type the new name right in the Layers palette. Click anywhere off the layer name to finalize the name change.

3. **Choose Edit⇨Fill.**

    You see the Fill dialog box, as shown in Figure 5-20.

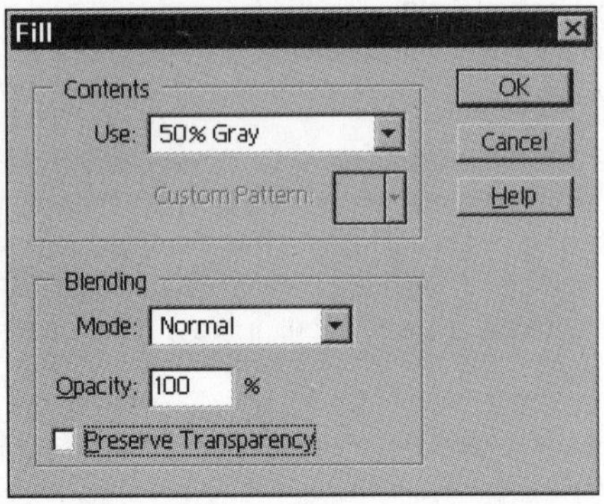

Figure 5-20:
After creating a new layer, fill the layer with 50 percent gray.

4. **Select 50% Gray from the Contents menu inside the dialog box.**

    Leave the other options at their default settings, shown in Figure 5-20.

5. **Click OK or press Enter to fill the new layer with gray.**

    Your image temporarily is hidden by all that gray.

6. **At the top of the Layers palette, select Overlay from the Blending Mode menu, as shown in Figure 5-21.**

    The gray layer becomes invisible, but remains the active layer.

7. **Grab the Burn tool, set the Range option (on the Options bar) to Highlights, and burn away on the Overlay layer.**

Notice that wherever you burn the image, the thumbnail for the burn layer darkens, as shown in Figure 5-21. If you want to bring any highlights back, just activate a painting tool, set the foreground color to 50 percent gray, and paint over the highlights. Wherever you paint, the original gray fill is restored, which removes the burn effect. You can even partially restore highlights by reducing the painting tool's Opacity value on the Options bar, which causes the tool to paint translucent strokes. Alternatively, adjust the layer's Opacity value (in the Layers palette) to reduce the impact of all of your burning.

Blending Mode menu

Figure 5-21: Apply the Burn tool on the gray layer after setting the layer blending mode to Overlay.

New Layer button

To set the foreground color to match that used in the original fill, set the burn layer's blending mode back to Normal to temporarily redisplay the gray fill. Then select the Eyedropper from the toolbox and click in any area of the new layer that hasn't yet been burned. Change the layer blending mode back to Overlay after you click. For more ways to set the foreground color, see Chapter 4.

Remember that if you want to preserve the burn layer as an independent layer, you must save the image file in a format that supports layers. For details about working with layers, see Chapter 3.

Note that not all Burn tools work exactly the same way as the one found in Elements (and Photoshop), so you may get different results than discussed here when you try the Overlay burning technique. If burning in this fashion doesn't work, trash the burn layer. Then flip to Chapter 8 to find out how to use your painting tools to restore color to washed out highlights. (The information you need is in the section related to bringing color back to washed out skin.)

Chapter 6

Covering Up Dust, Scratches, and Other Flaws

*W*hen I first heard the term "lazy perfectionist," I thought the phrase was the ideal description of my approach to housekeeping. When I'm in my kitchen cooking, for example, my eye wanders around the room and makes an inventory of tiny flaws, such as a barely noticeable cobweb high in the corner behind the refrigerator. These bits of imperfection bug the heck out of me, yet I'm rarely inspired to put forth the effort to remove them.

When it comes to photo retouching, however, I'm the perfectionist's perfectionist. I'm willing to spend hours dabbing at problems that no one else can see and that likely won't reproduce in print, anyway. In this chapter, you can read about some of my favorite tools and techniques for removing small flaws such as scanner dust and negative scratches. You also find information about how to repair more significant damage, such as a hole in an antique print.

After discovering how easily you can bring photographs to perfection, you may say that I'm still being lazy, especially given that I do this work sitting down, listening to my favorite CDs. I say, toss me the remote control for the CD player on the way out the door, okay?

Blurring Away Imperfections

You can make many small imperfections disappear by applying a slight blur. This technique works best when a small to moderate degree of contrast exists between the flaw and the surrounding pixels.

As discussed in Chapter 5, blur filters and tools reduce contrast along edges — areas where two colors meet. By making the color transition between a flaw and the neighboring pixels less abrupt, you make the flaw less noticeable. Of course, blurring also makes your image, well, blurry. So if you're not careful, you can wind up destroying details as well as defects.

The next two sections show you how to safely blur problems away by using two tools found in Elements and many other photo editors.

Dust and Scratches filter

To say that the image in Figure 6-1 has a few problems is an understatement. This photo, which dates to the early 1960s, shows my sister and I about to take a dip in Lake Erie — and from the looks of things, one of us is about to get in trouble for forgetting that you're supposed to change into a bathing suit before wading into the water. You'd have thought older sister would have taken me aside and reminded me, huh? I'm sure I paid her back for this oversight at some point.

Figure 6-1: To remove imperfections from large, flat areas of color, such as the sky in this photo, try the Dust and Scratches filter.

Aside from the wardrobe issue, this photo is plagued with small white scratches and other bits of flotsam. The problems are especially noticeable in the sky. In other areas, the natural imperfections of the sand and surf help to disguise the damage.

Pictures like the one in Figure 6-1 offer a perfect opportunity to try the Dust and Scratches filter. Found in Elements and many other programs, this filter is designed to remove specks of dust and scratches — hence its name.

Because the filter fades small flaws by blurring the image, however, you shouldn't apply it wholesale to your picture. Instead, limit the filter to problem areas by selecting them before you apply the filter. In Figure 6-1, I selected just the sky, as shown in Figure 6-2.

Figure 6-2:
Start with the Threshold value at 0, then raise the Radius value until blemishes disappear.

To keep from blurring details at the edges of the area you want to correct, keep your selection outline a few pixels shy of those details. If you look closely at Figure 6-2, for example, you can see that I drew the selection outline so that it doesn't come right up to my sister's head. That's because I wanted to preserve the strands of hair that are whipping around in the wind.

After applying the Dust and Scratches filter, you can use the Blur tool, described in the next section, to touch up any areas near the details. If you apply the filter on a duplicate layer — a highly recommended option — you also can use the Eraser tool to rub away the blur from spots where it affected the photo in ways you don't like.

The following steps walk you through the process of using the Dust and Scratches filter:

1. **Select the area that contains the flaws you want to eliminate.**

2. **Copy the selected pixels to a new layer.**

   By putting the copied pixels on a new layer, you can apply the filter without fear of permanently harming the original image. If you need help understanding this approach to image correction, see Chapter 4.

   In Elements, you can copy a selection to a new layer by pressing Ctrl+J (⌘+J) or by choosing Layer⇨New⇨Layer via Copy.

3. **Choose Filter⇨Noise⇨Dust & Scratches.**

   The Dust & Scratches filter appears, as shown in Figure 6-2. Be sure to select the Preview check box in the dialog box so that you can monitor the filter's effect in the image window. You can also refer to the thumbnail preview inside the dialog box; click the plus and minus signs under the thumbnail to zoom the preview in and out.

   You can use the thumbnail preview to get a close-up view of things and then zoom the view in the image window to show the entire photo, as shown in Figure 6-2. In this image, I wanted to monitor those hair strands around my sister's head, so I focused on that area in the thumbnail preview.

4. **Set the Threshold value to 0.**

   When you apply the filter, the program looks for areas of contrast and applies the blur along the boundaries between them. The Threshold value tells the program how much contrast must exist before the blur is applied. When you set the value to 0, the entire area that you selected in Step 1 is fair game. You adjust this value in Step 6, but start at 0.

5. **Raise the Radius value until you get the desired amount of blurring.**

   The higher the value, the stronger the blur. Use the lowest Radius value that eliminates the flaws.

6. **Raise the Threshold value as high as possible.**

   Stop when the flaws start to reappear. By raising the Threshold value, you keep the blurring to a minimum, preserving as much detail as possible.

7. **Press Enter or click OK to apply the blur and close the dialog box.**

To achieve the corrected image in Figure 6-3, I used a Radius value of 5 and a Threshold value of 3. Notice that a dark streak remains in the upper-left corner of the image. When I raised the Radius value enough to make this streak disappear entirely, the rest of the sky became totally flat, and I lost the little bit of cloud detail that was present in the original image. You can clean up leftover flaws like this dark streak by using the Blur tool, described next, or the Clone tool, explained later in this chapter.

Figure 6-3: I applied the filter just enough to remove most of the tiny scratches without making the sky totally flat.

Rubbing out spots with the Blur tool

If you've come to this part of the book after exploring Chapter 5, you may already be aware that the Blur tool can be a handy spot cleaner; I used the tool to remove the small, dark specks that marred the original image in Color Plate 5-2. Because this technique is so useful, I want to provide a little more detail about it here.

The key to taking advantage of the Blur tool for cleaning purposes lies in the Mode menu, which appears on the Options bar when you activate the tool. (If you don't see the Options bar, choose Window⇨Show Options.)

- ✔ By choosing Darken from the Mode menu, you can use the Blur tool to fade light defects that mar a dark area of a photo.

- ✔ Select Lighten to make dark specks disappear.

To understand how the Mode option affects the tool, see Figure 6-4. I drew a thin black line down the image, as shown in the left third of the figure. I did the same in the center and right thirds. Then I dragged down the center and right lines ten times with the Blur tool, using the Normal mode on the center line and the Lighten mode on the right line.

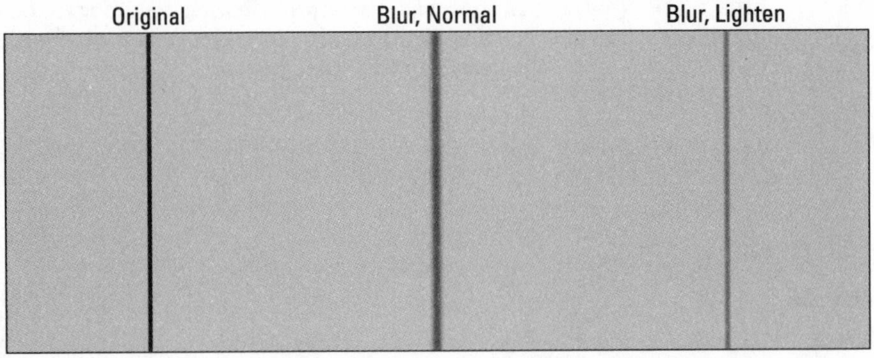

Original	Blur, Normal	Blur, Lighten

Figure 6-4:
To fade dark defects on a light background, set the Blur tool to Lighten mode.

In Normal mode, the Blur tool reduces contrast by adjusting the color and brightness of all pixels touched by your cursor. When I dragged down the center line in Figure 6-4, the black line got lighter and the surrounding pixels got darker, resulting in a smudge that's lighter but larger than the original defect.

If you set the Blur tool to Darken or Lighten mode, it achieves reduced contrast by adjusting either the light pixels or the dark pixels, but not both.

- ✔ In Darken mode, the Blur tool darkens the lightest pixels, leaving the darkest pixels alone.

- ✔ In Lighten mode, the opposite happens, as shown in the right example in Figure 6-4. When I dragged down the black line with the Blur tool set to Lighten, the black line got lighter, but the lighter, bordering pixels didn't change. With several more swipes of the Blur tool, the line would fade completely into the background.

Note a few important things about this technique, however. You can successfully blur away small flaws only. If the defect is too large, you wind up with an area that's noticeably blurry when compared to the surrounding regions. In areas that have a rough, grainy texture, you also may destroy the continuity of the image by applying the Blur tool, no matter what the size of the defect.

For times when the Blur tool doesn't do the job, turn to the cloning or patching techniques discussed later in this chapter. And to remove simple lines like the one in Figure 6-4, use the painting tools as described in the upcoming section "Applying Touch-Up Paint." I used the line in the figure because it provides a clear illustration of the Blur tool modes, but you can remove defects from an expanse of solid color much more quickly by simply matching the foreground paint color to the surrounding area and painting over the flaws.

With those caveats in mind, follow these steps to try cleaning a photo with the Blur tool in Photoshop Elements. The steps are the same in Photoshop and should also work in any other photo editor that offers a Blur tool and the Lighten or Darken tool modes.

Before you start working, you may want to open a second window so that you can see your image from a zoomed-out view and close-up perspective, as shown in Figure 6-5. In Elements, open a second window by choosing View➪ New View. The new window just provides a second view of your image; the program doesn't actually open the image file a second time. When you're done with your edits, you can close either of the windows and continue working with the one open window.

1. **Create a new, empty layer to hold your blurring strokes.**

   The fastest way to create the layer is to click the New Layer button at the bottom of the Layers palette, labeled in Figure 6-5. Position the new layer above the layer that contains the pixels you want to edit.

   If you need help working with the Layers palette, see Chapter 3.

2. **Activate the Blur tool by clicking its toolbox icon, labeled in Figure 6-5.**

3. **Select the Use All Layers check box on the Options bar.**

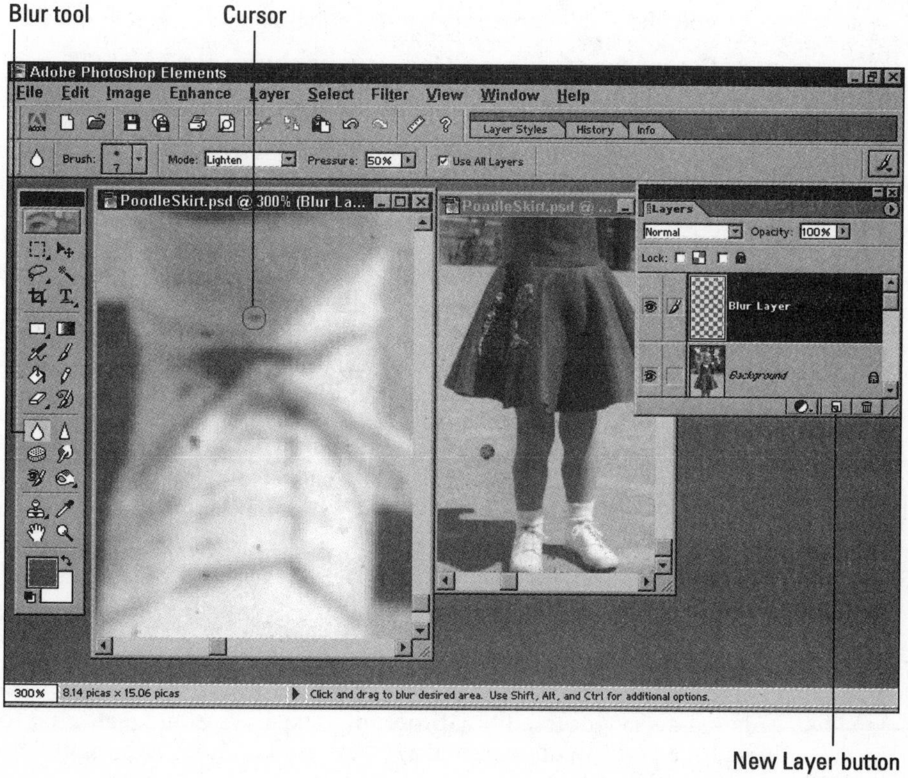

Blur tool   Cursor

Figure 6-5: Do your blurring on a separate image layer to protect the original photo.

New Layer button

When you select this option, the Blur tool "sees" pixels on all visible image layers. If you don't want the tool to affect a particular layer, hide the layer by clicking its eyeball icon in the Layers palette.

4. **Select Darken or Lighten from the Mode menu on the Options bar.**

    • Choose Darken if you want to hide a light defect on a dark background.

    • Select Lighten to hide a dark flaw on a light background.

5. **Select a brush that's slightly larger than the flaw you're trying to hide.**

    See the section "Choosing a brush size and shape," near the end of the chapter, if you need help with this step. For this job, a soft brush usually works best because the resulting blur fades out toward the edges of the brush.

6. **Set the Pressure (or Strength) value to 50 percent.**

    The option is named Pressure in Elements 1.0 and Strength in 2.0.Whatever the name, the option determines how much blurring the tool applies when you click on your image. You can use whatever value you like — 50 percent is a good starting point in most cases.

7. **Center the cursor over the flaw, as shown in Figure 6-5.**

8. **Press and hold down the mouse button to blur the defect.**

    The longer you hold down the mouse button, the more blurring occurs. You also can keep dragging over or clicking on the defect until it disappears.

If you go too far, you can use the Undo and Step Backward commands, discussed in Chapter 2, to undo your changes. Or you can use the Eraser tool to wipe the blurring strokes off the blur layer or just trash the layer and start over. Alternatively, lower the opacity of the blur layer using the Opacity control in the Layers palette to diminish the blur.

When you save your image file, remember that you have to use some special saving options if you want to keep the blur layer separate from the rest of the image. See Chapters 2 and 3 for information about saving files and preserving image layers.

Cloning Good Pixels over Bad

Almost every photo-editing program these days offers a **cloning tool.** Using this tool, you can copy undamaged areas of a photo and "paint" the copies over problem areas.

To see a perfect application of the Clone tool, look at the left photo in Color Plate 6-1, shown in grayscale in Figure 6-6. My mother took this picture on a cruise in Chile. Her camera offers a time/date stamp feature, and she turned the option on when shooting this image. In addition, something — likely a hard bit of dirt that made its way onto the film plane — caused a bright yellow scratch across the entire length of the photo. To make the picture suitable for framing, I removed both the line and time/date stamp by cloning nearby pixels onto the defects. Total repair time: less than five minutes.

Figure 6-6: To remove the scratch and time/date stamp (left), I cloned surrounding pixels onto the flawed areas (right).

Cloning tools go by several different names, depending on which software you're using. In Photoshop, the tool started life with the name Rubber Stamp, but was renamed the Clone Stamp in recent editions of the program as well as in Photoshop Elements. The tool's original name is reflected in its toolbox icon, which still looks like a rubber stamp. In this book, I'm using the briefer but clearer name Clone tool.

Enough preamble, on to some specifics. The next section explains the fundamentals of cloning; following that, you can find step-by-step instructions for applying the tool.

Cloning basics

No matter what photo-editing program you're using, the cloning process consists of these two main steps:

1. **First, click to set the *clone source*.**

The clone source marks the spot where you want to begin copying pixels. How you indicate this location varies from program to program. In Elements, you set the clone source by Alt+clicking (Option+clicking) with the Clone tool, as shown in the left image in Figure 6-7. I clicked just to the right of the time/date stamp.

2. **Click or drag over the defect.**

   When you click or begin to drag, most programs display two cursors. One cursor, the tool cursor, indicates where your cloned pixels will appear. The other cursor, which I call the clone source cursor, shows the current clone source. In Elements, the tool cursor is a circle and the clone source cursor is a plus sign, as shown in Figure 6-7.

If you click with the Clone tool, the program copies one cursor-full of pixels from the clone source onto the defective pixels. If you drag, however, the clone source shifts in tandem with your tool cursor, and you get a continuing stream of cloned pixels over the course of your drag.

Alt (Option) + click
to set clone source

Tool cursor

Clone source cursor

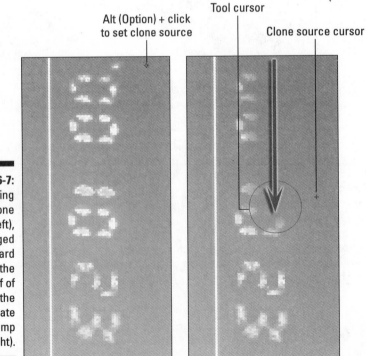

Figure 6-7: After setting the clone source (left), I dragged downward over the right half of the time/date stamp (right).

I'm pretty sure that last sentence left you about as confused as I was the first time I read about the Clone tool. So look at the right image in Figure 6-7, which may clarify things for you. I positioned the tool cursor at the top of the time/date stamp and dragged downward, as indicated by the arrow. (The arrow doesn't appear on-screen; I added it for illustration here.) As I dragged, the clone source also shifted downward, so that I always cloned the pixels that were just to the right of my tool cursor.

The next few sections provide more details about using the Clone tool.

Aligned versus non-aligned cloning

In some programs, you can choose from two cloning modes: **aligned** and **non-aligned.** You make this choice in Elements via the Aligned check box that appears on the Options bar when you activate the Clone tool. (See Step 2 in the next section.)

What's the difference between the two modes? Here's the deal:

✔ **Aligned:** When you work in this mode, the clone source always moves in tandem with your tool cursor, no matter how many times you click or drag after setting the clone source. This setting prevents you from cloning the same area more than once. If you want to re-clone an area, you have to set the clone source again.

✔ **Non-aligned:** With this mode, the clone source cursor returns to its initial position after you click or drag once.

To get a better idea of what the two modes do, see Figure 6-8. The top image shows an antique novelty cup. I set the clone source at the position marked by the X. In the lower-left image, I turned on the Aligned option and then dragged from left to right three times. The clone source moved in alignment with the tool cursor, so the result of the cloning is a perfect reproduction of the pattern at the top of the cup.

In the lower-right image, I turned off the Aligned option and again dragged three times from left to right. Each time I started a new drag, the clone source returned to its original position (marked by the X in the top image). As a result, I created three copies of the same area.

There's no right or wrong setting — the cloning option you choose simply depends on what you want to do to your image. For information on other tool options, see the next section.

Clone source

Figure 6-8:
After setting
the clone
source at
the X (top), I
dragged
three times
with the
Aligned
option
selected
(lower left),
and
deselected
(lower
right).

Aligned

Non-aligned

Step-by-step cloning tips

You can use the Clone tool to cover up just about any defect, providing that
your image contains enough good areas to clone. The following steps explain
how to work the tool in Photoshop Elements; if you're using another photo
editor, the process should be similar although the specific tool and command
names may be different.

1. **Create a new layer above the layer that contains the problem area.**

   To do this, click the name of the problem layer in the Layers palette and
   then click the New Layer button at the bottom of the palette. (Refer to
   Figure 6-9.)

   By cloning on a separate layer, you protect the original image from being
   permanently altered. You also can take advantage of some additional
   options to make your cloned pixels blend in with their surroundings
   better, as explained following these steps.

Clone tool   Tool cursor

Brushes palette   Clone source cursor   Brush Dynamics button

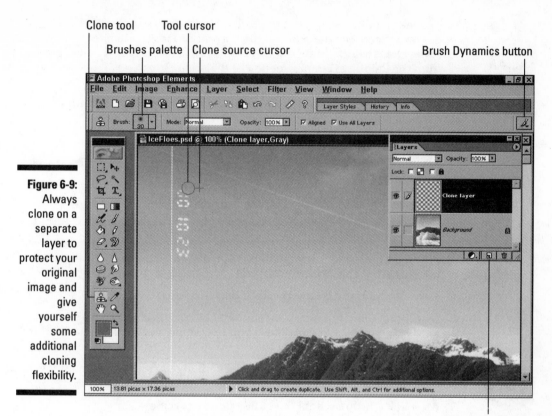

Figure 6-9:
Always
clone on a
separate
layer to
protect your
original
image and
give
yourself
some
additional
cloning
flexibility.

New Layer button

2. **Activate the Clone tool by clicking its toolbox icon, labeled in Figure 6-9.**

   Be sure to grab the regular Clone (Stamp) tool and not the Pattern
   Stamp tool, which resides on the same toolbox flyout menu.

3. **Choose a brush from the Brushes palette, labeled in Figure 6-9.**

   If you're using Elements 2.0, your Brushes palette looks a little different
   than the one in the figure, which features Elements 1.0.

   When cloning, a small brush usually works best. Select a soft brush if
   you're trying to hide defects that fall in an area of the photo that's in soft
   focus or has little detail. Use a harder brush to clone over flaws in
   sharply focused, detailed areas. You can swap out brushes as you go if
   needed. For example, to clone over the line in the sky area in Figure 6-6, I
   used a soft brush, but I switched to a harder brush when I got to the ice
   and mountain areas.

To make cloning easier, use the Brush Size cursor style, so that the cursor reflects the diameter of the current brush. To change the cursor style, choose Edit➪Preferences➪Display & Cursors. Select Brush Size from the Painting Cursors section of the dialog box.

See the section "Choosing a brush size and shape," later in this chapter, for more details about selecting a brush. Also check out "Painting dynamically" to read about other brush options.

 4. Set the tool mode and opacity using the Options bar controls.

For standard cloning, set the Mode option to Normal and set the Opacity value to 100 percent.

You can read more about these options in the next section.

 5. Turn the Aligned check box on or off, depending on how you want to work.

My, that's a helpful instruction, eh? See the preceding section if you're not sure what this option does.

 6. Turn on the Use All Layers check box.

By turning this option on, you enable the Clone tool to see pixels from all visible image layers. Because you're cloning on a separate layer, this option should always be on.

If you don't want the clone tool to pick up pixels from a particular layer, hide the layer by clicking its eyeball icon in the Layers palette.

 7. Alt+click (Option+click) to set the clone source.

Your click establishes the spot at which the Clone tool will begin to copy pixels when you apply the tool in the next step. When you release the Alt (Option) key, you see two cursors, as shown in Figure 6-9.

Remember, the round cursor is the tool cursor, and the crosshair cursor indicates the clone source. The tool cursor's appearance may be different from the one in the figure depending on the shape and size of the brush you use.

 8. Position the tool cursor over the defect you want to hide.

 9. Click or drag to clone the pixels under the clone source cursor onto the defect.

You can click or drag as many times as needed, changing the brush size and any other options as you go. Remember that if you turn off the Aligned option, the clone source cursor returns to its original position each time you click or start a new drag. If needed, you can Alt+click (Option+click) to set a new clone source.

If you're not happy with the results of your cloning, see the next section for ways that you can tweak the cloning layer or further adjust the Clone tool's performance.

More cloning tips

Because the Clone tool is so darned useful, I feel compelled to ramble on about it a little more. When you're cloning, keep the following tricks in mind to make the tool an even better performer:

✔ Adjusting the opacity of the cloned pixels can sometimes help them blend in with their new surroundings. As you lower the opacity of the cloned pixels, more of the original pixels show through. At 100 percent opacity, the cloned pixels completely obscure the originals.

You can adjust opacity by using the Opacity controls on the Options bar and in the Layers palette, as follows:

- The control on the Options bar affects the original transparency of the cloned pixels that you lay down with the Clone tool.

- The control in the Layers palette affects the opacity of all existing pixels on the clone layer.

In addition, if you're using Elements 1.0, you can use the Brush Dynamics options to vary the tool opacity and brush size on the fly. For details about this option, see the section "Painting 'dynamically'" later in this chapter.

✔ By varying the blending mode for the cloning layer or the Clone tool itself (via the Mode control on the Options bar), you can change the way that pixels on the clone layer blend with those on the underlying layer. See the upcoming section "Using blending modes" for information on what some of the most useful modes do.

✔ If cloned pixels appear slightly lighter or darker than their new neighbors, you can use the Levels command to fix things. But when you make this correction in Elements, don't apply Levels via an adjustment layer as you normally do (or should, at any rate). Instead, click the clone layer in the Layers palette and then press Ctrl+L (⌘+L) to open the Levels dialog box without creating an adjustment layer. (Or choose Enhance⇨Brightness/Contrast⇨Levels in Elements 1.0 or Enhance⇨Adjust Brightness/Contrast⇨Levels in Version 2.0.) This way, the filter affects only the clone layer.

To find out more about using Levels, see Chapter 5.

✔ One of the biggest mistakes that people make when cloning is not matching the texture of the cloned pixels with that of neighboring pixels. The edit then becomes obvious because it appears either grainier or blurrier than the surrounding area. You can see an example of this cloning gaffe in Color Plate 8-2 and find some tips for avoiding it in Chapter 8.

✔ You can reposition the cloned pixels by using the Move tool techniques outlined in the next section. In addition, you can use the techniques covered in Chapter 7 to rotate and resize the cloned area.

- ✔ You can remove cloned pixels by applying the Eraser tool to the clone layer. Just drag over pixels that you want to eliminate. By setting the Eraser tool opacity to less than 100 percent, you can even fade some pixels to partial opacity while leaving others at full opacity. As an alternative, you can draw a selection outline around the pixels you want to remove and then press Delete.

- ✔ If you totally screw up your cloning and want to start over, drag the clone layer to the Trash button at the bottom of the Layers palette.

- ✔ Remember that in order to keep the clone layer separate from the rest of the image, you must save the picture in a format that supports layers and turn on the Layers option in the Save As dialog box. For more information, see the section related to preserving layer masks in Chapter 3. If you need additional help with the file-saving process, refer to Chapter 2.

Creating Seamless Patches

Although the Clone tool is a terrific feature, it may not be the easiest or fastest way to do some types of touch-up work. If you need to cover a large defect or if the defect goes through an area that features strong geometric lines or patterns, you may want to create a patch to hide the problem instead of using the Clone tool.

Consider the left image in Color Plate 6-2, shown in much more boring grayscale form in Figure 6-10. I took this picture in a market on the island of Antigua. I love everything about the image except the white blob that's jutting into the lower-left corner — the blob is a portion of a large flowerpot. I'd love to return to Antigua to reshoot the picture, but alas, my schedule and budget don't allow that any time soon. But I can easily cover up the rogue flowerpot by copying some of the surrounding sidewalk tiles onto the white area, as I did to produce the right image in the figure and color plate.

Making this repair using the Clone tool would have been a tedious job. In order to make the alteration invisible, I needed to maintain the strong geometric pattern found in the sidewalk tile. That kind of work isn't easy with the Clone tool because it requires absolute precision when you position the clone source and clone tool cursor. If you're a hair off, the cloned tiles don't line up with the neighboring tiles, creating an obvious interruption in the pattern.

For this type of job, try the patching method outlined in the following steps. With this technique, you create a digital "patch" by drawing a selection outline around a good portion of the image and then copying the selection to a new layer. Then you drag the patch over the area you want to cover. I used this method to make the alteration to the Antigua photo.

Follow these steps to create and position your patch:

Figure 6-10: To cover up an intruding flowerpot in the lower-left corner (left), I created a patch from the surrounding sidewalk (right).

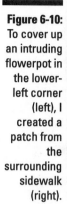

1. **Select the area that you want to use as a patch.**

   First, open the Layers palette and click the name of the layer that contains the patching pixels. Then draw a selection outline around the area you want to turn into a patch. In Figure 6-11, I used the Lasso tool to select an irregular area of the sidewalk.

   Chapter 3 explores different techniques for drawing selection outlines and also introduces you to the Layers palette.

   You don't have to be terribly precise with your selection outline, and the patch doesn't have to be the same size as the defect. If you have only a small area of good pixels to use as a patch, you can duplicate the patch as many times as needed to cover up the entire problem area. By the same token, if the patch winds up being too big, you can use the Eraser tool to rub away unneeded portions.

2. **Feather the selection outline.**

   As discussed in Chapter 3, feathering helps a copied selection blend more naturally into the surrounding pixels. To feather a selection outline in Elements, choose Select⇨Feather and then enter a Feather Radius value in the resulting dialog box.

   How much feathering you need depends on the image area you're trying to patch, and you may need to do some experimenting. For a detailed, sharply focused area like the sidewalk area in Figure 6-11, use a small Feather Radius value. I chose a value of 3 for my patch. In a soft-focus area, raise the Feather Radius value slightly. Remember, though, that feathering eats away a little bit of the outside edges of a selection, so you may need to draw your initial selection outline a little bigger than you otherwise would in order to wind up with the size of patch you want.

3. **Copy the selected area to a new layer.**

   In Elements, you can do this by pressing Ctrl+J (⌘+J) or choosing Layer➪New➪Layer via Copy. The program creates a new layer immediately above the layer that was formerly selected in the Layers palette.

   Your image appears unchanged in the image window because the patch is floating directly above the pixels that you copied to create it.

4. **Move the patch into place.**

   To move the patch in Elements, activate the Move tool by pressing V or clicking the tool's icon in the toolbox, labeled in Figure 6-11.

   You can move the patch by dragging it or, for precise positioning, by pressing the arrow keys. Each press of an arrow key moves the patch one pixel in the direction of the arrow. Press Shift and an arrow key to move the patch ten pixels in the direction of the arrow.

Move tool

Figure 6-11: To create the patch, I selected a section of sidewalk and copied the selection onto a new layer.

If you select the Show Bounding Box check box on the Options bar, a box appears around the selection outline, as shown in the figure. You can drag the square handles around the perimeter of the box to rotate and resize the patch if necessary. The handles work the same way as the handles around a transformation box, explained in Chapter 7.

If the patch didn't completely cover the defect, you can create an entirely new patch by repeating these steps. Or you can duplicate the patch layer as many times as needed, dragging each duplicate over a different part of the defect.

In addition, you can modify a patch using the same techniques outlined in the preceding section, "More cloning tips." (The tips regarding adjusting the Clone brush don't apply, of course.)

After you get your patch just right, you may want to merge the patch layer with the original, defective layer. That way, you can't accidentally move the patch out of position.

If your image contains just the background layer plus the patch layer, merge them by choosing Layer⇨Flatten Image. If your image contains many layers, hide the Layers palette eyeballs for all but the patch layer and the layer into which you want to merge the patch layer. (Click an eyeball to hide the layer; click again to redisplay the layer). After hiding the layers you don't want to merge, click the name of one of the other layers. Then choose Layer⇨Merge Visible. You can then redisplay the hidden layers.

If you do want to preserve the patch layer's independence, follow the instructions for saving layers outlined in Chapter 3.

Applying Touch-Up Paint

For flaws that interrupt an area of flat color, don't mess with any of the methods covered heretofore. Instead, match the foreground color to the surrounding area and then dab some paint over the problem, just as you would use touch-up paint to hide scuff marks on a wall.

As an example, see the left photo in Figure 6-12, which shows my sister and nephew posed in front of a fireplace (that's a tongue of fire in the background area just above my sister's shoulder). I wanted to cover up that bit of flame and also tone down the other prominent details of the fireplace, like the brass trim that runs horizontally behind my sister's head.

Figure 6-12:
To remove distracting background details (left), I loaded up my paintbrush and dabbed over them (right).

To make these changes, I just painted over the flame, the other bright background spots, and the brass trim. Before each paint stroke, I matched the paint color to the color of the surrounding area. I did my painting on a new layer, as shown in Figure 6-13, so that I could paint freely without worrying about damaging the original image. After completing my painting, I set the paint layer's opacity to 90 percent so that I could retain a little of the original texture found in the background.

In addition covering up flaws like the ones in this photo, you can use the paint tools to alter colors in your image. For example, you can turn red eyes back to their natural colors or add color to a grayscale image.

Chapter 8 shows you how to paint away red eye and other portrait problems, such as blown facial highlights. Chapter 9 provides the formula for adding color to grayscale photos.

The remaining sections of this chapter provide a brief introduction to the ins and outs of painting in a photo editing program. As is the case throughout the rest of this book, the screen shots and step-by-step instructions feature Photoshop Elements, but things work pretty much the same in Photoshop and in other photo-editing programs that offer painting tools.

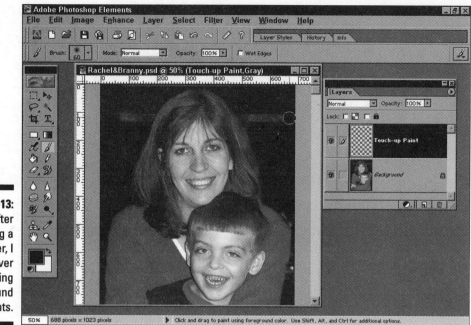

Figure 6-13:
After creating a new layer, I painted over distracting background elements.

Choosing a paint tool

The Photoshop Elements toolbox contains several tools that apply either the foreground or background paint. For touch-up purposes, however, only three serve you well: the Paintbrush (renamed the Brush tool in Elements 2.0), Pencil, and Eraser, all labeled in Figure 6-14. If you're using some other photo editing software, you likely have access to tools that work the same as these three, although the tool names may be different.

✔ **Paintbrush (Brush tool, in Version 2.0) :** Labeled in Figure 6-15, this tool enables you to create a variety of paint strokes, depending on the tool options you select. You can paint using a soft, fuzzy brush to create strokes that are blurry at the edges, as I did to paint the top line of text in the figure. With a hard-edged brush, your strokes have precise edges, as in the lower line of text.

Regardless of brush style, the Paintbrush always applies the foreground color.

✔ **Pencil:** Like the Paintbrush, the Pencil applies the foreground color. But the Pencil can paint only hard-edged strokes. As a result, it's less useful in photo retouching because few subjects in a photo have perfectly hard edges. I do use the Pencil for doing things like fixing a break in a border, however, or touching up sign lettering.

✔ **Eraser:** When you're working on any layer but the background layer, the Eraser becomes a digital paint remover. It rubs away existing pixels, enabling you to wipe away any paint that spills on an area you didn't intend to alter. By adjusting the tool's opacity, you can set the Eraser to completely eradicate pixels or to just make them more translucent, so that pixels on the underlying layer become partially visible.

On the background layer, the Eraser applies the background color. I think I've hammered home the importance of always doing your retouching and restoration work on a separate layer rather than on the original background layer, so I'm confident that you'll never turn to the Eraser as a way to apply the background color except when you're editing an adjustment layer mask. (See Chapter 4 for details on that process.)

If you want to paint with the background color, press X or click the Swap Colors icon in the toolbox to make the current background color the foreground color. Then paint with the Paintbrush or Pencil.

Figure 6-14:
For retouching, stick with the Paintbrush, Pencil, and Eraser.

Color Plate 3-1:
When a picture contains a mix of too-bright and too-dark areas, adjust the exposure of shadows, midtones, and highlights independently. Here, I brightened the shadows and midtones just enough to bring the faces out of the shadows and then toned down the strongest highlights a notch.

Tolerance, 10; Contiguous

Tolerance, 10; Not contiguous

Color Plate 3-2:
To select the lightest parts of this image, I clicked at the spot marked by the red X with the Photoshop Elements Magic Wand tool. The dotted outlines show the area that the tool selected at two Tolerance settings and with the Contiguous option on and off.

Tolerance, 40; Contiguous

Tolerance, 40; Not contiguous

Red feathers

Info			
R :	213	H :	6°
G :	62	S :	79%
B :	44	B :	84%

Blue feathers

Info			
R :	52	H :	225°
G :	78	S :	67%
B :	156	B :	61%

Yellow feathers

Info			
R :	160	H :	68°
G :	186	S :	100%
B :	0	B :	73%

Green feathers

Info			
R :	142	H :	95°
G :	208	S :	55%
B :	94	B :	82%

Color Plate 4-1:
Like all digital images, this photo is made up of red, green, and blue light. The R, G, and B values shown in the palettes on the right indicate the amount of red, green, and blue light present in the areas marked by the white boxes.

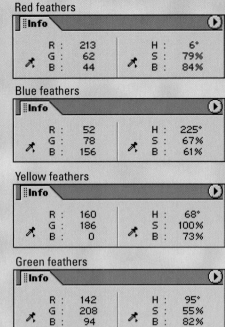

Photoshop only

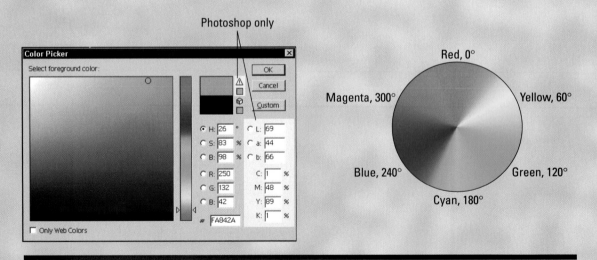

Color Plate 4-2:
In most photo editors, you can mix custom colors by using a variety of formulas, also known as color models. For example, the Adobe Photoshop Color Picker, shown on the left, enables you to blend colors using the R, G, B (red, green, blue) model; the HSB (Hue, Saturation, Brightness) color model, which is based on the 360-degree color wheel shown on the right; and the Lab and CMYK color models, which are designed for high-end professional imaging and print production uses.

Color Plate 4-3:

An RGB image consists of three channels, or storage vats, one each for the red, green, and blue color data. In some photo editors, you can view the individual channels, as shown here. Bright areas in a channel image indicate high amounts of the channel color; dark areas indicate low amounts. For example, the neck feathers in the red channel appear very bright because those feathers consist mostly of red light, as seen in the composite image and indicated by the R, G, and B values in the top palette in Color Plate 4-1.

Color Plate 4-4:
To bring out-of-whack colors into line, you can use a color balance filter such as the Photoshop Elements Variations filter. Click on a thumbnail to add more of one color and subtract an equal amount of the opposite color.

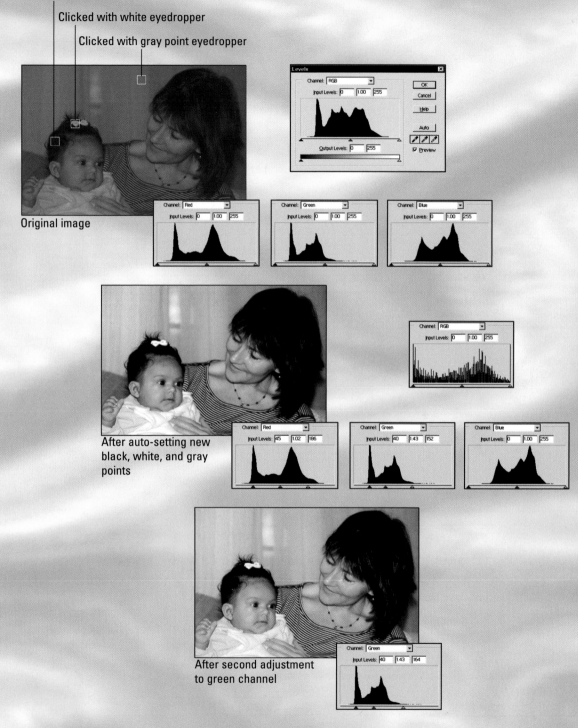

Clicked with black eyedropper

Clicked with white eyedropper

Clicked with gray point eyedropper

Original image

After auto-setting new black, white, and gray points

After second adjustment to green channel

Color Plate 4-5:
You also can correct color problems by using a Levels filter. After you click on areas that should be black, white, and neutral gray, the filter automatically adjusts the image according to those color cues. For this photo, the automatic adjustment worked pretty well, but the image was a touch too green for my liking. I used the other filter controls to remove a little green.

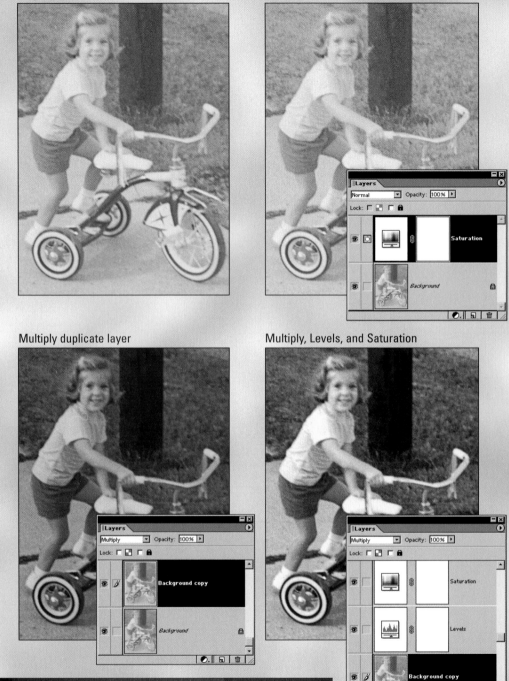

Original

Saturation filter

Multiply duplicate layer

Multiply, Levels, and Saturation

Color Plate 4-6:
Raising the saturation of this old, faded photo brought new life to the scene but also turned the subject's skin orange. For a better result, I duplicated the original image layer and selected Multiply as the layer blending mode, which makes colors darker and more intense. Then I used the Levels filter to brighten the multiplied image and applied the Saturation filter to boost the colors slightly. Although this process sounds complicated, it takes just minutes to do.

Original

Multiply once

Multiply twice

Selected areas erased

Desaturate and Levels adjustment

Original

Amount, 100; Radius, 2; Threshold, 2

Amount, 200; Radius, 1; Threshold, 4

Amount, 300; Radius, 3; Threshold, 0

Color Plate 5-1:
Applying the Unsharp Mask filter takes a bit more time than using automatic sharpening filters but gives you better results. I applied Unsharp Mask using slightly different settings to create the two effects shown in the top-right and lower-left image. However you sharpen your images, avoid overdoing. Too much sharpening results in ugly, glowing halos along the borders between contrasting areas, as shown in the final image.

Color Plate 5-2:
To make a busy background less intrusive, apply a blur filter to the background only.

Color Plate 5-3:
The Levels filter enables you to adjust the brightness of shadows, midtones, and highlights independently. To fix this image, I brightened the highlights and midtones, and darkened the deepest shadows slightly.

Original

Shadows, midtones burned

Highlights burned

Burned on gray layer

Color Plate 5-4:
With a Burn tool, you can darken an image by dragging over the areas you want to adjust. On color images, the tool does a good job darkening shadows and midtones, as illustrated by the top right image. But when you try to burn highlights, you often get gray streaks, as shown in the lower-left image. The secret is to apply the tool to a separate layer that's filled with gray and set to the Overlay layer blending mode — another technique that sounds difficult but is in fact very easy.

Color Plate 6-1:
You can easily remove scratches and small flaws like the time/date stamp in this travel photo. Just use your photo editor's Clone tool to copy good pixels from surrounding areas over the problem pixels.

Color Plate 6-2:
To cover up larger image defects, like the white flower pot that juts into the lower left corner of this image, create a patch from a surrounding area. Then move the patch into place over the element you want to remove.

Color Plate 7-1:
Photos shot with a wide-angle lens often suffer from convergence problems, which is a fancy way of saying that structures that should be vertical tilt toward the middle of the frame. You can straighten out such images by using perspective or distortion filters, as I did with this courthouse image. (Yes, that's a tree in the tower, and no, it didn't cause the courthouse to lean.)

Color Plate 7-2:
To turn this holiday photo into a nice portrait, I first deleted the Santa Claus figure that originally came between the couple. (The white areas show Santa's original body and hand). After moving the pair together, I dropped in a plain background and added shadows behind each subject. I also flipped the man's eyes so that he would be looking into the frame and removed the name badge, pearls, and purse strap from the woman's outfit.

Original

Red areas desaturated

Color restored

Flare removed

Color Plate 8-1:
To eliminate red eye, bypass automated red-eye filters, which hardly ever work well. Instead, desaturate the eye pixels and then paint back in the original eye color where needed. In this photo, I also used the Clone tool to remove the small white flare at the corner of the left eye.

Original

Cloned with soft brush

Cloned with hard brush

Cloned with medium brush

Color Plate 8-2:
Although the Clone tool works makeover miracles, be careful not to destroy skin texture when using it. If you use a too-soft clone brush, you get a blurry look, as shown in the upper right image; use a too-hard brush, and you wind up with a distinct border along the repaired area, as shown in the lower-left example. For this image, as in most portraits, a brush set to medium softness worked best.

Original

Color Plate 8-3:
You can fix over-exposed facial areas by simply dabbing flesh-colored paint on the image. Match the paint color to the surrounding skin and lower the paint opacity slightly so that you retain some of the original brightness. After painting, give the new skin some texture by applying a noise or grain filter.

Skin painted

Grain added

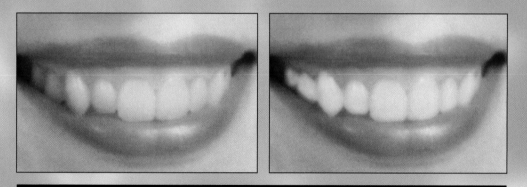

Color Plate 8-4:
To brighten teeth, brush over the surface with the Dodge tool, which lightens the pixels under your cursor, or select the teeth and use the Levels filter to make the change. Aim for a subtle lightening, as shown here, and not glow-in-the-dark teeth.

Original

Best-effort correction

Sponge special-effect filter

Grayscale

Hand-tinted

Color Plate 9-2:
For this casual portrait of mother and daughter, I replaced the distracting background with a fun, blue-sky-and-white-clouds backdrop. I created the sky by using the Clouds filter, a special-effects feature found in many photo editors.

Original

Background, gradient; Cloth, Overlay fill

Background, Texturizer filter; Cloth, Desaturate and Levels filters

Background, Grain filter; Cloth, Hue/Saturation filter with Colorize option

Color Plate 9-3:
Chapter 9 shows you several ways to replace a plain background with something more interesting and also explains how to alter the color of an object in a photo. I used a variety of techniques to create three different backgrounds and shift the color of the tablecloth in this product shot.

Uncompressed TIFF
300 ppi, 723K

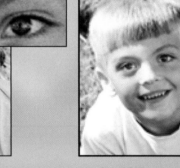 

Uncompressed TIFF
75 ppi, 50K

Compressed JPEG
300 ppi, 47K

256-Color GIF
300 ppi, 94K

 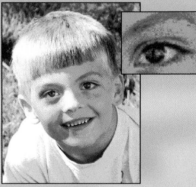

To work with any of these tools, click its icon in the toolbox. Note that the Paintbrush and Eraser are both located on flyout menus with related tools.

What about the remaining paint tools — Airbrush, Gradient, and Paint Bucket — found in Elements, Photoshop, and other programs? My take is this:

✔ The Airbrush pumps out paint much like a real airbrush, only without the mess. The longer you hold down your mouse button, the more paint the tool sprays onto your image.

In my experience, the tool is too hard to control to make it a good option for precise retouching work, although it can be fun to use when creating special effects. I sometimes use the Airbrush for adding streaks of color to a sunset, too. (Oh, don't look so shocked. It's not like I'm falsifying court evidence or anything — just adding a few touches to a pretty picture that I want to hang on my wall.)

If you're using Elements 2.0, you may be searching high and low for your Airbrush tool. Adobe took the tool out of the toolbox in Version 2.0 and instead provides an Airbrush button on the Options bar when you work with the Brush tool (the tool formerly known as Paintbrush). Clicking the button toggles the tool between regular painting mode and airbrush mode.

✔ The Gradient tool fills an area with a spectrum of colors, something you'll almost never find a reason to do when eradicating flaws from a photo. However, the Gradient tool may provide an answer if you have a subject set against a plain background and want to make things more interesting. I explain how to use the Gradient tool to create a new background in Chapter 9.

✔ The Paint Bucket, known as the Fill tool in some programs, is of no use at all. When you click with the Fill tool, the program automatically applies the foreground color to pixels that are similar to the one you clicked. Predicting which pixels will be colored is nigh on impossible, so you hardly ever get the results you expect. If you want to fill an area with color, draw a selection outline and then use the Fill command. Chapter 9 shows you how.

For information on changing the foreground and background colors, including how to use the Eyedropper to lift a color in your photo to use as a paint color, see Chapter 4.

Basic painting techniques

After activating any paint tool but the Eraser, you can apply the foreground color to your photo as follows:

✔ **To lay down a single drop of color:** Click once. The size and shape of the drop depends on the brush you selected. (The next section shows you how to choose a brush.)

- ✔ **To create a stroke of color:** Drag across the image.
- ✔ **To quickly paint a straight line in any direction:** Click at the point where you want the line to begin and Shift+click at the spot where you want the line to end.
- ✔ **To paint a horizontal or vertical line:** Press Shift as you drag. To create a vertical line, press Shift and drag up or down. To create a horizontal line, press Shift and drag right or left.

These last two tricks also work when you're working with any of the Elements editing tools (Blur, Clone, Burn, and so on). If you use another photo editor, check the program's Help system for information about creating straight lines.

Choosing a brush size and shape

You can adjust the diameter and shape of the stroke that a paint tool creates by changing the tool's brush. Although the way that you select a brush varies depending on what photo editor you're using, most programs that offer paint tools at least give you the option of setting the brush softness and size.

In Photoshop Elements, you change out brushes by using the Brushes palette, which appears on the Options bar whenever you activate a tool that offers a choice of brushes. (If you don't see the Options bar, choose Window⇨Show Options.) Figure 6-15 shows the palette as it appears in Elements 1.0; the Version 2.0 palette features a slightly different design.

You display the available brushes and choose the one you want to use as follows:

- ✔ **To display the Brushes palette:** Click the triangle next to the brush icon on the Options bar, as indicated in Figure 6-15. (In Elements 2.0, you also can display the palette by clicking the brush icon next to the triangle.)
- ✔ **To select a brush:** Click its palette icon. In Elements 1.0, the icons show you the shape and approximate size of brushes; however, for very large brushes, the icons don't reflect the real brush size. The number below each icon indicates the exact brush size, in pixels. As you pause your cursor over a brush, you see a small label that gives the brush name, as shown in Figure 6-15.

  In Elements 2.0, the Brushes palette icons look like an actual paint stroke. If you prefer the Version 1.0 design, click the right-pointing triangle near the top of the palette to display a pop-up menu. Then choose Small Thumbnail from the menu.

Click to display menu

Click to display palette

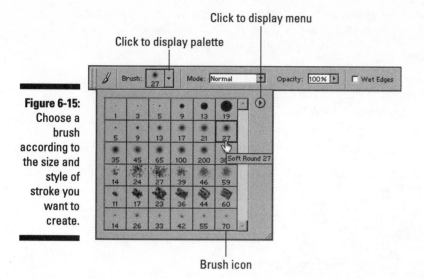

Figure 6-15: Choose a brush according to the size and style of stroke you want to create.

Brush icon

Don't forget that you can set your tool cursor to reflect the size of the current brush. To do so, choose EditÍPreferencesÍDisplay & Cursors. Then select the Brush Size option in the Painting Cursors section of the dialog box. While you're in the dialog box, choose General from the menu at the top of the dialog box and check the setting of the Show Tool Tips option. If it's turned off, you don't get the little brush labels when you pass your cursor over the Brushes palette.

✔ **To adjust the properties of the current brush:** In Elements 1.0, click the brush icon on the Options bar, as shown in Figure 6-16. The dialog box shown in the figure drops down, offering options that enable you to adjust the size, hardness, angle, and roundness of the current brush. You can also tweak the brush spacing, but for ordinary retouching, you probably shouldn't. If you raise the value, you can wind up painting a dotted or dashed line instead of a smooth stroke. To find out more about this or any of the other options, check out the program's Help system, which offers an excellent overview of all of them.

In Version 2.0, you an access the brush customization options only while the Brush tool is active. Click the More Options button at the right end of the Options bar to display the available brush controls. Again, check the program Help system to find out what how each control affects brush performance.

✔ **To load a different assortment of brushes into the palette:** In Elements 1.0, display the Brushes palette menu by clicking the arrow in the upper-right corner of the palette. (Refer to Figure 6-15.) Then select one of the brush collections from the bottom of the menu. You have a choice of calligraphic brushes, natural-texture brushes, and square brushes, among others. To return to the original brush assortment, choose Reset Brushes from the menu.

In Elements 2.0, you can select a brush collection from the Brushes pop-up menu at the top of the Brushes palette. Choose Default Brushes to reload the original brushes.

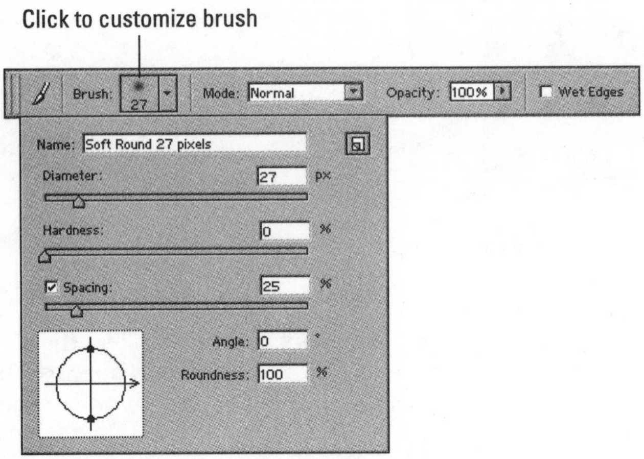

Click to customize brush

Figure 6-16: Click the brush icon on the Options bar to adjust the size, softness, and other attributes of the current brush.

Adjusting paint opacity

By tweaking the Opacity value on the Options bar, you can adjust — big surprise — the opacity of your paint strokes. When you set the value to 100 percent, you paint fully opaque strokes. Reduce the value to make your strokes translucent. The lower the value, the more translucent the paint.

If you're working with the Eraser, the Opacity value affects the strength of the tool, as it does with the Clone tool and some other editing tools. Set the value to 100 percent to erase at full strength, returning the layer areas that you touch with the tool to complete transparency. At lower values, the pixels you swipe with the Eraser become translucent. The lower the value, the less you affect the pixels.

Don't forget that you can also use the Opacity value in the Layers palette to adjust the opacity of all existing pixels on a layer. For an introduction to layers, see Chapter 3.

Painting "dynamically"

Depending upon your photo software, you may be able to adjust certain aspects of your paint strokes on the fly. In Elements 1.0, for example, you can vary the opacity, size, and color of a paint stroke by using the options on the Brush Dynamics menu, shown in Figure 6-17. To display the menu, click its button, which appears at the right end of the Options bar whenever you work with a tool for which the settings are available.

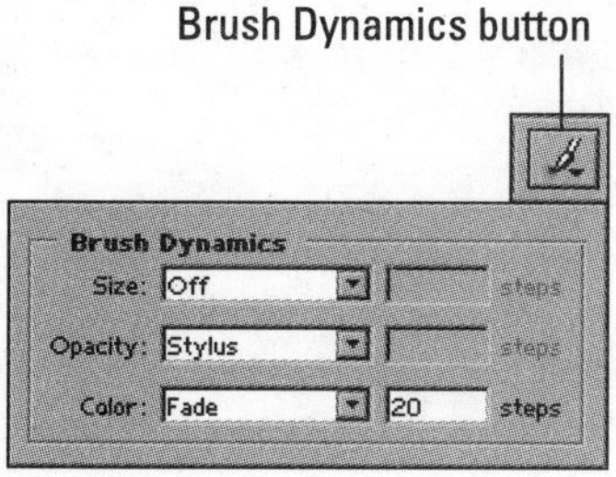

Brush Dynamics button

Figure 6-17:
Use the Brush Dynamics options in Elements 1.0 to alter a stroke as you paint.

When a paint tool is active, you see the Size, Opacity, and Color options, as shown in the figure. When the Eraser is active, only the Size and Opacity options are available. For each option, you can choose from three settings:

- **Off:** The paint tool behaves normally.

- **Fade:** The stroke changes gradually along the length of your stroke. For example, if you choose this option for Color, the stroke starts out in the foreground color and then shifts to the background color. If you select the Fade option for Opacity, your stroke fades to full transparency at the end of your drag. With Size, the Fade option creates a tapering stroke, with the stroke narrowing along the course of your drag.

  You specify how abruptly you want the transition to take place by entering a value in the Steps box. The higher the value, the more gradual the transition.

- **Stylus:** If you're working with a pressure-sensitive drawing tablet, the Stylus option enables you to vary your strokes according to how hard you press down with the stylus. With Size and Opacity, pressing harder increases brush size and opacity, respectively. With Color, light pressure applies the background color, while full pressure applies the foreground color.

For retouching and restoration, the only one of these options I ever use is Opacity, which I sometimes set to Stylus. Working in this mode, I can increase the intensity of a correction by simply pressing harder with my drawing tablet's stylus. If I want to get consistent results with every drag, though, I turn the option off. Then I adjust the opacity of the edits by tweaking the Opacity value for the entire layer, via the Layers palette. (Yet another reason to always separate your important editing phases into individual layers, as discussed in Chapter 4.)

If you're using Elements 2.0, the Brush Dynamics menu is gone, as are some of the original brush dynamics options. To explore the remaining options, click the More Options button at the right end of the Options bar. The Brush tool must be active to access the options.

Two of the options translate to the Version 1.0 Brush Dynamics controls, as follows:

- ✔ If you're working with a drawing tablet, select the Pen Pressure check box to adjust both opacity and stroke size according to the amount of stylus pressure you apply.

  Although you can access this option only while the Brush tool is active, the setting affects all the paint and edit tools. So if a tool isn't responding the way you expect, switch to the Brush tool to check the status of the Pen Pressure setting.

- ✔ The Fade option works like the 1.0 Fade option except that it fades both the opacity and size of the stroke over the course of your drag. This setting affects the Brush tool only.

The Color Jitter and Scatter settings create special-effects strokes; you can read about them in the program Help system. The remaining options correspond to the brush features formerly found in the Brushes palette. See the earlier section "Choosing a brush size and shape" for details.

Using blending modes

Chapters 4 and 5 introduce you to layer **blending modes,** a feature that enables you to mix the pixels on one layer with those on the underlying layer in different ways. When you work with the paint tools and some editing tools, you also have access to blending modes. The section "Rubbing out spots with the Blur tool," earlier in this chapter, shows you how to use the Lighten and Darken blending modes to remove small blemishes from an image.

Layer blending modes affect all pixels on a layer. Tool blending modes affect just the strokes that you're about to apply.

Photo-editing programs that offer layers and blending modes typically offer the same core assortment of blending modes. Some of these modes are useful for creating special effects only, while others can be helpful for various retouching and restoration tasks.

The following list provides a brief introduction to a few of the more practical blending modes as they apply to painting tools.

- ✔ **Normal:** Your paint strokes obscure underlying pixels, according to the tool opacity setting. In Figure 6-18, I used the Paintbrush to paint a medium-gray stroke over a black-to-white gradient, with the tool opacity set at 100 percent. The gray stroke completely covers everything underneath.

- ✔ **Lighten:** In this mode, the tool affects the underlying pixels only if doing so will make the pixels lighter. As an example, see the second stroke in Figure 6-18. I applied the same paint color, at full opacity, as in the Normal example. But this time, only the darker half of the gradient changes color because pixels in the lower half are lighter than the medium-gray paint color.

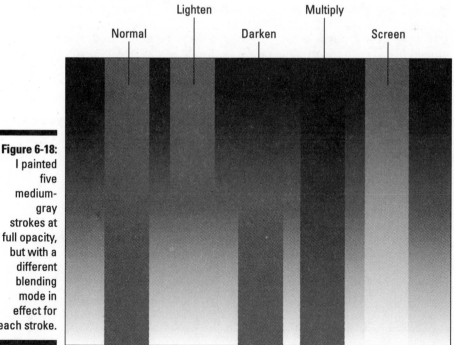

Normal   Lighten   Darken   Multiply   Screen

Figure 6-18: I painted five medium-gray strokes at full opacity, but with a different blending mode in effect for each stroke.

✔ **Darken:** This mode is the opposite of Lighten. With Darken, the tool changes only pixels that will become darker as a result of the edit. In Figure 6-18, my paint stroke darkened the light half of the gradient, but any areas that were darker than medium gray didn't change.

✔ **Multiply:** The Multiply mode multiplies the brightness value of the original pixel with that of the paint color, resulting in a pixel that's darker than both, as shown in Figure 6-14. If you multiply any color with black, you get black; multiplying any color with white produces no color change.

✔ **Screen:** The opposite of Multiply, Screen always results in a color that's lighter than the original pixel and the paint color. In this case, multiplying any color with white produces white and multiplying any color with black results in no color change. The last paint stroke in Figure 6-18 provides a look at the screen mode.

✔ **Color:** With Color, you wind up with a pixel that takes its hue from the paint color but retains the brightness value and saturation of the original pixel. The Color mode is useful for changing the color of objects in a photo.

For an example of the Color mode in action, see the section on removing red eye in Chapter 8. Also check out the hue-spinning section of Chapter 9.

When you're working with the Clone tool, these blending modes mix the cloned pixels with the original pixels in the same way as when you apply paint. You can read more about the Clone tool in the section "Cloning Good Pixels over Bad," earlier in this chapter. Also check out "Rubbing out spots with the Blur tool" for details on using the Lighten and Darken blending modes while blurring.

Chapter 7

Improving Composition

- -

- -

Earlier chapters in this book show you how to refine a photograph through minor changes — tweaking exposure and contrast, covering up small flaws, and fixing color problems. This chapter takes you a step further, showing you how to drastically alter the composition of an image by cutting away parts of the picture, shifting elements within the frame, or both.

Purists may say that these types of changes go beyond the realm of retouching or restoring because you're altering what the photographer saw through the viewfinder. That's true, I suppose, and I certainly don't advocate editing the composition of photos intended for scientific, legal, or other use where your audience expects that what they see is exactly what the photographer got.

If your goal is to improve an image, however, I see no reason not to explore every way to do so, especially when you're working with family photos or other favorite images from your personal collection. If you have the opportunity to recompose and reshoot the picture, by all means, grab your camera. Otherwise, take advantage of the techniques presented in this chapter to create the composition that you wish you'd captured when you pressed the shutter button.

Cropping a Photo

When preparing fresh asparagus for a gourmet meal, a good chef snaps off the woody lower stems and sends only the tender upper portion of each stalk to the dinner table. Similarly, you can serve up just the best parts of a photo by cropping away unsightly or unimportant areas around the perimeter of the picture.

Consider the picture in Figure 7-1, for example. I shot this photo of my nieces and nephews several years ago at a King family gathering. This was one of those "everybody grab their cameras and shoot quick!" situations. Although the older cousins made a valiant attempt to keep the toddler-age twins from squirming away, I could tell right away that I wasn't going to have more than a few seconds to snap the picture. So I didn't pay much attention to framing at all — just centered the kids in the viewfinder and hoped for the best. (First rule of photography: If the picture isn't perfect, blame the subjects!)

Given the circumstances, the picture turned out better than I expected — the focus is sharp and four out of five youngsters are making eye contact. By snipping away the excess background in my photo editor, I was able to correct my original compositional mistake and produce a much better summer memory, shown in Figure 7-2.

Figure 7-1:
An excess of background distracts from the main subject.

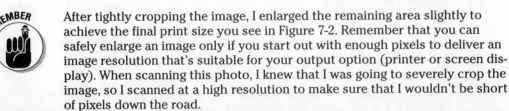

After tightly cropping the image, I enlarged the remaining area slightly to achieve the final print size you see in Figure 7-2. Remember that you can safely enlarge an image only if you start out with enough pixels to deliver an image resolution that's suitable for your output option (printer or screen display). When scanning this photo, I knew that I was going to severely crop the image, so I scanned at a high resolution to make sure that I wouldn't be short of pixels down the road.

Figure 7-2:
To improve
the
composition,
I cropped
the photo
and then
enlarged the
remaining
image area.

Of course, if you're scanning a photograph, your scanner software probably offers a crop tool that enables you to scan just the areas of the image you want to keep. I scanned the entire picture for this example just as an illustration of how you can improve composition by cropping.

Choosing a cropping method

Photoshop Elements offers several ways to cut off unwanted areas from the perimeter of a picture. Which method works best depends on the specific cropping result you want.

- **To crop to approximate photo dimensions:** Work with the Crop tool, covered in the next section. You can crop your photo to any width or height, and you can even rotate the remaining image area at the same time.

- **To crop to specific dimensions (such as 4 inches by 6 inches):** You can use the Crop tool, but a safer option is to use the Rectangular Marquee selection tool in conjunction with the Crop command. For details, see "Cropping to a specific size," later in this chapter.

- **To shave a precise amount off one or more sides of the image:** Turn to the Canvas Size command. The upcoming section "Resizing the image canvas" tells all.

If you're using a photo editor comparable to Elements, you likely have access to at least the first and last options. Check your software Help system to find out whether the second cropping approach is possible.

Working with the Crop tool

When you're not concerned with achieving a precise image size, use the Crop tool to cut away the junk at the outer edges of your pictures. The following steps explain the process in Photoshop Elements — most Crop tools in other programs work similarly.

Before you begin, save a backup copy of your image. After you crop, you may not be able to get the original pixels back, depending on how your software handles cropping.

In some programs, including recent versions of Photoshop, you *can* restore cropped areas by taking advantage of an advanced cropping function. Check your software's Help system for information about the availability of this feature and what precautions you need to take to store the cropped pixels so that you can access them later.

1. **Activate the Crop tool by clicking its toolbox icon, labeled in Figure 7-3.**

   Note that in Elements 2.0, the Crop tool appears on the opposite side of the toolbox, next to the new Selection Brush tool.

   In both versions of the program, the Options bar presents the controls shown in the figure when the Crop tool is active. For normal cropping, leave these options at their default settings, also shown in the figure. (The next section explains more about these options.)

2. **Drag to enclose the area you want to keep inside a crop boundary, as shown in the figure.**

   The dotted outline represents the crop boundary, as shown in Figure 7-3.

   If the program restricts the crop boundary to a certain width/height ratio, click the Clear button on the Options bar. The Crop tool may be working according to the Width, Height, or Resolution settings that you previously used.

   After you release the mouse button, small squares appear around the perimeter of the crop boundary, as shown in Figure 7-4. (If you want to sound like a digital imaging pro, refer to the squares as *crop handles.*) The Options bar controls also change. If you select the Shield Cropped Area check box (renamed Shield in Elements 2.0), a translucent overlay covers the area outside the crop boundary, as in the figure. You can use the controls next to the check box to adjust the color and opacity of the overlay.

3. **Adjust the crop boundary as needed.**

   You can refine the boundary as follows:

   • **To enlarge or reduce the crop boundary:** Drag a crop handle. To enlarge the boundary proportionally, Shift+drag a corner handle.

Crop tool   Crop boundary

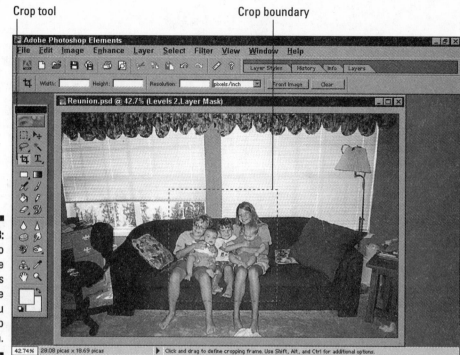

Figure 7-3:
Drag to
mark the
boundaries
of the image
area you
want to
retain.

- **To reposition the boundary:** Drag inside the boundary. Or press the arrow keys on your keyboard to nudge the boundary. Press an arrow key once to shift the boundary one pixel in the direction of the arrow. Press Shift plus and arrow key to move the boundary ten pixels.

- **To rotate the boundary:** You can position your cursor outside the boundary, near one of the corner crop handles, and then drag up or down to rotate the boundary. However, when you do this, you rotate the image by a corresponding amount when you apply the crop. For more information about this feature, see the section "Rotating while cropping," later in this chapter.

4. **Click the Apply button or press Enter to crop the photo.**

   Figure 7-4 shows the Apply button as it appears in Elements 1.0. If you decide not to go forward with the crop after you create the crop boundary, click the Cancel button or press the Esc (Escape) key. (In Elements 2.0, the Cancel button sports a new design and appears to the left of the Apply button.)

   To reverse the crop after the fact, use any of the undo techniques I outline in Chapter 2.

Cancel

Crop handle   Apply

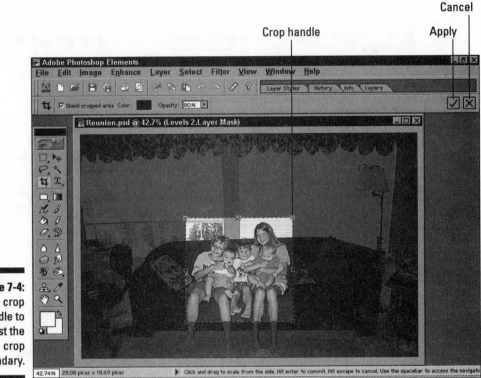

Figure 7-4:
Drag a crop
handle to
adjust the
crop
boundary.

Cropping to a specific size

Some photo editors enable you to constrain the Crop tool to drawing a crop boundary that has a specific aspect ratio. You may even be able to use the tool to establish both the image print size and output resolution simply by cropping.

These features may seem like the perfect way to adjust your picture so that it fits a certain picture frame. Unfortunately, using these crop options can leave you with fewer pixels than you need to produce a suitable print. In some cases, the program may add or delete pixels automatically in the course of applying the crop, and that's a job that you, and not some automatic software control, should handle.

For a review of how pixels and resolution affect printed pictures, head for Chapter 2. To find out how to change the number of pixels in an image, flip to Chapter 10.

The following steps show you a safer way to achieve a specific output size in Photoshop Elements. This technique involves drawing a selection outline with the Rectangular Marquee tool and then applying the Crop command. (You can use the same steps in any program that offers similar features.)

1. **Save a backup copy of your original image.**

2. **Grab the Rectangular Marquee tool, labeled in Figure 7-5.**

Rectangular Marquee tool

Figure 7-5:
Use the
Rectangular
Marquee
tool in Fixed
Size mode
to crop a
photo to a
specific
output size.

3. **On the Options bar, set the Style option to Fixed Size, as shown in the figure.**

4. **Figure out how many pixels you need for your final output.**

   Again, Chapter 2 provides the background information that will help you do this math. To briefly recap, though, you calculate these numbers differently depending on whether you want to print your picture or use it on-screen:

   - **For print output:** Multiply your desired output size by the optimal output resolution your printer needs. For example, if your printer manual says that the printer does its best work when an image has an output resolution of 300 ppi (pixels per inch), and you want a final print size of 4 inches wide by 6 inches tall, you need 1200 pixels horizontally and 1800 pixels vertically.

- **For screen display:** Match the pixel count to the amount of screen real-estate you want the picture to consume. Remember that a monitor uses one screen pixel to display each image pixel. So on a monitor set to a screen resolution of 800 x 600, an image that's 800 pixels wide by 600 pixels tall fills the screen.

If you want to use your picture both ways, crop with the print requirements in mind. Then make a copy of the image for use on-screen and follow the steps laid out in Chapter 10 to eliminate excess pixels and get the screen display size you need.

5. **Enter the pixel values you calculated in Step 4 in the Width and Height boxes on the Options bar.**

Elements assumes that you want to use the same unit of measurement as the rulers that appear alongside the image window. If you don't see the rulers, choose View⇨Show Rulers or press Ctrl+R (⌘+R). You establish this measurement unit by choosing Edit⇨Preferences⇨Units & Rulers and selecting an option from the Rulers menu in the resulting dialog box.

If the rulers aren't set to pixels, be sure to type the letters **px** after the value that you enter in the Width and Height boxes. For example, to set the width to 600 pixels, type **600 px**. Press Enter after you enter the value.

6. **Click in the image window.**

A selection outline appears, as shown in Figure 7-5. The dimensions of the outline match those you set in the Width and Height boxes.

7. **Move the selection outline to frame the portion of the picture you want to keep.**

To move the outline, drag inside it. You also can nudge the outline by pressing the arrow keys. Press a key once to move the outline one pixel; press Shift plus an arrow key to move the outline 10 pixels.

8. **Choose Image⇨Crop.**

9. **If you're printing the photo, establish the output dimensions.**

At this point, you've established the number of horizontal and vertical pixels, which is the end of the line if you're preparing a photo for on-screen use. But if you're printing the picture, you still need to specify the final output resolution (pixels per inch) and print size.

Chapter 10 explains this process in detail, so I won't duplicate the information here.

In some cases, the selection outline that you create in Step 6 may be smaller or larger than the portion of the picture you want to retain. In Figure 7-5, for example, my outline includes too much of the background at the top of the picture. What to do? The answer depends on the way you plan to use the photo and whether you want to cut away less of your picture or crop the image more tightly.

✔ **To retain more of the photo:** If you enlarge the selection outline to retain more of the picture, you will wind up with more pixels than you need (because you capture more pixels than your original formula suggested). That means that you can crop to any size — as long as it's larger than your original outline — without worry.

To make your life easier, press Ctrl+D (⌘+D) to get rid of the existing selection outline. Then abandon the Fixed Size tool setting and instead set the Style option to Constrained Aspect Ratio (renamed Fixed Aspect Ratio in Elements 2.0). With this option, the values you enter in the Width and Height boxes establish just the proportions of your outline. If you want a picture to fit a 4 x 6-inch frame, for example, you simply enter 4 and 6 as the Width and Height values. You also can enter a specific pixel count, but you're limited to a top value of 999.999 pixels.

After entering the values, drag in your image to create a new selection outline. You can make the outline as large as necessary to surround the parts of the picture you want to keep. No matter what the size of the outline, the Constrained Aspect Ratio feature ensures that the proportions of the outline remain the same as the one you originally drew.

After you apply the Crop command, you can *downsample* — that is, dump excess pixels — to arrive at the right output resolution or screen size. Chapter 10 explains how to take this step.

✔ **To crop the photo more tightly:** I'm afraid there is no perfect solution for this one. If you retain less of the original photo than indicated by the marquee you created in Step 6, you wind up with fewer pixels than you need to achieve the output resolution or display size you want.

For a print picture, you can try reducing the resolution value you used to calculate the pixel dimensions in Step 4. This results in a smaller selection outline when you click in Step 6. But remember that using an image output resolution lower than your printer suggests may reduce the quality of the print.

For an on-screen image, you can select the Constrained Aspect Ratio option and draw the selection outline as explained in the preceding bullet point. This time after you crop, you need to *upsample* — add pixels — to wind up at the display size you want. However, upsampling typically results in lower image quality, too.

To be honest, in this situation, I usually draw the selection outline with the Constrained Aspect Ratio option regardless of whether my photo is meant for screen or printer. After I choose the Crop command, I see where I'm at in the pixel department. If I'm not too far off, I just move along, recognizing that I'm sacrificing a little bit of image quality in order to arrive at a certain picture size.

Of course, if you're working with a scanned image, you can always rescan the picture. When you rescan, use your scanner software's crop function to scan just the area of the photo you want to retain, making sure to set the input resolution high enough for your planned output.

Resizing the image canvas

You can also trim away the edges of a picture by reducing the size of the image *canvas*. The canvas is like a transparent backing on which every digital image rests. When you cut away the edges of the canvas, you cut off part of the photo, just as you would if you sawed a few inches of canvas off an oil painting.

You also trim the canvas whenever you use the Crop tool, but if you want to slice off a very small section of the photo — say, a 5-pixel-wide border — getting the cut just right can be difficult to do with that tool. Some programs, including Elements, provide an easier option. You enter precise canvas width and height values in a dialog box, and then the program does the trimming for you.

The following steps show you how to reduce the canvas size in Elements:

1. **Choose Image⇨Resize⇨Canvas Size.**

    You see the Canvas Size dialog box, shown in Figure 7-6. The dialog box looks slightly different in Elements 2.0; the changes are mostly cosmetic, though.

Figure 7-6:
The Canvas Size dialog box enables you to clip away a precise amount from any side of your image.

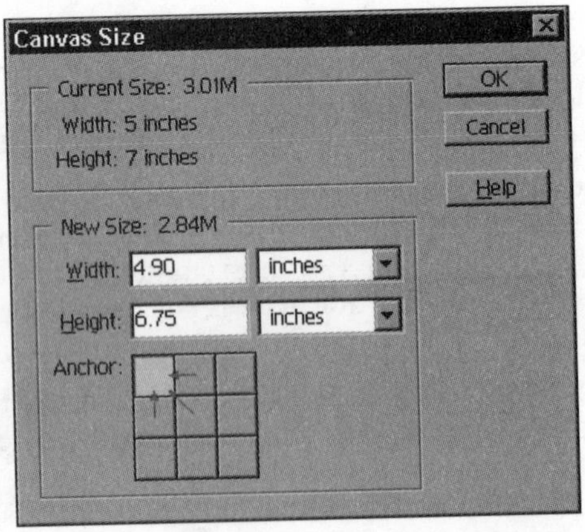

> **Canvas Size**
>
> Current Size: 3.01M
> Width: 5 inches
> Height: 7 inches
>
> New Size: 2.84M
> Width: 4.90   inches
> Height: 6.75   inches
> Anchor:
>
> OK
> Cancel
> Help

2. **Enter the desired canvas dimensions in the Width and Height boxes.**

    You can select a different unit of measurement from the drop-down lists next to each box.

    In Elements 2.0, the Relative option enables you to take another approach to reducing the canvas. You can select the Relative option and enter negative values in the Width and Height boxes to indicate the amount of canvas that you want to eliminate. For example, to trim the image width by 2 inches, enter –2 in the Width box and select Inches as the unit of measurement.

3. **Click an Anchor tile to indicate the placement of the image with respect to the new canvas.**

   For example, if you click the center square, the program lops equal amounts off both sides of the canvas according to the Width value you specified in Step 2. Likewise, equal amounts are removed from the top and bottom of the canvas according to your Height specification. To look at it another way, the program places your image smack dab in the middle of the new, smaller canvas. Areas that fall off the edges of the new canvas get tossed in the dumpster.

   To trim the top of the canvas only, click a bottom square; to chop the image off at the knees instead, click a top square. To trim the left side of the canvas only, click one of the right squares; to trim the right side, click a left square.

   In Figure 7-6, I clicked the top-left square, which trims the bottom and right sides of the image. (Of course, the trimming occurs on both sides only if you reduce both the Width and Height values in Step 2.)

4. **Press Enter or click OK to trim the canvas and close the dialog box.**

   You see an alert box telling you that a portion of your image will be lost; press Enter or click Proceed to go forward with the change.

You also can enlarge the canvas to add empty areas around the perimeter of the image — think of this as stapling a clean section of new canvas to the edge of a painting. You may need to do this when combining several images into a photo collage, for example. To enlarge the canvas, follow these same steps but raise the Width and Height values in Step 2.

When you increase the canvas size, the new canvas areas are filled with the current background color. That means that you can use the Canvas Size command to add a border around one or more edges of your photo. Just change the background color to the color you want to use for the border and set the Width and Height values according to how much border you want to add.

Chapter 10 explores more ways to add borders around a photo.

Leveling the Horizon Line

Unless you're trying to achieve some special photographic point of view, the rules of good composition require a level horizon line. When the line tilts up or down, the subject looks as though it's about to slide off the page.

Even if your composition doesn't show the actual horizon, as in the old photo in Figure 7-7, you should level the subject with respect to where the horizon line *would* be if the scene stretched to that point. Otherwise, elements that should be perfectly vertical or horizontal lean one way or another. In this photo, for example, the sides of the house lean to the right, and the siding boards tip downward. This scene reminds me of an amusement park attraction — "Come inside and explore the fabulous tilting house!"

Figure 7-7:
Among other problems, this old photo suffers from a framing that tilts the horizon line.

You can easily straighten a tilting horizon line by using the techniques explored in the next few sections. Be aware that when you level a picture, however, some of your original image areas move off the canvas, and empty canvas areas appear along the edges of the image, as shown in Figure 7-8. Because of this result, you should take this step before making any other edits. You may need to crop your photo differently as a result of the image shift that occurs when you level the picture.

Figure 7-8:
Leveling the horizon line reveals empty canvas and moves some image areas off the edge of the canvas.

Chapter 1 discusses the right order to follow when you undertake a retouching or restoration project and also describes the other steps I took to repair this picture after righting the house.

Straightening the image automatically

Photoshop Elements and some other programs geared toward the novice photo editor offer a feature that's supposed to automatically straighten an image. This feature — called the Straighten Image command in Elements — works very well on some pictures. But on some images, the result is totally off.

When you apply the command, the program looks for strong, straight lines across the image and then rotates the image to make those lines level. But when your photo contains many different straight edges, the program doesn't always pick the right ones to use as a basis for the leveling, and you don't get the right amount or direction of rotation.

Still, if the feature works, you save yourself some time, so it's worth a try. Choose Image⇨Rotate⇨Straighten Image and wait for the program to do its stuff. After the rotation occurs, empty canvas areas are filled with the current background color. If you're not happy with the outcome, undo the change and then use the manual straightening technique outlined in the next section.

Leveling with precision

Most programs offer a selection of Rotate commands, and the natural assumption is that these commands will fix a tilting image. However, Rotate commands typically are meant for changing the orientation of a photo. For example, if an image is lying on its side when you open it in your photo editor, you use the Rotate command to set the image upright. In some programs, you also can rotate an image layer to any angle, although you normally can't do so to the bottom (background) layer.

To level a horizon line, you need to be able to rotate the background layer with respect to the image canvas. In Elements, you do this via the Free Transform command, like so:

1. **Choose Select⇨All or press Ctrl+A (⌘+A) to select the entire image.**

   As I warned in my earlier introduction to leveling, you should tackle your tilt problem as the very first step in your editing project. If your image already contains layers, you must either rotate each layer individually or flatten the image (merge all layers into one), a topic discussed near the end of this chapter. You can also link layers; see the program Help system for information on that process, which is a bit beyond the scope of this book.

2. **Choose Image⇨Transform⇨Free Transform or press Ctrl+T (⌘+T).**

   After you choose the command, a transformation box appears around the perimeter of the image, as shown in Figure 7-9. Small squares, known as *transformation handles,* rim the box. The Options bar also changes to offer the controls shown in the figure.

   If you don't see the handles, you may need to enlarge the image window to reveal them. Just drag a side of the window to do so.

3. **Position your cursor outside the transformation box, near one of the corner handles.**

   Your cursor should take on a curved appearance, as shown in Figure 7-9.

   No curved cursor? Check the status of the three Options bar buttons just to the right of the Rotation Angle box, which is labeled in Figure 7-9. Click the first button, labeled Rotate in the figure, to kick the program into rotate mode. (If none of the buttons is active, something else is wrong — see my note in Step 2 related to enlarging the image window.)

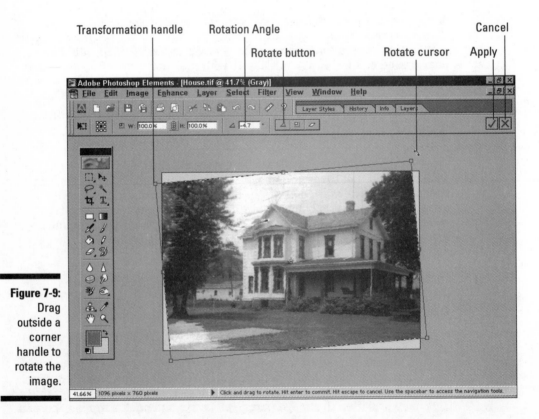

Figure 7-9:
Drag outside a corner handle to rotate the image.

4. **Drag up or down to rotate the image with respect to the image canvas.**

   Some empty canvas areas should appear around the edges of the image, as shown in the figure. Empty areas get filled with the current background color.

   For small moves, abandon the transformation handles and instead adjust the angle of rotation by raising or lowering the value in the Rotation Angle box on the Options bar. Double-click the box to highlight the value and then press the up and down arrow keys to raise and lower the value.

5. **Press Enter or click the Apply button at the right end of the Options bar to apply the rotation for good.**

   Before taking this step, you can cancel out of the transformation by clicking the Cancel button or pressing the Esc (Escape) key. (Note that the Apply and Cancel buttons have swapped positions in Elements 2.0.)

If your software offers a window grid feature, as shown in Figure 7-10, turn it on to serve as a visual guide when you're setting the rotation angle. To display the grid in Elements, choose View➪Grid. You can adjust the appearance of the grid by choosing Edit➪Preferences➪Grid and using the controls in the resulting dialog box.

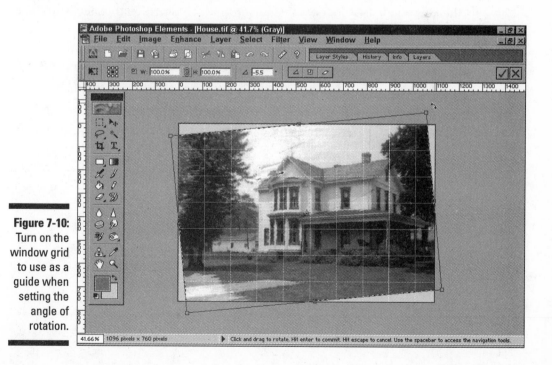

Figure 7-10: Turn on the window grid to use as a guide when setting the angle of rotation.

Rotating while cropping

Some Crop tools enable you to level and crop an image at the same time. In Elements, for example, you can drag outside one of the corner handles on the crop boundary to set the rotation angle, as shown in Figure 7-11. When you apply the crop, the program applies the transformation and trims the image canvas accordingly.

The drawback to this method is that the image preview doesn't update to show you the rotated image as it does when you use the Free Transform command. However, you can use the crop boundary to provide a guide when you're setting the rotation angle. Drag one of the center crop handles inward, so that the edge of the crop boundary aligns with an element that should be level. For example, in Figure 7-10, I dragged the bottom edge to the foundation line of the house and then adjusted the rotation angle until the foundation and edge aligned. Before you apply the crop, return the edge of the crop boundary to its original position.

Notice that in Figure 7-11, the angle of rotation is different than in Figure 7-10. When you rotate while cropping, the program tilts the canvas with respect to the image, rather than the other way around. Then it straightens both canvas and image together when you apply the crop. Don't spend too much time thinking about it — your eyes will tell you which direction the image needs to go when you start rotating.

Figure 7-11:
Use a side of the crop boundary as a guide when leveling an image while cropping.

Righting Leaning Towers

When you shoot pictures using a wide-angle lens, you sometimes wind up with a *convergence* problem. The perspective of the lens distorts the scene in a way that makes vertical lines near the outer edges of the picture tilt inward. The further an object is from the lens, the more pronounced the effect. Objects closer to the lens, on the other hand, may appear larger than they should.

The photo in Figure 7-12 and on the left side of Color Plate 7-1 illustrates an extreme convergence problem. In case you're wondering, that *is* a tree growing out of the tower, which tops the Greensburg, Indiana, courthouse. No one's sure why the tree decided to grow there, but the townsfolk are quite proud of it, nonetheless.

Figure 7-12: Pictures shot with a wide-angle lens often exhibit convergence problems.

You can buy special lens filters, known as shift/tilt filters, to help prevent convergence. But if your camera doesn't accept add-on filters or you're working with an existing photo, you can fix minor convergence problems in your photo editor. To get the job done, you need an image editor that enables you to warp a picture so that it's no longer a perfect rectangle — to make it wider at the top than at the bottom, for example.

In Elements, the tool for the job is the Free Transform command, introduced in the preceding section. If you're using another photo editor, look in the help system for details about distortion or transformation filters, which likely work similarly to the Elements Free Transform feature.

Don't crop your picture before correcting convergence. Depending on the image, you may want to trim away a part of the picture after correcting it. If you crop beforehand, you limit your options at the trimming stage.

The following steps show you how to use the Free Transform command to tackle a convergence problem.

1. **Enlarge the image canvas by about 25 percent horizontally and vertically.**

   You need the extra canvas room because you stretch the image in the upcoming steps. Follow the instructions provided earlier in this chapter, in the section "Resizing the image canvas," to enlarge the canvas.

2. **Choose Select⇨All or press Ctrl+A (⌘+A) to select the entire image.**

   This step assumes that you're working with a single-layer image. If your image contains multiple layers, you need to perform the transformation on each layer independently or else flatten the image to a single layer or link the layers. (Again, I don't cover layer linking in this book, but the Elements manual and online Help system tell you what you need to know.)

   Chapter 3 introduces you to layers; for details on flattening an image, see the last section in this chapter.

3. **Press Ctrl+T (⌘+T) or choose Image⇨Transform⇨Free Transform.**

   A transformation box appears around the selected area, as shown in Figure 7-13, and transformation handles appear around the perimeter of the box.

Transformation handle

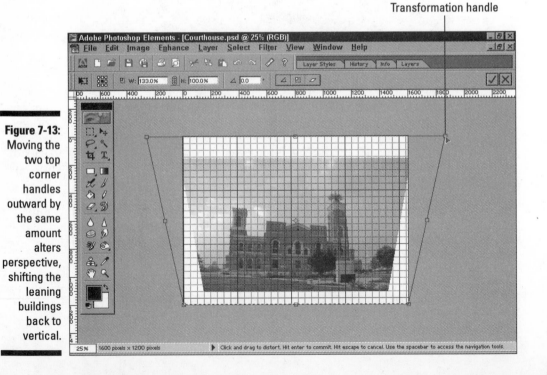

Figure 7-13: Moving the two top corner handles outward by the same amount alters perspective, shifting the leaning buildings back to vertical.

4. **Press Ctrl+Alt+Shift (⌘+Option+Shift) as you drag the top-left or top-right handle outward, as shown in Figure 7-13.**

   When you drag either handle, the opposite handle should move in tandem. If you don't press Ctrl+Alt+Shift (⌘+Option+Shift), only one handle moves. How far you need to drag depends on the degree of the convergence. Drag the handle a short distance, let the image-editor redraw the picture, and assess the results. Keep dragging until you're satisfied.

   If your software enables you to display a grid atop your image, as shown in Figure 7-13, turn the grid on. Then use the lines in the grid to gauge how far you need to stretch the image to get things into proper position. In Elements, you display the grid by choosing View➪Grid.

5. **Increase the image height if needed.**

   Inspect the lower half of the picture. Most likely, objects now look shorter and fatter than they should. To get them back into shape, you need to stretch the picture vertically by dragging a top-center or bottom-center handle.

6. **Refine the image by distorting the image further, if needed.**

   With some images, you may need to distort your picture a little more to get everything completely square.

   Use the following techniques:

   - To adjust image width, drag a center side handle.

   - To adjust height, drag a top or bottom center handle.

   - To distort the image without any restrictions, Ctrl+drag (⌘+drag) any handle.

   - To skew (slant) the image, Ctrl+Shift+drag a side handle. (⌘+Shift+drag on a Mac.)

   At any point during your distortion session, you can press Ctrl+Z (⌘+Z) to undo the last drag of a handle. To cancel out of the transformation entirely, click the Cancel button on the Options bar or press the Esc (Escape) key.

7. **Press Enter or click the Apply button on the Options bar to apply the transformation.**

8. **Crop away the excess canvas.**

   Your corrected scene, although no longer falling in on itself, is now non-rectangular. You can fix that by trimming the image with a Crop tool. Of course, because your image is wider at one end than the other, you wind up trimming away some of the original scene when you crop, as you can see when you compare the corrected image in Figure 7-14 and on the right side of Color Plate 7-1 with the original.

Figure 7-14:
The courthouse stands upright again, although some areas at the edge of the frame are lost in the process.

As you can see, even with all my manipulations, I couldn't completely square up my courthouse picture. You may not be able to entirely correct extreme convergence problems such as this either, but you should at least be able to make a noticeable improvement, as I did for this image.

Rearranging Picture Elements

Clipping away unwanted objects from the edge of a photo is a breeze, as the first part of this chapter shows. Covering up small flaws here and there rarely involves much effort, either; with the Clone tool and other techniques discussed in Chapter 6, you can clean up even the messiest photos in no time.

Eliminating a large area from the center of a photo or rearranging objects within the frame — or both — present more difficult challenges, especially when you're working with portraits. For example, a good friend sent me a picture of her parents at a Christmas party. Both parents looked great in the shot. The only trouble was, Santa Claus sat between the two. After my friend's father passed away, she asked whether I could remove Santa and move her parents together to create a nice portrait.

Figure 7-15 and the top image in Color Plate 7-2 show the original photo after I took the step of deleting Santa. (The deleted areas appear white; the deleted area behind the man's back was Santa's hand.) With Santa out of the way, I studied the picture to figure out how I could fit the couple together. I could see that this shuffling would be relatively easy because of the couple's original postures. I wouldn't have to reshape an arm or anything else to make a natural pairing. (By the way, if you do want to reshape an arm, try using the Free Transform command discussed in the preceding section.)

Figure 7-15: Deleting the middleman in this photo made it easier to study how I might be able to move the other two subjects closer together.

Figure 7-16 and the lower image in Color Plate 7-2 show the finished image. After I slid the woman over into the seat previously occupied by Santa, I decided to also slip a more attractive background behind the couple. In addition, I used the cloning and patching tricks covered in Chapter 6 to remove the woman's purse strap and name badge. I took the easy way out and also removed the pearls because I wasn't confident in my ability to fill in the gaps in the necklace that were left after I removed the purse. Finally, I flipped the man's eyes so that he would be looking into the frame. A little sharpening and exposure correction provided the finishing touches.

Figure 7-16: In the final image, husband and wife are together again, sans Santa, and set against a new background.

The remaining part of this chapter breaks down the steps involved in removing large objects from the interior of a photo, joining the remaining areas, and rotating, flipping, and otherwise transforming selected areas, such as the eyes in Figure 7-15.

For information on creating and adding a new background, check out Chapter 9.

Deleting a picture element

To banish an unwanted person or thing from a photo, you use virtually the same process that you use to get rid of data in any computer program: After selecting the area you want to eliminate, you just press the Delete key.

When you're working with digital images, however, pressing Delete creates a slightly different result than when you're working in a word processor or producing some other type of text-based document. Delete a selected bit of text in a document, and the surrounding letters move over to fill in the hole. But in a digital image, remaining picture areas don't move a muscle when you delete a selection. The photo editing software leaves the job of filling the hole to you.

What becomes visible through the hole depends on the position of the layer that contains the hole.

> ✔ If you delete a selection from the bottom layer of an image, the hole becomes filled with the current background color. In Figure 7-17, I had the background color set to white, which is the default background color.

Figure 7-17:
Deleting a
selection
from the
bottom layer
creates a
background
-colored
hole.

✔ If you delete something from any other layer, the deleted area becomes transparent, and pixels on the layer immediately below show through the hole. For example, in Figure 7-18, I created a two-layered image, putting a textured background on the bottom layer and then adding the image from Figure 7-17 on top. This time, the textured background shows through the Santa-shaped hole. In the Layers palette, the checkerboard pattern in the top layer's thumbnail represents the transparent area.

Figure 7-18:
When you delete a selection from an upper layer, the underlying layer shows through the hole.

To fill a hole on an upper layer with a solid color instead of making the hole transparent, use the Fill command, explained in Chapter 9. If you're unfamiliar with the concept of image layers, see Chapter 3 for an explanation.

Rearranging subjects within the frame

When you move an object in a photo, you get the same result as when you delete an object — that is, you create a hole where the object used to be. To keep this hole-cutting to a minimum, the best course of action is to put the object on its own layer before repositioning it. That way, you cut just one hole in the image. After the object is on its own layer, you can move it around as much as you want without making more holes.

The following steps explain how to do this pixel rearranging in Elements. The process is the same in other programs, although the specific commands may be slightly different.

1. **Select the area that you want to move.**

   Chapter 3 shows you how to create a selection outline.

2. **Place the selected area on a new layer.**

   In Elements, you can do this by pressing Ctrl+Shift+J (⌘+Shift+J) or choosing Layer➪New➪Layer via Cut. In Figure 7-19, I selected the woman and placed her on a new layer.

   When you take this step, you cut a hole in the original layer, as shown in the figure. As explained in the preceding section, the hole becomes filled with the background color if you removed the selection from the background (bottom) layer. Otherwise, the hole becomes transparent, and the underlying layer becomes visible through the hole.

   If you prefer, you can duplicate the area and place the duplicate on a new layer by pressing Ctrl+J (⌘+J) or choosing Layer➪New➪Layer via Copy. In this case, you don't create a hole. Instead, you wind up with two objects instead of one (the original and the copy).

3. **Activate the Move tool by clicking its toolbox icon or pressing Ctrl+V (⌘+V).**

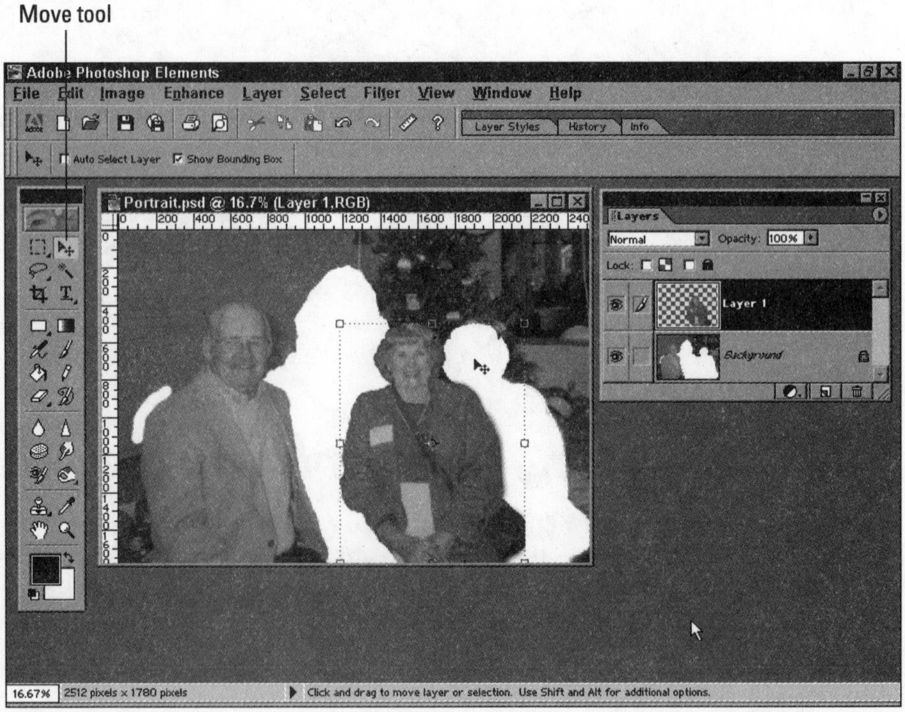

Move tool

Figure 7-19: After moving the woman to a new layer, I used the Move tool to shift her closer to her husband.

If you turn on the Show Bounding Box check box on the Options bar, as shown in the figure, a box appears around the selection. You can drag the handles of the box to rotate, stretch, and otherwise transform the selection. For details, see the upcoming section "Transforming a selected area." The handles on the bounding box work just like those on a transformation box. In fact, when you drag a bounding box handle, the program assumes that you want to use the Free Transform command and displays the Options bar controls associated with that feature.

If you turn on the Auto Select Layer option, the program automatically selects the layer that contains the object that you touch with the Move tool. When I'm working with a multilayered image, I find this option more trouble than it's worth, so I usually leave it off and select the layer that I want to edit by clicking the layer name in the Layers palette.

4. **Drag or nudge the layer contents into place.**

   Because you put the selection on a layer, it exists independently of the rest of the image, which means that you can move it around at will to get the positioning of the element just right. To move the element, drag it or use the arrow keys to nudge the elements small distances. Press an arrow key once to move everything on the layer one pixel in the direction of the arrow; press Shift plus an arrow key to move everything 10 pixels.

Keep your moved pixels on their own layer until you're completely, absolutely happy with their new position in the image. You can then merge the moved pixels with the underlying layer by following the instructions given in the section "Merging layers" later in this chapter. If you merge the layers and then decide that you want to shift the moved pixels a little more, you cut a new hole in the image. Until you're ready to merge the layers, you may want to lock the layer that contains the moved pixels to avoid accidentally moving them out of place. See the upcoming section "Locking layers" for details.

If you have trouble positioning the moved pixels exactly where you want them in Elements, open the View menu and check the status of the Snap feature (named Snap to Grid in Elements 2.0). A check mark means that the option is active. When you move things around your picture, this feature automatically snaps the pixels into alignment with the nearest point on the window grid, the alignment aid introduced earlier in the section "Leveling with precision." Although helpful in some situations, the snapping behavior can prevent you from precisely positioning an object, so you may want to turn it off.

Adjusting composition by changing layer order

Another way to rearrange people or things in a photo is to change the order of the layers that contain those elements. In this case, you create no new holes in the image.

Chapter 3 provides a full explanation of layers, but for this discussion, the important concept is this: When you have a multilayered image, pixels on one layer obscure pixels on the underlying layer. In spots where the upper layer is empty — transparent — the underlying pixels become visible. By repositioning layers within the layer stack, you can hide objects that were previously in full view and vice versa.

For example, in Figure 7-20, the woman exists on the top layer of the image, so her arm obscures a part of the man, who lives on the layer below. But when I swap the layer order, the woman's arm slips behind the man, as shown in Figure 7-21.

Figure 7-20: Because the woman resides on the top layer of the image, her arm partially obscures her husband, who occupies the underlying layer.

The method of changing layer order depends on what photo-editing software you use. In Elements, you simply drag a layer up or down in the Layers palette to change its position in the layer stack. Couldn't be simpler.

To reposition the background layer, however, you must first turn it into an ordinary layer — for some reason, the background isn't an "official" layer, even though it looks just like the others. Double-click the layer name in the Layers palette or single-click the layer name and choose Layer⇨New⇨Layer from Background. Either way, the New Layer dialog box appears. Accept the default settings and click OK to close the dialog box. Now your background layer works like any other layer. I took this step to create the version of the image shown in Figure 7-21.

Figure 7-21: Reversing the layer order slips the woman's arm behind her husband's back.

Note that if you convert the official background layer to a regular layer, deleting something from the bottom layer in the image no longer results in a background-colored hole. Instead, the layer becomes fully transparent, just as it does when you delete something from upper layers. When you print the image, the hole will be the same color as your paper. If you want to fill the hole with some other color, select it and use the techniques outlined in Chapter 9 to pour in the color. (Keep in mind that most home and office printers can't print white areas on colored paper.)

If you're creating an image for on-screen use, see Chapter 10 for information on filling transparent areas with solid color when you save the file in the JPEG format.

Transforming a selected area

On occasion, you may need to rotate, flip, stretch, or otherwise manipulate a relocated area so that it fits into its new surroundings better. For example, in the portrait of my friend's parents, I flipped her father's eyes on the horizontal axis so that he would appear to be looking into the frame, instead of out of the frame. After I flipped the eyes, I had to rotate them slightly to match the original eye shape.

In Elements, you do this via the same Free Transform command that I introduced earlier in this chapter, in the section "Righting Leaning Towers." Here's the drill:

1. **Select the area you want to transform.**

   • To transform everything on an upper image layer, click the layer name in the Layers palette.

   • To transform everything on the background layer, press Ctrl+A (⌘+A) to create a layer-wide selection outline.

   • To transform only part of a layer, background or otherwise, create a selection outline as explained in Chapter 3.

2. **Choose Image⟹Transform⟹Free Transform or press Ctrl+T (⌘+T).**

   After you choose the command, the Options bar offers the controls shown in Figure 7-22, and a transformation box appears around the selected area. If you don't see the handles around the edge of the box, as shown in the figure, enlarge the image window by dragging an edge of the window.

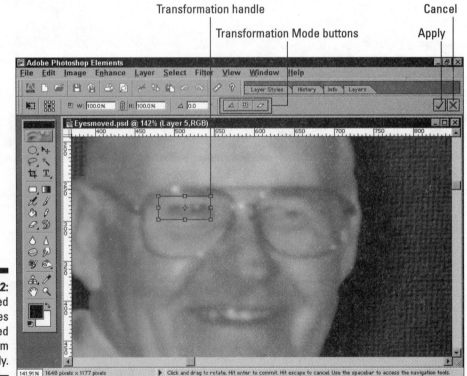

Figure 7-22: I selected the eyes and flipped them horizontally.

3. **Drag the transformation handles to adjust the selected area's shape, size, and angle.**

   You can adjust the selected pixels as follows:

- **To change the width only:** Drag a side handle.

- **To change the height only:** Drag a top or bottom handle.

- **To adjust size proportionately:** Press Shift as you drag a corner handle.

- **To rotate the selection:** Place the cursor outside any corner handle to display the curved rotate cursor. Then drag up or down. Alternatively, you can choose any available command on the Image➪Rotate menu.

- **To flip the selection horizontally or vertically:** Choose one of the Flip commands from the Image➪Rotate submenu. The transformation box remains visible and active even after you choose this command.

- **To distort the shape of the selection:** Ctrl+drag (⌘+drag) any handle.

- **To skew (slant) the image:** Ctrl+Shift+drag a side handle. (⌘+Shift+drag on a Mac.)

- **To alter the image perspective:** Press Ctrl+Alt+Shift (⌘+Option+Shift) as you drag the top-left or top-right handle outward.

You also can enter specific values in the boxes on the Options bar. If you're not sure what a particular control affects, pause your cursor over it to display a flag that labels the control. (The Show Tool Tips option on the General panel of the Preferences dialog box must be enabled for the flags to appear. To check the setting, choose Edit➪Preferences➪General.)

At any time, you can undo the last drag or change you made by using the Undo command. (See Chapter 2 for help.) To completely cancel out of the operation and start over, click the Cancel button, labeled in Figure 7-22. (If you're using Elements 2.0, the Apply and Cancel button are in the opposite order on the Options bar.)

4. **Click the Accept button or press Enter to apply the transformation.**

The instructions in Step 3 assume that you haven't clicked the Rotate, Skew, and Slant buttons on the Options bar (collectively labeled Transformation Mode buttons in Figure 7-22). If you click one of the buttons, you're locked into making that type of transformation only. To reset the buttons, cancel out of the transformation and start over.

Rebuilding shadows

When you rearrange people or things in a photo, pay close attention to the shadows that they cast. You don't want to wind up with one object that casts a strong shadow and a close neighbor that creates no shadow at all. A strongly lit subject that casts no shadow at all would also look funky, as would a dimly lit object that creates a strong shadow. Use your original photo as a reference point to see the direction and intensity of the light source, and then create any needed shadows accordingly.

As an example, see the edited portrait in Figure 7-23. At this stage in the project, I've completely cut away the original background and created a new, textured background to place behind the couple. But without any shadows behind the subjects, the result looks flat — an obvious indication that the background isn't the original. My friend had asked me to add the new background, but because it's so obviously fake, it draws attention to itself, which I didn't want. Referring to the original photo, I created a soft shadow behind the couple to add some separation between them and the new background and to restore the shadows that would have been present given the original lighting conditions.

Figure 7-23:
What's wrong with this picture? (Hint: The answer's in the shadows, or lack thereof.)

You can create a shadow in two ways, either painting it in by hand or applying an automatic shadow filter. The next two sections show you how to do both.

Painting in a shadow

If you're a skilled painter, just grab a painting tool, select a soft, fuzzy brush, and paint the shadow, as follows:

1. **Select the area to which you want to add a shadow and send the selection to a new layer.**

Use the techniques outlined in Chapter 3 to create your selection outline. In Elements, choose Layer⇨New⇨Layer via Copy or press Ctrl+J (⌘+J) to copy the selected area and put it on a new layer.

2. Create a new layer to hold the shadow.

   Put this layer directly underneath the layer you created in Step 1.

3. Paint your shadow on the shadow layer.

   Play with the layer opacity and blending mode controls in the Layers palette to refine the shadow's appearance. The Multiply blending mode is especially good for creating natural-looking shadows. You also can apply a blur filter to the shadow layer to make the shadow softer and use the Levels filter to make the shadow darker or lighter. If you need to reposition the shadow, you can drag it into place with the Move tool.

Note that the layer that you create in Step 1 — the layer that holds the object or person getting the shadow — must be completely transparent in the areas where you want the shadow to appear. Otherwise, the layer obscures the shadow.

Chapter 6 provides details about working with painting tools and blending modes.

Applying an automatic shadow

Many programs offer a special effect that applies a shadow automatically for you. In most cases, you can adjust the size, angle, and opacity of the shadow to fit the scene

In Elements, you create shadows by applying a layer *style,* as follows:

1. Select the area to which you want to add a shadow.

2. Copy the selection to a new layer.

   To do this, just press Ctrl+J (⌘+J) or choose Layer⇨New⇨Layer via Copy.

3. Display the Layer Styles palette by clicking its tab in the palette well or choosing Window⇨Show Layer Styles.

   The Layers Styles palette appears, as shown in Figure 7-24.

4. Select Drop Shadows from the menu at the top of the palette, as shown in the figure.

   The palette contains icons that represent various shadow styles.

5. Click the Soft Edge shadow icon.

   For most photographs, this option creates the most realistic shadows. When you click the icon, a tiny letter *f* (for *ef*fects, popularly abbreviated to *fx*) appears next to the layer name in the Layers palette, as shown in Figure 7-24.

Figure 7-24: I applied the drop shadow layer style to create some separation between the subjects and the background.

6. **Adjust the shadow angle and placement, if needed.**

   If you're not happy with the look of the shadow, double-click the *f* in the Layers palette or choose Layer⇨Layer Style⇨Style Settings to display the dialog box shown in Figure 7-25. Use the Lighting Angle and Shadow Distance control to adjust the angle and placement of the shadow.

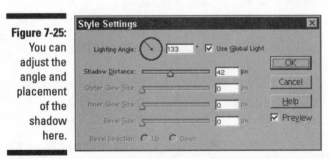

Figure 7-25: You can adjust the angle and placement of the shadow here.

The Use Global Light option ensures that the same light direction is maintained for all shadows that you create. You don't need to worry about the option if you're applying the shadow to just one layer, but if you're adding multiple shadows, I recommend that you keep the option turned on.

7. To adjust the shadow size, choose Layer➪Layer Style➪Scale Effects.

In the resulting dialog box, lower the Scale value to shrink the shadow; raise the value to make the shadow larger. Click OK after you're happy with the shadow.

To remove a shadow — or any other layer style effect — click the layer's name in the Layers palette and then choose Layer➪Layer Style➪Clear Layer Style. In Elements 2.0, you also can clear a layer style by clicking the Cancel button that's located near the top right corner of the Layer Styles palette.

Locking layers

For extra editing protection, you may want to lock image layers after you're happy with their appearance in your photo. Elements enables you to do this via the Layers palette. You have two locking options:

✔ **To lock just the layer's transparency:** Click the layer name and then select the Lock Transparency box at the top of the Layers palette, as shown in Figure 7-26. In Elements 2.0, the check box has been replaced by a simple button; clicking the button toggles the lock open and shut. When the transparency is locked, you can still move the layer contents, but you can't do anything to the transparent areas of the layer.

Lock Transparency

Lock All

Figure 7-26: After you get the placement of a layer just right, protect it by locking the layer.

✔ **To fully lock the layer:** In Elements 1.0, select the Lock All check box, also labeled in the figure. In Elements 2.0, click the Lock button to toggle the lock open and shut.

When a layer is fully locked, the only change you can make to it is to change its order in the Layers palette. To do any other editing, you must first unlock the layer.

Notice that the little lock icon that appears next to the layer name appears hollow if only the transparency is locked; the lock appears solid if everything is locked down tight. Of course, you can also just look at the check boxes (Elements 1.0) or buttons (Elements 2.0) to see the status of a layer.

If you're using a photo editor other than Elements, check your program's Help menu to find out whether any locking options are available to you.

Merging layers

Although layers provide you with a wealth of editing flexibility, each layer that you add increases the size of the image file and puts additional strain on your computer's resources. So after you're finished working on a particular set of layers, you may want to combine them into a single layer.

Remember that after you merge layers, you can no longer manipulate them independently of each other. For safety's sake, you may want to save a backup copy of your fully layered image before you merge layers. Save the backup under a different name so that when you save the merged image, you don't overwrite the file that contains the layered image. You also must take some special steps when saving the file; see Chapter 3 for a review.

In Elements, you can use the following techniques to combine layers:

✔ **To merge one layer with the layer immediately below:** Click the upper layer and then choose Layer➪Merge Down or press Ctrl+E (⌘+E).

✔ **To merge multiple layers while leaving some layers intact:** In the Layers palette, hide the eyeball icons of the layers that you *don't* want to merge. (Click the eyeball icon to hide the icon and the layer; click again to bring both back into view.) Then choose Layer➪Merge Visible or press Ctrl+Shift+E (⌘+Shift+E).

✔ **To merge all layers into one:** First make sure that all layers are visible; check the Layers palette to see that each layer's eyeball icon is displayed. If not, click the eyeball column to bring the layer back into view. Then choose Layer➪Flatten Image. If you choose the command while a layer is hidden, the program asks whether you want to discard the hidden layers or cancel out of the flattening operation.

If you're an experienced layer user, you may also want to investigate some of the advanced layer management options that Elements offers, such as layer groups and layer linking. The Help system tells you more about what these options enable you to do.

Chapter 8

Fixing Faces

• •

In This Chapter

▶ Removing red eye

▶ Adding sparkle and intensity to eyes

▶ Covering flaws without destroying skin texture

▶ Toning down facial shine

▶ Bringing color back to washed-out skin

▶ Softening wrinkles

▶ Whitening teeth

▶ Removing glasses flare

▶ Selecting hair

• •

*O*f all the projects that you may tackle in your photo editor, retouching facial areas in portraits presents the biggest challenges. Why? Because people who view your work will have great familiarity with how a human being is supposed to look, especially from the neck up — after all, they see an example every time they look in the mirror. You may be able to get away with sloppy editing when you're working on a landscape or still life, but if you're not careful when doing portrait work, most people can easily spot where the picture has been altered.

This chapter shares special techniques that can help you achieve the retoucher's ultimate goal: a perfect portrait that doesn't look as though it's been retouched. Note that I'm not going to show you how to create the kind of absolutely flawless face that you see in fashion magazines (which, in case you didn't know, *is* a result of photo editing). We're talking realistic portraits here, not some cover-girl appearance that's never seen in the mirror by anybody.

Removing Red Eye

Taking a flash picture with a point-and-shoot camera often results in a problem known as *red eye*. Because of the position of the flash with respect to the subject, the eyes reflect the flash and appear glowing red in the photograph, as shown in the top left image in Color Plate 8-1. Even using the red-eye reduction flash mode found on many cameras often doesn't prevent this phenomenon. (That's why the flash setting is called red-eye *reduction* mode, not a *prevention* mode.)

Because red eye is such a common problem, nearly every photo editor aimed at the consumer market offers an automatic red-eye removal feature. Photoshop Elements, for example, offers a red-eye brush that's supposed to automatically replace the red pixels with a proper color. Unfortunately, automated red-eye tools typically don't work very well. They either alter too much or too little of the eye or change the eye color to some unnatural shade.

If your photo editor offers such a feature, go ahead and give it a whirl. Hey, maybe you'll get lucky and find the one picture that the automated tool can handle. If not, use the following technique to paint out red eye. I think you'll be surprised at how easy this job is to do on your own; in fact, in many cases, doing the job "manually" involves less effort than working with automated tools. More important, the results are always superior.

The technique involves two main steps: First, you desaturate the red pixels, turning them all shades of gray. Then you paint in the original eye color where necessary. I used this approach to fix the red-eye problem in Color Plate 8-1.

Here are the steps in Elements, which you can use in any program that offers the features mentioned:

1. **Select the eye area and copy the selection to a new layer.**

   You can copy a selection to a new layer by pressing Ctrl+J (⌘+J) or choosing Layer⇨New⇨Layer via Copy. For an introduction to selecting an area of a picture and working with layers, flip to Chapter 3.

   You don't have to be precise with your selection outline; just draw a loose outline around the general eye area. If you prefer, you can simply duplicate the entire layer that contains the eyes. (Duplicating just the eye area helps keep the image file size down, however.)

2. **Activate the Sponge tool by clicking its toolbox icon, labeled in Figure 8-1.**

3. **On the Options bar, set the Mode option to Desaturate.**

4. **Set the tool pressure control to 100 percent.**

   In Elements 1.0, the control is called Pressure; in Elements 2,0, Flow. In both versions of the program, the control is found on the Options bar.

5. **Select a small, soft-edged brush.**

   Turn off Brush Dynamics options for this project. (Chapter 6 explains everything you need to know about choosing brushes and working with the Brush Dynamics features.)

Sponge tool

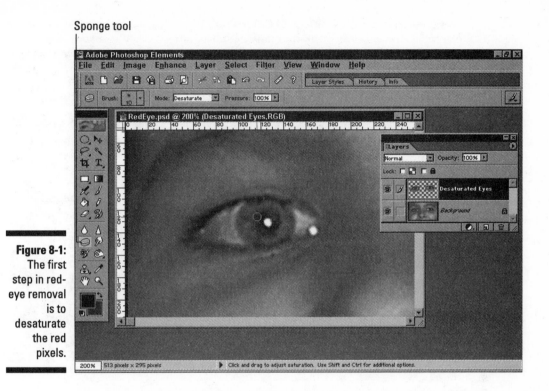

Figure 8-1:
The first step in red-eye removal is to desaturate the red pixels.

6. **Dab at the red pixels on the duplicate layer you created in Step 1.**

    Keep clicking or dragging over the pixels until all hint of red is gone. Try not to desaturate eye pixels that aren't affected by the red eye problem, but if you do, don't fret too much. You can restore the color later.

    If the red-eye pixels are limited to just the pupil, desaturating may fix your problem entirely. For example, see the top right image in Color Plate 8-1, which shows my red-eye photo after the desaturation step. The desaturated eyes look pretty good, but some areas of the iris lost a bit of color, which I wanted to restore.

7. **Create two new empty layers and set the layer blending mode for each to Color.**

    I'm assuming here that both eyes suffer from the red eye problem; if you have to retouch one eye only, you need just one layer.

    To add a new layer, click the New Layer button at the bottom of the Layers palette. (Refer to Figure 8-2). Set the layer blending mode via the menu at the top of the palette, as shown in the figure.

Paintbrush   Blending Mode menu

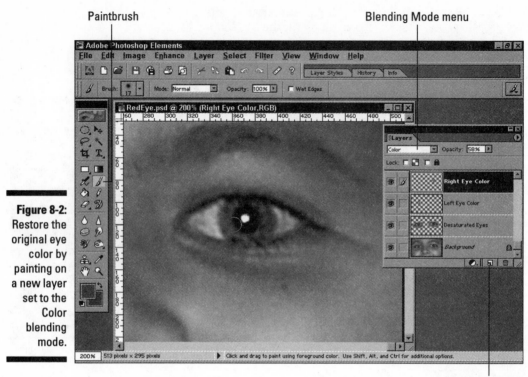

Figure 8-2:
Restore the
original eye
color by
painting on
a new layer
set to the
Color
blending
mode.

New Layer button

8. Set the foreground color to match the original eye color.

Chapter 4 explains how to change the foreground color.

If any part of the original eye color is intact, you can click the area with the Eyedropper to make that color the foreground color.

9. Restore the original eye color by painting over the eye where needed.

You can use any painting tool that suits your fancy; I usually work with the Paintbrush, labeled in the figure, using a small, soft brush. (This tool goes by the name Brush in Elements 2.0.)

On the Options bar, set the Opacity value to 100 percent and set the Mode option to Normal, as shown in Figure 8-2. You can turn on Brush Dynamics features if you like. You may need to switch among a few different colors to restore both the pupil and iris color.

As you paint, notice that although the colors of the eye pixels change, the original highlights and shadows are maintained, as illustrated in the lower left image in Color Plate 8-1. This effect is a result of setting the layer blending mode to Color. Chapter 6 explains more about blending modes.

If you don't like the results, try altering the foreground color or the eye layer's Opacity setting (in the Layers palette). Another option is to change the layer blending mode to Normal and lower the layer Opacity setting enough to allow some of the desaturated eye pixels to show through the paint layer. By painting each eye on a separate layer, you can tweak each eye individually.

10. **Merge the new eye layer(s) with the original image layer.**

   See the last section in Chapter 7 for information on merging layers.

As you remove red eye, be sure not to remove the tiny white catchlights that appear in the eye — in the example photo, the highlights appear smack dab in the middle of the pupils. Those catchlights give the eye life. If you do destroy the catchlights, use the Eraser to rub away the mistake on the paint layer.

The big white square at the corner of the left eye in Color Plate 8-1, however, is not a natural catchlight, but a blown highlight — a severely overexposed area that is completely white and lacking in any detail. In the color plate, the blown highlight looks pretty much like the catchlight, but it occurs in an area that should not be reflecting light to such a high degree. To remove the flaw, I used the Clone tool techniques discussed in Chapter 6. The lower-right image in the color plate shows the result of this part of the eye repair.

Emphasizing Eyes

In any portrait, the eyes are the most important element. They draw the viewer in, revealing much about the subject's mood and personality. To focus your audience even more on a subject's eyes, try using the following tricks to boost eye color, brightness, and sparkle.

Always do this kind of retouching work on a duplicate layer. In Elements, you can copy just the eyes to a new layer by selecting the eye area and then pressing Ctrl+J (⌘+J).

✔ **Boost the saturation of the iris:** In Elements, use the Sponge tool, labeled in Figure 8-3, for this step. Choose a very small, soft brush, set the Mode control on the Options bar to Saturate, and click all the way around the iris. Don't overdo — you don't want the eye color to look unnatural.

✔ **Brighten the whites of the eyes:** Dab at the whites of the eyes with the Dodge tool, also labeled in the figure. Which Range setting you use depends on the original eye, so you need to do some experimenting here. Again, don't go too far. You just want to make the whites slightly lighter, not glow-in-the-dark bright.

If the eyes are bloodshot, your best bet is to clone good portions of the eye over the blood vessels.

✔ **Sharpen the eyeball:** To make the eyes sparkle, pick up the Sharpen tool, labeled in Figure 8-3. Choose a soft brush that's slightly larger than the size of the eyeball. Then click once or twice to sharpen just that area.

If your photo editor doesn't offer a Saturation, Dodge, or Sharpen tool, you can select the portion of the eye that you want to alter and then use the program's standard saturation, exposure, and sharpening filters to make these changes.

For more details about saturation, see Chapter 4. For information about adjusting exposure and sharpening focus, refer to Chapter 5. And for help with cloning and selecting tool brushes, head for Chapter 6.

Removing Blemishes

Chapter 6 shows you how you can use the Blur tool to remove tiny flaws from an image. However, that technique doesn't work well for most skin repairs because the blurring can destroy skin texture, creating a noticeable alteration.

The Clone tool, also covered in Chapter 6, typically provides a better way to remove blemishes from skin areas. Always clone on a separate layer, using a brush size slightly larger than the blemish. For brush softness, a medium setting usually works best. With a very soft brush, the cloned area may appear blurrier than the surrounding skin; with a very hard brush, you may be able to detect the edges of the brush stroke.

As an example of how brush softness can impact your photo, see Color Plate 8-2. I wanted to remove the light stripe running across the cheek area. (A reflection from a nearby mirror caused the stripe.) In the upper-right image, I cloned nearby skin over the stripe, using a brush set to maximum softness. I successfully removed the stripe, but the edited area of the cheek looks much softer than the rest of the face. Compare the inset area of this image with the one accompanying the original image to see just how much texture I destroyed with my cloning.

In the lower-left image, I cloned using a brush set to maximum hardness, which produced an even less successful result. The hard edge created a distinct line within the cloned area. Changing the brush to medium hardness enabled me to blend the cloning strokes successfully, as shown in the lower-right image.

Of course, the right brush setting depends on the original texture of the skin. For very rough skin, you need a brush that's a little harder than you do when working on soft skin.

Clone tool
Sponge tool
Sharpen tool
Dodge tool

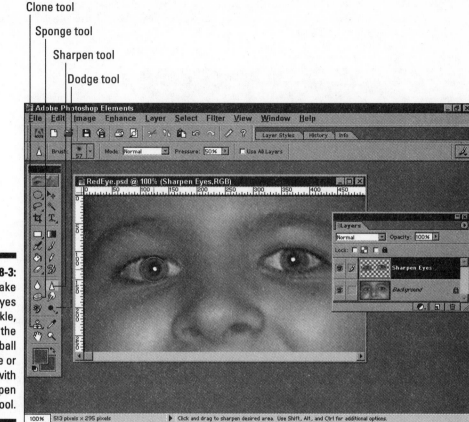

Figure 8-3:
To make eyes sparkle, click on the eyeball once or twice with the Sharpen tool.

To hide larger flaws, use the patching technique outlined in Chapter 6. If needed, you can adjust the color and brightness of a patch of cloned pixels by using the tools discussed in Chapters 4 and 5. And if you destroy too much skin texture despite your best cloning efforts, see the upcoming section "Restoring Skin Texture."

Repairing Overexposed or Shiny Skin

Portraits taken in very bright sunshine or shot with a strong flash may have some areas that are so overexposed that they are completely white, without the subtle color variations and texture details that should be present. (Photo nerds refer to such areas as *blown highlights*.) Reflections from oily skin are another cause of blown highlights. Skin color and texture can also be lost as a photographic print fades over time.

Color Plate 8-3, shown in grayscale in Figure 8-4, shows an example of this problem. The nose and cheek areas on the left side of the photo are completely washed out.

Figure 8-4:
An incorrect exposure drained the color out of the cheek and nose on the left side of this picture.

You can tackle the problem in several ways, depending on the scope of the problem and whether you're working with a color or grayscale photo. Here are the best options I know:

✔ To correct small blown highlights in a grayscale photo, use the Burn tool, covered in Chapter 5. You may also have success burning a color photo if the problematic skin area has any hint of color. But in most cases, burning highlights causes the skin to turn gray, a phenomena discussed at the end of Chapter 5. You can try the workaround method described in that chapter or abandon the Burn tool and try one of the techniques presented next.

Also note that burning alone won't restore skin texture, just darken the skin color. The section "Restoring Skin Texture" helps you tackle the rest of the repair.

✔ For both grayscale and color images, you also can cover blown highlights by cloning surrounding skin areas onto the bad spot. As always, clone on a separate layer. For the most natural results, reduce the opacity of the cloned layer slightly. That way, you retain some of the original brightness of the area, so the portrait lighting looks more natural. See Chapter 6 for details about working with the Clone tool.

✔ If you have a large area of blown highlights, as in the example in Figure 8-4 and Color Plate 8-3, you may be able to use the patching technique discussed in Chapter 6 to fix the face. However, simply painting in the missing skin color may prove easier. I used this technique to make the repair on the example image. After restoring color, you can add in texture. The next section explains this technique in detail.

Adding Color to Washed-Out Skin

The following steps show you how to paint in skin color in Elements. As always, you can easily adapt these steps to another photo editor that offers layers and layer blending modes.

1. **Create a new, empty layer.**

2. **In the Layers palette, set the blending mode for the new layer to Normal and set the Opacity value to 50 percent.**

3. **Set the foreground color to match the surrounding skin area.**

   Remember that you can click in the image window with the Eyedropper to match the foreground color to a color in your picture.

4. **Paint over the blown highlights.**

   Work with the Paintbrush using a soft brush. (The tool is named Brush in Elements 2.0.)

   On the Options bar, set the tool opacity to 100 percent and the mode to Normal, as shown in Figure 8-5. As you paint, reset the foreground color as needed to match the color of the nearby pixels. If you accidentally get paint on the surrounding areas, use the Eraser tool to rub it away or just use the Undo or Step Backward commands to undo the errant paint strokes.

5. **Refine the color and opacity of the painted layer as needed to match the surrounding skin.**

   After painting over the problem area, you can tweak your new skin color as follows:

   • Raise or lower the Opacity setting in the Layers palette to adjust the amount of original skin that's visible through the paint layer.

   • Experiment with different layer blending modes. When the highlights are totally blown, Normal usually works best. If some original skin color exists, try the Multiply and Color modes.

   Be sure that you select this option in the Layers palette, not on the Options bar. The Options bar control affects strokes you're about to paint; the Layers palette control affects existing strokes on the current layer.

   • Shift the color and saturation of the painted layer by using the Hue/Saturation filter, found under the Enhance⇨Color submenu in Elements 1.0 and the Enhance⇨Adjust Color submenu in Version 2.0. In this case, you want the filter to affect your new paint layer only, so don't apply the filter via an adjustment layer. (Chapter 9 discusses the Hue control; Chapter 4 explains the Saturation control and adjustment layers.)

Paintbrush

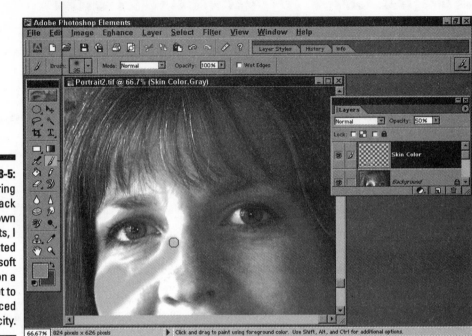

Figure 8-5:
To bring color back to the blown highlights, I first painted with a soft brush on a layer set to reduced opacity.

Again, the goal of these steps is simply to get the skin color and brightness correct. The painted skin will have a flat, unnatural look when you're done because it won't have any texture, as illustrated by the lower-left image in Color Plate 8-3. Compare the inset area in that image, which shows a section of the painted cheek, with the inset in the top image, which shows a section of the original, "good" cheek area that exists on the right side of the picture. To find out how to complete the skin repair job, move on to the next section.

Restoring Skin Texture

When you retouch skin areas, make sure that the texture of the repaired area matches the surrounding skin. Otherwise, you create a discrepancy that makes your retouching job obvious. As an example, see the lower-left image in Color Plate 8-3, which shows the result of painting in lost skin color using the technique outlined in the preceding section. The color looks fine, but the skin looks flat and lifeless.

Rebuilding skin texture is easier than you may expect. All you need is a special-effects filter that adds grain, or noise, to an image.

Noise refers to small color defects that occur as a result of interference in the electronic signal that generates a digital image. In plain English, noise gives the image a speckled look. In most cases, you want a noise-free image — in fact, many people apply a slight blur to their photographs to get rid of noise. But the effect is perfect for creating skin texture.

Elements offers two filters that suit this purpose:

- The Add Noise filter creates very tiny speckles, which works well for subjects with very small pores.

- With the Grain filter, you can vary the size and style of the speckles. I used this filter to rebuild the skin texture in the example photo in Color Plate 8-3.

The following steps, which show you how to texturize skin, assume that you restored lost skin color by painting on a new layer as described in the preceding section. Apply the Add Noise or Grain filter to a duplicate of that new, painted layer, as follows:

1. **In the Layers palette, click the name of the layer on which you painted the new skin color.**

2. **Duplicate the layer.**

3. **Zoom the image display so that you can get a close-up view of the original skin texture.**

   You need to be able to inspect the skin closely so that you can match the texture effect to the original skin texture. If you're new to portrait retouching, you may be surprised to see just how many different shades are present in skin.

4. **Choose the filter that you want to apply.**

   - To apply the Noise filter in Elements, choose Filter⇨Noise⇨Add Noise.

   - To apply the Grain filter, choose Filter⇨Texture⇨Grain.

   With either filter, a dialog box appears, offering controls that adjust the size and color of the effect.

5. **Tweak the filter controls until the skin texture matches that of the surrounding skin.**

   - The Add Noise filter typically produces the most natural results when you select the Uniform option and deselect the Monochromatic check box, as shown in Figure 8-6. Lower the Amount value to produce a more subtle effect; raise the value to generate more noise. Be sure to turn on the Preview check box inside the dialog box so that you can monitor the results of the filter in the image window as well as in the dialog box preview.

• The Grain filter enables you to adjust the size and style of the speckles that you create. In the filter dialog box, shown in Figure 8-7, select a style from the Grain Type menu; try the Clumped, Enlarged, Contrasty, and Speckled styles. After choosing a grain style, adjust the Contrast and Intensity values until you create an effect that works. (The appropriate settings will depend on the skin color and original texture you're trying to match.) I used the settings shown in Figure 8-7 to produce the texture for the final image in Color Plate 8-3. Unfortunately, the Grain filter doesn't offer a live image preview; you have to rely on the thumbnail preview inside the dialog box.

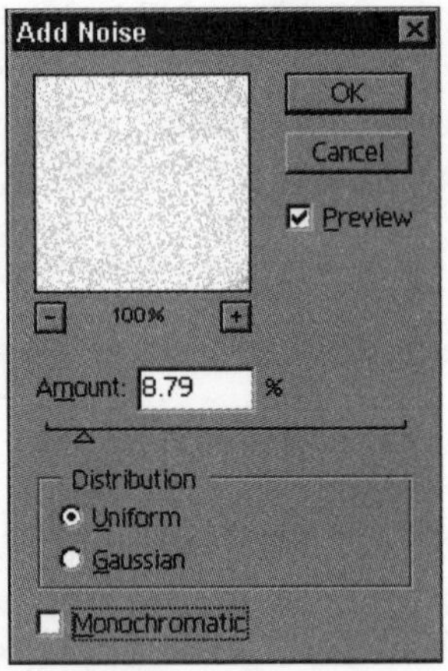

Figure 8-6: If the subject has small pores, try applying the Add Noise filter to recreate skin texture.

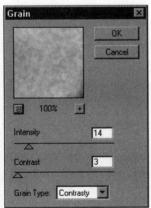

Figure 8-7: For skin with larger pores, the Grain filter typically does the best job because you can adjust the size and style of the speckles that the filter adds.

Because you're applying the filter on a duplicate skin layer, you also can vary the look of the texture by adjusting the layer opacity and blending mode in the Layers palette.

6. **Merge the textured layer with the painted skin layer.**

   After you're happy with your total skin repair, you also can merge the combined repair layer with the original image layer. But remember that after you do so, you can't manipulate the skin layer independently of the underlying layer.

For more on merging layers, see the end of Chapter 7.

In the sample image in Color Plate 8-3, the Grain filter did a pretty good job of recreating the original skin texture, as you can see by comparing the inset area in the final image with that in the original image. The inset for the original image is darker because it shows the opposite side of the face, which wasn't lit as brightly as the side that needed the repair. In painting and texturizing the blown highlights, I maintained a slight difference in lighting between the two sides of the face to retain the depth of the original portrait.

Softening Wrinkles

Skin care companies haul in boatloads of cash every year by selling products that promise to "soften the appearance of fine lines and wrinkles." Plastic surgeons net plenty more when people discover that all those creams and potions don't give them the baby-fresh skin they desire.

If you're in pursuit of unlined, un-aged skin, you'll be happy to know that your photo editor can deliver the goods absolutely free of charge. Pick up your software's Blur tool, dab a little here, drag a little there, and you can look decades younger in minutes — well, in photographs, anyway.

For best results, use the Blur tool either in the Lighten or Darken mode. As first explained in Chapter 5, the Blur tool softens focus by reducing contrast along edges (areas where dark pixels meet up with light pixels). In Normal mode, the tool lightens the dark pixels and darkens the light pixels, which creates a lighter, but larger, edge — not a good result for wrinkle removal. In Lighten mode, the tool simply makes the darker pixels lighter, leaving the lighter pixels alone, which makes lines fade away. In Darken mode, light lines fade into a dark background.

Before I run through the steps involved in this technique, I want to caution you to step lightly when you make this kind of change to a portrait. First off, a line-free face on anyone who's older than 25 just looks unnatural. Second, you're going beyond fixing up photographic errors to "fixing" the subjects themselves. I never make this kind of change to someone's appearance without being asked by the subject to do so. Most people won't react well if you show them the altered picture and say, "I thought you'd look better without all those wrinkles."

With those caveats in mind, follow these steps to apply your digital line reducer in Elements:

1. **Add a new, empty layer above the layer that contains the area that needs the facelift.**

2. **Activate the Blur tool, labeled in Figure 8-8.**

3. **Turn on the Use All Layers control on the Options bar, as shown in the figure.**

4. **Set the tool mode to Lighten or Darken, depending on the shade of the line you want to soften.**

   • If the line is darker than the surrounding skin, select Lighten.

   • If the line is lighter than the surrounding skin, select Darken.

Blur tool

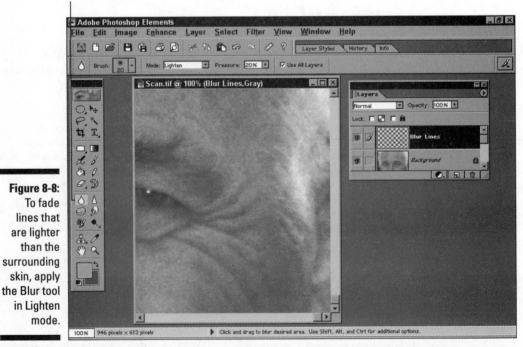

Figure 8-8:
To fade lines that are lighter than the surrounding skin, apply the Blur tool in Lighten mode.

Be sure to select Lighten or Darken from the Mode menu on the Options bar, not in the Layers palette. The Mode control on the Options bar sets the mode for the tool itself, while the one in the Layers palette adjusts existing pixels on a layer.

5. **Choose a soft, small brush.**

6. **Drag over the line.**

   You can adjust the impact of the tool by varying the Pressure setting in Elements 1.0 and the Strength setting in Elements 2.0. If you're working with a drawing tablet, you can also use the Brush Dynamics options to increase or decrease the blur effect according to stylus pressure. (See Chapter 6 to find out more about the Brush Dynamics options and how they differ between Elements 1.0 and 2.0.)

   Additionally, because you blurred on a separate image layer, you can use the Opacity control in the Layers palette to lessen the impact of blurring that you've already done.

   If the blurring effect creates a noticeable break in skin texture, try applying the filters discussed in the preceding section to the blur layer.

7. **Merge the blurred layer with the underlying layer after you finish your wrinkle reduction.**

   You may want to print your image first to make sure that your edits aren't noticeable. Saving a backup copy of the layered image also is a good idea.

In grayscale photos, you also can lighten lines by dragging over them with the Dodge tool. Set the Range option to Shadows so that you lighten the darkest areas of the line. To erase lines a little more, drag again with the Range option set to Midtones. For more about the Dodge tool, see Chapter 5.

Brightening Smiles

Whitening stained or dingy teeth is a simple retouching job — just dab at the teeth with the Dodge tool. I used this technique to brighten the teeth in Color Plate 8-4. If your photo editor doesn't have a Dodge tool, you can select the teeth and then apply an exposure adjustment filter to them.

The following steps walk you through the process of dodging teeth in Elements. But before you begin, I want to reiterate the warning I raised in the preceding section: You should make this alteration only at the request of the subject, as is the case with any edit that alters the person's appearance. Also, aim for a subtle brightening effect like the change made in Color Plate 8-4. Going further looks unnatural; even cosmetically whitened or capped teeth aren't solid white.

1. **Copy the mouth area to a new layer.**

   In Elements, you can do this by drawing a loose selection outline around the mouth and then pressing Ctrl+J (⌘+J) or choosing New⇨Layer⇨Layer via Copy.

2. **Select the Dodge tool, labeled in Figure 8-9.**

3. **On the Options bar, set the Range control to Midtones and set the Exposure value to 20 percent.**

4. **Choose a soft brush that's smaller than a single tooth.**

5. **Drag over each tooth to lighten the darkest areas.**

6. **Switch the Range option to Shadows and drag over any very dark areas on the surface of the tooth.**

   Keep dodging until you're happy with the look of the teeth. Be careful not to lighten the shadows and midtones so much that you end up with teeth that are all one brightness value — you want to retain some tonal variety for a natural look.

7. **Merge the dodged mouth layer with the underlying layer.**

   For information on merging layers, see the end of Chapter 7.

Dodge tool

Figure 8-9: To brighten a smile, stroke the teeth with the Dodge tool.

Removing Reflections from Glasses

Light bouncing off a subject's eyeglasses can create reflections that are distracting at best and obscure part or all of the eye area at worst.

If the reflection is limited to the frame of the glasses, you can remove the problem fairly easily. Either clone some nearby frame pixels over the reflection or set the foreground color to match the frame color and paint over the bad spot, using the technique discussed in "Repairing Overexposed or Shiny Skin," earlier in this chapter.

As mentioned in that section, do the repair job on a separate layer and reduce the layer opacity slightly so that you retain some of the original highlights. Make sure that the brightness of the repair matches that of the surrounding pixels so that you don't create a noticeable break in the photograph's lighting.

Fixing reflections that fall over the eye area, like those shown in Figure 8-10, prove trickier. If enough "good" eye pixels are available, you can clone over the reflection. You may need to clone from the opposite eye and then transform the cloned area to match the shape and size of the original eye.

To fix the photo in Figure 8-10, I had to clone back and forth between both eyes. Fortunately, the area that had the reflection on the left side of the photo was intact on the right side of the picture, and vice versa. So I just kept selecting a good area from one eye, copying it to a new layer, flipping the layer horizontally, and then nudging the copy into place over the other eye. All told, I had to repeat the process about ten times.

If your original photo doesn't have enough good eye pixels and you have another photograph of the subject, you can try copying the eye area from that picture and pasting it over the reflected area of your current photo. Chapter 9 shows you how to cut and paste picture elements from one photo to another.

Figure 8-10:
To remove eyeglass flare (left), I cloned good eye areas over the reflections (right).

You can use these same techniques to remove reflections from any shiny object, by the way.

Selecting Hair (And Fur)

Because of its irregular, wispy nature, hair is extremely difficult to select with precision, whether you're working with the human variety or the furry-animal variety. Unfortunately, a sloppy selecting job can make edits instantly obvious, especially when you cut and paste the selection into a new background.

For example, suppose that you wanted to select the dog in Figure 8-11 and then place it into a new image, setting the animal against a plain background. If you grab some of the background along with the fur when drawing your selection outline, you wind up with a halo around the dog, as shown in the left example in Figure 8-12. On the other hand, if you fail to include small strands of fur along the edge of the pup, you get the sharp-edged, "helmet head" — helmet fur? — look shown on the right side of the figure.

Selecting hair and fur is such a selection dilemma that software products have been developed just for tackling the job. Perhaps the best known is ProCreate KnockOut, which sells for $329 — not a small sum for a one-trick tool, even if the trick is pretty darned impressive.

Fortunately, you don't have to shell out extra cash to select hair or fur with success. You do, however, need to spend a bit more time and attention when creating the selection outline. The following steps show you some tricks that make the job easier:

Figure 8-11:
Fur and hair present tricky selection challenges.

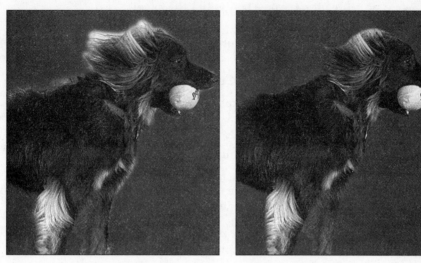

Figure 8-12: An imprecise selection outline can result in a halo of background pixels (left) or give the subject a sharp-edged, unnatural shape (right).

1. **First, create a mask that covers the background.**

   Create your mask on a new, empty layer, following the steps laid out in Chapter 3. For this selection project, you want the mask paint to cover everything but the subject you're ultimately trying to select.

   When working near the subject, paint with a very small brush, zooming in tightly on the image so that you can see exactly where to put the paint.

2. **Generate a selection outline from the mask.**

   Again, Chapter 3 explains this process, but here's a quick recap of how to do this in Elements: Ctrl+click (⌘+click) the mask layer in the Layers palette to create the dotted selection outline.

   The dotted lines of the outline may not perfectly reflect the actual boundaries of the selection. Trust your mask painting job, not the dotted outline.

3. **Invert the selection outline so that the subject becomes selected instead of the background.**

   To invert the outline, choose Select⇨Inverse or press Ctrl+Shift+I (⌘+Shift+I).

4. **In the Layers palette, click the name of the layer that contains the subject that you want to edit.**

   Now the selection outline that you created in Step 2 affects the layer you clicked.

5. **Copy the selected area to a new layer.**

   Press Ctrl+J (⌘+J) to do the job quickly in Elements.

6. **Hide all the other layers in the image.**

   Click the eyeball icons in the Layers palette to hide the layers. Now you see just the selected subject that you copied to the new layer. Inspect the layer to see how well you did with your selection outline.

7. **Touch up the edges of the subject if needed.**

   Use the techniques explained in the next two sections to either rub away stray background pixels or add more hair strands around the edge of the subject.

8. **Continue with your editing project.**

   If you're done with the layer that held your subject in its original background, you can delete the layer. You can then redisplay any other image layers that you hid in Step 5.

To put your selected subject into another picture, use the cut-and-paste techniques outlined in Chapter 9.

Rubbing away background halos

To rub away stray background areas that exist between strands of hair after you separate a subject from its original background, use the Eraser tool. Work with a very small, soft brush, as shown in Figure 8-13. (In the figure, I left a white background layer visible so that you could easily see where I was erasing.)

You can vary the performance of the Eraser tool in Elements by playing with the Mode control on the Options bar. For this tool, the Mode control doesn't relate to blending modes but to brush types that you can use while erasing. For more about the Eraser tool, see Chapter 6.

If you're working with Elements, you may also want to check out the Background Eraser tool, which shares a flyout menu with the regular Eraser. This tool is designed to assist you with erasing background pixels around an object. As you drag with the tool, it analyzes the pixels at the center of your cursor and then erases similarly colored pixels underneath the entire cursor.

Unlike the standard Eraser, the Background Eraser erases pixels to transparency even on the background image layer. The tool automatically converts the background layer to a standard image layer for you in order to erase to transparency. (Chapter 7 shows you another way to make this change.)

Space limitations prevent me from discussing this tool in depth here, but if you want to try it out, the Elements manual and Help system explain how to use it. I personally prefer the regular Eraser because it's more predictable.

Eraser tool

Figure 8-13:
Use the
Eraser to
rub away
stray
background
pixels
between
strands of
hair along
the edges of
the subject.

Recreating hair

If you clipped away the ends of the hair with your selection outline, you can draw a new outline and then copy the missing hair to the subject layer. But I have a faster fix if your photo editor offers a Smudge tool, as does Elements. This tool, labeled in Figure 8-14, creates an effect similar to dragging a brush through a wet oil painting. By dragging outward along the edges of your subject, you can create natural-looking bits of hair, as shown in Figure 8-14. (In this example, I set the dog against a dark background to make the hair restoration process easier to see.)

After selecting the Smudge tool, create a new layer to hold your smudge strokes. Choose a very small, soft brush and select the Use All Layers box on the Options bar. In the Layers palette, hide any layers except your new layer and the layer that contains your subject. That way, the Smudge tool only draws paint from the subject layer even though the Use All Layers option is active.

To control the distance over which you smear paint as you drag, adjust the Pressure setting in Elements 1.0 and the Strength option in Version 2.0. At a low setting, you smear only near the start of your drag. I used a setting of 67 percent and started dragging just inside the edge of the dog's head to create the flying bits of fur shown in Figure 8-14. You also can use the Brush Dynamics options to vary the impact of the tool.

When you're happy with your hair implants, merge the smudge layer with the subject layer, following the process explained at the end of Chapter 7. Chapter 6 explains the Brush Dynamics controls; be aware that these controls are significantly different in Elements 1.0 and 2.0.

Smudge tool

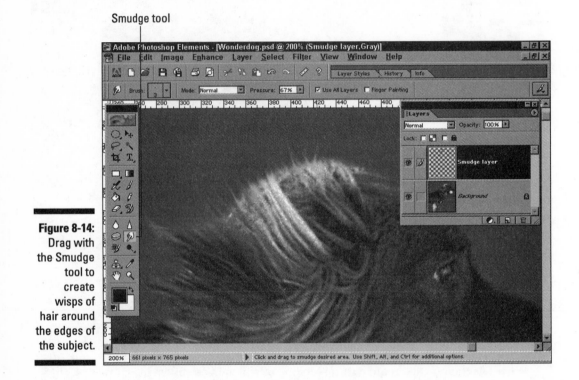

Figure 8-14:
Drag with the Smudge tool to create wisps of hair around the edges of the subject.

Part III
Finishing Touches

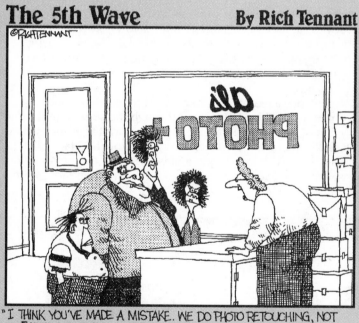

The 5th Wave   By Rich Tennant

"I THINK YOU'VE MADE A MISTAKE. WE DO PHOTO RETOUCHING, NOT FAMILY PORTRAI... OOOH, WAIT A MINUTE-I THINK I GET IT!"

In this part . . .

*I*f you're looking for creative inspiration, you've come to the right place. Chapter 9 shows you how to add interest to your pictures by applying special effects, playing with image colors, and combining multiple pictures into a collage.

When you're ready to show off your work, check out Chapter 10, which guides you through the sometimes tricky steps of preparing your picture for the printer or for online use. To help you add one more special touch, Chapter 10 also shows you how to put a digital "matte" around an odd-sized picture so that you can display it in a standard photo frame.

Chapter 9

Exploring Creative Imagery

● ●

In This Chapter

▶ Making a photo collage

▶ Copying things from one picture to another

▶ Using special effects to hide defects

▶ Hand-tinting a grayscale picture

▶ Replacing an ugly background

▶ Adding an antiqued effect

▶ Changing the color of a photo element

● ●

*M*ost aspects of photo retouching and restoration involve mechanical, logical thinking, which scientists tell us happens on the left side of the brain. Sure, I suppose you could say that drawing a perfect selection outline is a creative endeavor of sorts — just not a sort that gives the artistically inclined, right side of your noggin a real workout.

To make sure that you don't neglect your head's creative hemisphere, this chapter explores some photographic projects and techniques that will get those right-brain synapses firing. Among other things, you can find out how to combine several pictures into a photo collage, give an image a nicer background, and change the color of an element in the scene. Just in case you're the type who has a hard time justifying pure creative enjoyment, this chapter also discusses a practical application of special-effects filters, showing you how to use artistic filters to disguise flaws in an image.

Creating a Photo Collage

Chapter 7 explains how to alter the composition of a picture by rearranging people and objects within the frame. You can use the same techniques discussed in that section of the book to create a photo collage that incorporates elements from several different photos. For example, I combined five pictures from my family's archive to create the collage shown in Figure 9-1. This kind of image would make a terrific banner on a family genealogy Web site. (See Chapter 10 for details on preparing images for the Web.)

Creating a collage is an easy job in most photo editors. The hardest part of the project is figuring out which photos to use and how to arrange them in your new composition. As you plan your collage, keep in mind that you don't have to use photos in their entirety. You can combine selected areas of different photos, and even have those elements float over a background image, as shown in Figure 9-2. For this collage, I placed portions of four photographs of famous Italian landmarks on top of a fifth image, which I faded slightly to create an interesting background.

Figure 9-1:
You can combine several photos into a collage such as this one.

Figure 9-2:
For this collage, I pasted portions of four photos on top of a fifth picture.

No matter what your collage design or how many photos it includes, you use the same general approach to putting the pieces together. The next several sections spell out the steps in detail.

Creating a new picture canvas

The first step in building a collage is to create a new, empty image file to hold the combined pictures. This part of the project is no different than creating a new document in a word processing or other computer program, except that in a photo editor, the new document is referred to as an image *canvas*.

When you create a new canvas, you specify the canvas dimensions as well as the initial output resolution — the number of image pixels per inch — that you want for your final image file.

To get an introduction to pixels and output resolution, check out Chapter 2.

Follow these steps to generate a blank canvas in Elements. (The process is very similar in other photo editors, although the dialog box in which you specify the canvas size and resolution may look different.)

1. **Choose File⇨New.**

   The New dialog box appears, as shown in Figure 9-3.

   New

   Name: Collage   OK

   ┌─ Image Size: 74K ──────────────┐   Cancel
   │   Width: 500   pixels   ▾ │
   │   Height: 150   pixels   ▾ │   Help
   │   Resolution: 300 pixels/inch ▾│
   │   Mode: Grayscale ▾   │
   └────────────────────────────────┘

   ┌─ Contents ─────────────────────┐
   │   ◉ White   │
   │   ○ Background Color   │
   │   ○ Transparent   │
   └────────────────────────────────┘

   Figure 9-3: Set the original canvas dimensions, contents, and output resolution in this dialog box.

2. **Enter a new image name in the Name box.**

3. **Set the canvas dimensions by entering values in the Width and Height boxes.**

You can enlarge or reduce the canvas size at any time, so don't worry if you're not yet certain how big you want your collage to be. Just enter approximate dimensions for now.

Elements 2.0 offers a new feature, the Preset Sizes drop-down list, which enables you to set the Width and Height by selecting from a list of standard sizes. To set the canvas to some other size, select Custom from the list and enter the dimensions in the Width and Height boxes.

If you're creating an image solely for on-screen use, establish the image dimensions using pixels as the unit of measure. Match the pixel numbers to how much of the screen you want the image to consume, as discussed in Chapters 2 and 10. Select the unit of measure from the drop-down lists next to the Width and Height boxes in the Canvas Size dialog box.

4. **For a print picture, set the output resolution in the Resolution box.**

   For an explanation of output resolution, see Chapter 2. When you set this value, the program adds or subtracts as many pixels as necessary to create the canvas at the dimensions and resolution that you specify. In this case, adding or deleting pixels doesn't affect the image quality, as it does after you put pictures on the canvas. At this stage, you don't *have* any image quality — the canvas is merely a bunch of transparent pixels.

   As discussed in Chapter 2, you don't need to pay any attention to the Resolution value at all if you're creating a screen image.

5. **Set the image color model.**

   You do this via the Mode option in the dialog box. For a grayscale image, select Grayscale; for a full-color image, choose RGB.

   Note that in Elements, choosing Grayscale creates a true grayscale image, which limits you to 256 colors, all of which are shades of gray. If you plan to use any other colors in your collage, select RGB. See Chapter 4 for more information about grayscale images.

6. **Select a Contents option to specify the initial canvas contents.**

   You can fill the canvas with white, with the current background color, or with transparent pixels.

   If you choose the Transparent option, the appearance of the canvas in the image window depends on the settings on the Transparency panel of the Preferences dialog box. By default, a transparent canvas appears as a gray-and-white checkerboard pattern. To change that setting, choose Edit⇨Preferences⇨Transparency.

7. **Click OK or press Enter to close the dialog box and open your new canvas.**

Combining pictures

Adding a picture to the collage is a simple matter of selecting the area of the photo that you want to use, making a copy of the selection, and then pasting the copy into the collage canvas. Follow these general steps:

1. **Open the picture that you want to use in the collage.**

2. **Select the area of the image that you want to include in the collage.**

   Chapter 3 discusses selection techniques.

   Note that in order to use the Copy command in the next step, Elements requires you to have an active selection outline. That means that if you want to select everything on a single layer in a multilayered image, simply clicking the layer name in the Layers palette isn't sufficient, as it is when you make some other edits.

   If you want to select an entire layer, click the layer name in the Layers palette and then press Ctrl+A (⌘+A) to create the selection outline. Use the same keyboard shortcut to select everything in a one-layer image; you don't have to click the layer name in the Layers palette in this case.

3. **Choose Edit⇨Copy or press Ctrl+C (⌘+C).**

   The Copy command, found in nearly every computer program, duplicates the selected area and sends the copy to a temporary holding tank known as the Clipboard.

4. **Open the destination picture (the picture into which you want to copy the selection).**

   In this case, the destination image is the collage canvas that you created in the preceding section. If that image is already open, click anywhere on the image to make it the active photo. Or choose the file name from the Window menu. (In Elements 2.0, choose Window⇨Images to display the file names.)

5. **Choose Edit⇨Paste or press Ctrl+V (⌘+V).**

   The follow-up to the Copy command, Paste takes the contents of the Clipboard and dumps them into the active document.

   In Elements, as in most other programs that offer image layers, your pasted selection goes on a new layer. This setup enables you to manipulate the pasted collage element independently of the rest of the image, using the techniques outlined in the next section.

You also can copy and paste a selection simply by dragging it from one image window to another. However, in most programs, you must drag in a special way or you move the selected element instead of copy it. In Elements, select the Move tool, labeled in Figure 9-4. If the Auto Select Layer box is checked, click it to deselect the option. Then press Alt (Option) to display the copy cursor, shown in the figure. Keep pressing Alt (Option) as you drag the selection to the other open window.

If you want to copy an entire layer from one image to another in Elements, you don't need the Move tool or the Alt (Option) key, however. Just open both images, display the Layers palette, and drag the layer from the palette into the destination image window. This technique works when any tool is active.

To display image windows side-by-side, choose Window⇨Tile in Elements 1.0; choose Window⇨Images⇨Tile in Elements 2.0.

Move tool   Copy cursor

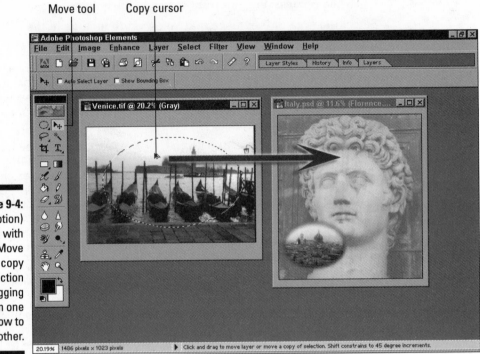

Figure 9-4:
Alt (Option)
+drag with
the Move
tool to copy
a selection
by dragging
it from one
window to
another.

Sizing collage elements

When you paste one picture (or part of the picture) into another image, the apparent size of the pasted picture may change. This happens when the two pictures are set to different output resolutions.

For a thorough introduction to output resolution, refer to Chapter 2. Remember that although your photo editor opens images as a default resolution value, you can change the value at any time. Chapter 10 explains how.

A pasted picture automatically takes on the output resolution of its new home. The number of pixels in the pasted photo remains the same; only the number of pixels per inch, which determines print size, changes.

Say that you start with a photo that's set to an output resolution of 150 ppi. If you place that photo into a picture that has an output resolution of 300 ppi, the print dimensions of the pasted picture get smaller, as illustrated in Figure 9-5. Conversely, when you copy a high-resolution image to a low-resolution image, the print size of the pasted image increases. Again, you haven't added or deleted any pixels, just altered the number of pixels per inch, which affects print size.

150 ppi

300 ppi

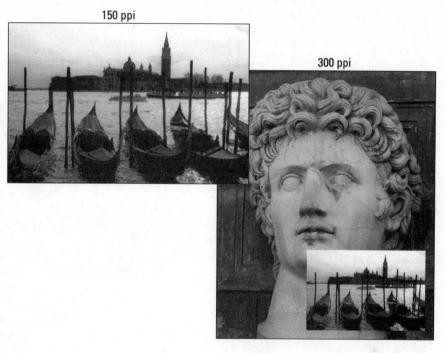

Figure 9-5:
The print size of a 150-ppi photo is reduced when the picture is placed into an image that has an output resolution of 300 ppi.

If necessary, you can resize a pasted photo after placing it into the collage. However, remember that if you enlarge a photo, you may lower image quality because in order to make your change, the program must add pixels. Depending on how your software works, you may not be able to see how much you're affecting image quality until after you save and reopen or print the image file. In some programs, you do further damage each time you change an element's size. For tips on maintaining image quality and for other methods of setting image size, see Chapter 10.

With that caveat in mind, you can adjust the size of a collage element in most programs by displaying transformation handles around the element and then dragging the handles, as shown in Figure 9-6. Alternatively, you may be able to enter specific width and height dimensions for the element.

In Elements, the steps are as follows:

1. **Select the element that you want to resize by clicking its layer in the Layers palette.**

   I'm assuming that you want to resize the entire layer contents; if not, create a selection outline as explained in Chapter 3.

2. **Press Ctrl+T (⌘+T) to display the transformation box around the selected element, as shown in Figure 9-6.**

   You also can choose Image⇨Transform⇨Free Transform to display the box.

Width

Maintain Aspect Ratio

Height

Cancel

Drag to resize

Apply

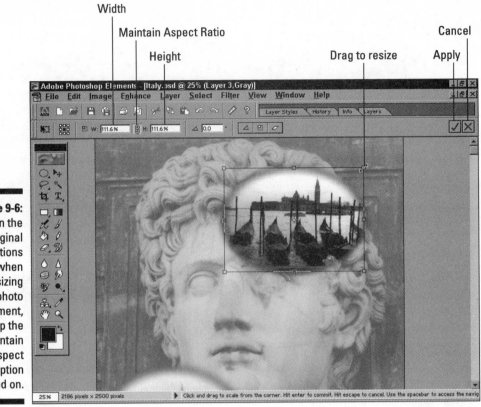

Figure 9-6:
To retain the original proportions when resizing a photo element, keep the Maintain Aspect Ratio option turned on.

3. **Turn on the Maintain Aspect Ratio control, as shown in Figure 9-6.**

   This option ensures that you maintain the original proportions of the element when you resize. Otherwise, you can easily distort the element.

   When active, the Maintain Aspect Ration button appears "pressed in," as shown in the figure. Click the button to turn the feature on and off.

4. **Drag a corner handle to resize the selected element.**

   If you drag a side, top, or bottom handle, the program automatically turns off the Maintain Aspect Ratio feature and allows you to distort the element. So be sure that you grab a corner handle.

5. **Click the Apply button, labeled in Figure 9-6, or press Enter to apply the size change.**

   If you decide not to go forward, click the Cancel button or press the Esc (Escape) key instead. (Note that in Elements 2.0, the Apply and Cancel button have switched positions on the Options bar.)

When I'm building a collage, I usually create a "rough draft" version in which I cut and paste the picture elements without much regard for resolution or size. While working on the composition, I shrink and enlarge elements willy-nilly without worrying about image quality.

After I decide on a final layout, I print a copy of the collage to use as a reference. Then I dump the rough draft and prepare each collage element again, setting the dimensions and output resolution according to my notes and saving the element under a new name (so that I can access the original later if needed.) If necessary, I rescan photos to generate the output resolution and size I need.

After each element is properly sized, I combine the photos into the collage. With this approach, I need only do minor resizing, if any, within the collage, which keeps image quality as high as possible.

Arranging collage elements

After pasting the various elements of your collage into the new image canvas, you can rotate and reposition them to refine the composition. Because the pieces of the collage live on separate layers, you can manipulate each component without affecting the rest of the image.

To adjust the placement or orientation of a collage element, use the same techniques outlined in the Chapter 7 sections related to rearranging objects within a photo. The following list provides a quick recap and introduces a few other compositional options that can create some interesting collage effects.

As with the rest of the instructions in this book, these provide specific tool names and techniques for Photoshop Elements. Things work pretty much the same in other photo editors that offer layers, however.

✔ **To move a collage element:** Click the element's layer in the Layers palette and then activate the Move tool. (Refer to Figure 9-4, earlier in this chapter, if you need help finding the tool.) Then drag the element in the image window.

While the Move tool is active, you can press the arrow keys on your keyboard to nudge the element into place. Pressing a key once moves the element one pixel in the direction of the arrow. Press Shift plus the arrow key to nudge the element 10 pixels.

If the Move tool doesn't seem to want to move the layer contents, check the status of the Auto Select Layer box on the Options bar. When the check box is selected, the Move tool automatically selects the layer that contains a visible pixel at the spot where you begin your drag. If the layer you want to move has transparent areas and you begin your drag in that transparent area, the tool grabs whatever layer has a visible pixel in that area instead. To force the Move tool to work with the layer you want to reposition, turn the check box off and re-click the layer name in the Layers palette.

✔ **To rotate an element:** Press Ctrl+T (⌘+T) or choose Image⇨Transform⇨ Free Transform command to display the transformation box, as shown in Figure 9-6 in the preceding section. Place your cursor outside a corner handle until the cursor looks like a curved, double-headed arrow and drag up or down to rotate the element. For more precise movements, you can enter a value into the Rotation Angle box on the Options bar.

Try to rotate only once. Every time you rotate an element, the program has to rebuild the pixels in the element. Repeated rotations can seriously degrade image quality.

If the Move tool is active and the Show Bounding Box check box on the Options bar is selected, you can just manipulate the handles on the bounding box instead of choosing the Free Transform command. As soon as you drag a handle, the program automatically chooses the Free Transform command for you and displays the standard transformation controls on the Options bar. For this technique, be sure to turn off the Auto Select Layer check box on the Options bar.

✔ **To shuffle the order of the elements in the composition:** Drag the layer names up and down in the Layers palette. Remember that wherever a layer contains pixels, it obscures pixels on the layer below. Where a layer is transparent, the underlying layer shows through.

Also remember that you can't move the original background layer until you turn it into a "normal" layer. Click the layer name in the Layers palette and choose Layer⇨New⇨Layer from Background to make the transformation. You also can just double-click the layer name to display the New Layer dialog box and then click OK or press Enter.

✔ **To fade one layer with another:** You can create some interesting effects by playing with layer opacity. For example, to create the image in Figures 9-7 and 9-8, I copied a butterfly from one of my nature pictures into a photograph of a leaf. In Figure 9-7, I left the opacity of the butterfly layer at 100 percent, so the butterfly completely covers the leaf below. In Figure 9-8, I set the opacity of the butterfly layer to 50 percent, which makes the butterfly appear as if it's part of the leaf. In both cases, the leaf image is completely visible through all transparent areas in the butterfly layer, represented by the checkerboard pattern in the Layers palette thumbnail.

Also play with the options in the Blending Mode menu, labeled in Figure 9-8, to explore other artistic choices for mixing layers in your collage. For an explanation of blending modes, see the end of Chapter 6.

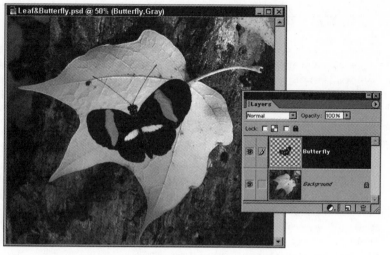

Figure 9-7:
When set to full opacity, areas of the butterfly layer that contain visible pixels completely obscure the underlying leaf image.

Blending Mode menu

Figure 9-8:
Reducing the opacity of the butterfly layer to 50 percent allows some of the underlying leaf pixels to be visible through the butterfly.

Before moving on, take another quick look at Figure 9-7. If you want a composition like this to look more lifelike, add a shadow underneath the top element to add some separation between it and the underlying layer. (I didn't do so here because a shadow has a reduced opacity, which may have confused the issue of layer opacity that I wanted to illustrate.) Chapter 7 explains how to add a shadow.

Saving the collage

Be sure to save your collage at regular intervals while you're creating it. Especially if you're working with high-resolution images, a multiple-photo composition puts a big strain on your computer, which means that your chances of experiencing a system crash are higher than normal. By saving the file often, you avoid losing hours of work if the computer throws a fit. At worst, you lose only the edits you made after your last save.

Remember that photo editors typically do not offer an auto-save feature like the one found in many word processing and other standard document-creation programs. Don't think of this as an oversight in the photo editor, though. If the program went about saving your image file automatically, without your permission, it would lock in whatever changes you had made since the last save, and you may not have decided yet whether you like those changes. To enable you to experiment freely, photo editors give you complete control of — and responsibility for — saving the file.

Chapter 2 provides the full story on how to save an image file, so I won't repeat the information here. Do remember that in order to keep your individual collage layers intact, you must save the file in a format that supports layers. In Photoshop Elements, use the native program format, PSD. You also must select the Layers check box in the Save As dialog box to retain layers.

After you're finished with your collage, of course, you may want to go ahead and merge all the image layers. Doing so reduces the file size and also prevents you from accidentally moving an object out of place. See the end of Chapter 7 for details on how to merge image layers.

Using Effects to Rescue a Lousy Image

As I hope the examples used throughout this book have made clear, you can't always turn a poor photo into a great one. The picture in Color Plate 9-1 illustrates this point. I spent hour upon hour with this image, using every technique and tool I know, and still couldn't produce anything better than the left image in the middle row of the color plate. Cropping out the bottom of the picture, which had degraded over time to a green fog, solved part of the problem. But the original image was so underexposed and poorly focused that the facial areas were seriously lacking in detail.

That's not to say that you should totally abandon photos like this, however. If the moment captured in the picture is a special one, you can apply artistic effects that preserve the essence of the event while playing down photographic flaws. For example, in the middle right example in Color Plate 9-1, I applied the Photoshop Elements Sponge filter to my best-effort correction to create a soft, impressionistic image. For another take on the same subject, I converted the corrected photo to a grayscale image and then painted on the image to create the appearance of an old, hand-tinted photo, as shown in the bottom row. Both effects are ideal for less-than-perfect images because people don't expect to see razor-sharp edges and high detail in the style of art that the effects produce.

These two effects are hardly the only options available to you; experiment with all the effects your photo editor offers to discover more artistic ways to make the best of a poor-quality image. To get you started, the next section breaks down the steps involved in applying a special effect. Following that, you can find specific steps for creating the hand-tinted photograph look.

Applying special effects

Most photo editing programs offer a variety of special effects filters. Some programs, including Elements, even offer a mini-browser that displays thumbnail previews of the effect that each filter produces. To display the Elements effects browser, shown in Figure 9-9, click its tab in the palette well or choose Window⇨Show Filters Browser. (In Elements 2.0, choose Window⇨Filters.)

Filters browser

Figure 9-9:
Apply special effects to a duplicate image layer so that you can experiment without worrying about destroying the original photo.

New Layer button

Elements also offers a second mini-browser, the Effects browser, which provides access to some additional effects. However, these effects are more suited to creating image backgrounds rather than applying to an entire photograph. Later sections in this chapter discuss backgrounds and the Effects browser.

Regardless of what special effect you want to use, apply the filter using the following general approach:

1. **Save a copy of the original image under a new name.**

   You may want the image without the effect later, so always apply the filter to a duplicate of your original image file.

2. **If you want to apply the effect to all layers in a multiple-layer image, flatten the image.**

   Of course, if you want to apply the filter to only one layer in the image, don't take this step. Chapter 7 explains how to flatten an image. If you're not ready to merge layers, you must apply the filter to each layer independently to alter the entire image.

3. **Duplicate the layer(s) to which you want to apply the effect.**

   In Elements, you can duplicate a layer by simply dragging it to the New Layer button at the bottom of the Layers palette, labeled in Figure 9-9.

4. **On the duplicate layer(s), select the area that you want to change.**

   If you want to alter the entire layer, there is no need to create a selection outline in Elements.

5. **Apply the special effect.**

   In Elements, you can apply a filter from the Filters browser by clicking the filter's thumbnail and then clicking the Apply button at the top of the browser. If you want to be able to adjust the effect that the filter creates, select the Filter Options box in the browser, as shown in Figure 9-9, before you click Apply. Otherwise, the program applies the filter at its default settings (in which case you can skip the upcoming Steps 6 and 7).

   Alternatively, you can choose the filter name from the Filters menu. If you go this route, you always get access to filter options if any are available for the selected filter.

6. **Tweak the effect, if desired.**

   For some filters, you're presented with a dialog box containing controls that enable you to vary the effect. The Sponge filter that I applied to my image in Color Plate 9-1 offers the options shown in Figure 9-10, for example. If the dialog box contains a Preview check box, turn on the option so that you can preview the effect in the image window. For some filters, including the one featured in Figure 9-10, you have to rely on the small thumbnail preview inside the dialog box.

To zoom the preview in and out, click the plus and minus signs underneath the thumbnail. Drag inside the thumbnail to scroll the display so that you can see another part of the image.

Figure 9-10:
Most filters
offer a
variety of
controls for
adjusting
the effect.

7. **Click OK or press Enter to close the filter dialog box and apply the effect.**

After applying the effect, you can vary its impact further by adjusting the blending mode and opacity of the filtered layer. For example, to ramp down the impact of an effect, lower the layer opacity, which allows pixels in the original image layer to become partially visible again.

If you decide you don't like the effect, you can use the undo options discussed in Chapter 2 to remove it. Because some filters involve several different actions, you may need to undo more than one level of edit. Alternatively, just delete the filtered layer. To try a different effect, create another duplicate layer and apply the filter to it.

After you're happy with the results, merge the filtered layer with the original, as outlined at the end of Chapter 7.

Creating a hand-tinted photo effect

Giving your photo the hand-tinted look shown in the last example in Figure 9-2 is an easy process. If you learned how to color inside the lines of a coloring book as a kid, you can do this, too. Actually, you'll find this project simple even if you weren't such a hotshot with the Crayolas.

The process involves two main steps. First, you replace every color with a shade of gray, white, or black — in other words, you desaturate the image. Then you paint on the tint colors in using your favorite painting tool in conjunction with the Color layer blending mode.

Here's a detailed look at the technique:

1. **Make a copy of your image and save the copy with a new name.**

   This project permanently alters the colors in your photo, so work on a copy of the image just in case you ever need the original again.

2. **If you're working with a color image, desaturate the image.**

   Look for your software's Saturation control, usually provided via a Hue/Saturation filter, and use the control to turn all colors to shades of gray.

   Some photo editors offer an automatic desaturation filter that accomplishes this step. In Elements, the Remove Color command does the job. However, I suggest that you bypass Remove Color and instead desaturate your image via a Hue/Saturation adjustment layer, for reasons that become clear in later steps.

   Choose Layer➪New Adjustment Layer➪Hue/Saturation and click OK when the New Layer dialog box appears. You then see the Hue/Saturation dialog box, shown in Figure 9-11. Select Master from the Edit drop-down list at the top of the dialog box. Then drag the Saturation slider all the way to the left, as shown in the figure.

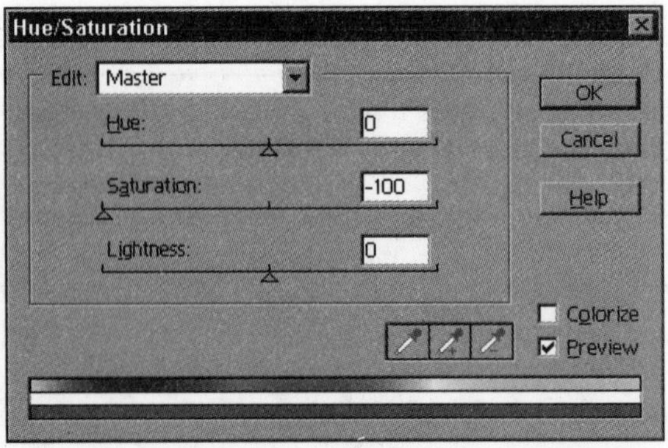

Figure 9-11:
Lowering
the
Saturation
value sucks
color from
an image.

3. **If you're working with a grayscale photo, convert the image to the RGB color model.**

   As explained in Chapter 4, a true grayscale image permits you to use only 256 colors, all shades of gray. In order to tint your photo with other colors, you have to convert the image to the RGB color model.

To check the current color model in Elements, choose Image⇨Mode and see what option is selected on the Mode submenu. Click RGB if it's not already selected. This step doesn't automatically add color to your picture; it enables *you* to add color via your software's paint tools.

Note that your image may already be in the RGB model even though the original photograph was a black-and-white picture. Some scanners output all images in RGB, regardless of whether the image is full color or not. In addition, some photo editing programs open all images as RGB images, regardless of the original color model.

For a review of color models and grayscale image characteristics, see Chapter 4.

4. **Create a new, empty image layer to hold your paint.**

   In Elements, just click the New Layer button at the bottom of the Layers palette. (Refer to Figure 9-12.)

Eraser

Paintbrush   Blending Mode menu

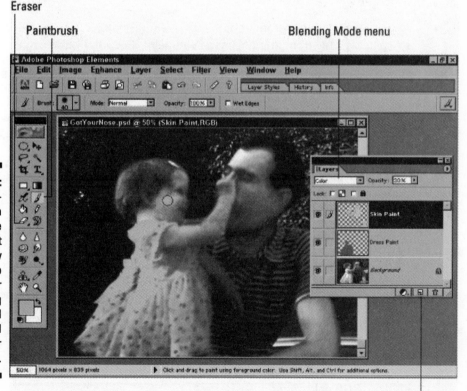

Figure 9-12:
To "hand-tint" a grayscale photo, paint on a new layer set to the Color blending mode and reduced layer opacity.

New Layer button

5. **Reduce the opacity of the new layer to 30 percent and set the layer blending mode to Color.**

   Make these changes in the Layers palette, as shown in Figure 9-12, if you're working with Elements.

6. **Select a paint color and painting tool, and paint on the new layer.**

   If you started with a color image, you may want to open it so that you can reference the original image as you select paint colors. In Elements, you can even click with the Eyedropper in the original image window to match the foreground color to a color in the image. If you desaturated the image via a Hue/Saturation adjustment layer, of course, your colors still exist on the original layer in the modified image. Hide the adjustment layer by clicking its eyeball icon in the Layers palette and then click the name of the original color layer. Click with the Eyedropper in the image window to set the foreground color. Click the adjustment layer's eyeball icon again to redisplay the desaturated version of the image. Finally, click the paint layer's name to make that layer active again and do your painting.

After you paint your first few strokes, you can adjust the layer opacity to achieve a blend of original image and paint that you like. In some programs, you can also reduce the opacity of the paint tool itself to affect new strokes that you paint. (In Elements, use the Opacity control on the Options bar and the Brush Dynamics options, all explained in Chapter 6.)

The Color blending mode enables you to add color to a photograph without changing the original brightness values. White areas remain white, and black areas remain black. If you want to change the color of a pure white or black area, create a new layer to hold the paint for those areas, this time setting the layer blending mode to Normal. In fact, you may want to create a new layer for each of the major objects you want to tint so that you can adjust the opacity and blending mode as needed for each element. If you can't get the results you want from the Color or Normal blending modes, try the Hue or Overlay mode.

As you paint, use the Eraser tool or the Undo and Step Backward commands to clean up any errant paint strokes. When you're done painting, merge the image layers to reduce the file size and make your color changes permanent.

For details on selecting a paint color, see Chapter 4. To find out more about working with painting tools and the eraser, check out Chapter 6. Chapter 7 shows you how to merge layers.

Creating Better Backgrounds

The background plays a huge role in the appeal of a photograph. A busy background distracts from the main subject, as illustrated by several examples in this book, including the image in Figure 9-13 and Color Plate 9-2. When you're shooting pictures in a family setting, you just can't worry about the background too much if you want to capture spontaneous moments like this one.

Figure 9-13: Replacing a busy background gives this image a fun, fantasy look and returns the focus to the subjects.

Fortunately, you can easily drop in a new background in any photo editor. I opted to replace the background in my image with an image of blue sky and fluffy clouds — which, incidentally, I made from scratch by using a special effects filter known as a Clouds filter. After replacing the background, I also adjusted the exposure, contrast, and sharpness of the original image to produce the "after" version of the picture.

The product shot in Figure 9-14, shown in color in the upper-left example in Color Plate 9-3, shows a background problem of a different sort. Although the background is plain and therefore doesn't compete with the glassware, its color doesn't provide enough contrast with the white ewer and the yellow dish, which has a white rim and interior. The white glass in both pieces literally disappears into the light background.

Figure 9-14:
This background is too bright, making the lighter pieces of glass difficult to distinguish in some areas.

For this kind of shot, a simple color change to the background can work wonders. In the top right image in the color plate, I replaced the background with a *gradient fill* that provides better contrast between glass and background. Figure 9-15 shows the grayscale version of the picture.

Figure 9-15:
A darker background makes the glassware shapes easier to distinguish.

A gradient is a band of color that fades from one hue to another — in the case of the example in the color plate, from light brown to dark brown. *Fill* is the imaging geek's word for a color or pattern that covers the interior of an object or selected area.

By making the background darker at the bottom of the picture, I was able to replicate the original lighting conditions in which the photo was taken. To add a bit more visual interest, I then applied a texture effect to the new background to create the variations shown in the bottom row of the color plate.

In addition to filling a background with another color or a texture, you can set your subject against a background from another photo. Just follow the steps outlined in the collage-building sections earlier in this chapter to copy and paste your subject into the background photo.

The next section explains the basic approach you should use to replace an ugly or inappropriate background. Following that, you can find out how to create the gradient, textured, and clouds backgrounds that I used in Color Plates 9-2 and 9-3.

Replacing the background

To swap out the background in a photo, follow these steps. (The instructions assume that you want to put the new background in your original photo, not copy your subject into a new background in a different photo. For that approach, follow the collage-building steps outlined earlier in the chapter.)

1. **Select everything but the background area that you want to replace.**

   Chapter 3 shows you all the techniques that you can use to select a portion of your photo.

2. **Copy the selected area onto a new layer.**

   In Elements, choose Layer⇨New⇨Layer via Copy or press Ctrl+J (⌘+J).

   To keep things clear, double-click the layer name in the Layers palette and name this new layer something like *Subject.* Be sure that the layer blending mode and opacity are set to Normal and 100 percent, respectively.

3. **Create a new, empty layer and position it directly underneath the new subject layer that you created in Step 2.**

   This layer will hold your new background. Set this layer's blending mode to Normal and the Opacity value to 100 percent as well. Name this layer *New Background.*

4. **Fill the new background layer with whatever you want to use as the new background.**

   The next few sections offer some ideas for creating backgrounds.

That's the basic process. Your new background shows through any transparent areas of the new subject layer. The original image layer underneath the two new layers should be completely obscured.

To refine the results, try these tricks:

✔ **To get rid of stray background pixels on the subject layer:** If you grabbed part of the original background when creating your original selection outline, click the subject layer name in the Layers palette to make it the active layer. Then use the Eraser tool on the Subject layer to wipe away those stray background pixels. As you erase, underlying pixels from the new background layer become visible.

See Chapter 6 for details about working with the Eraser tool; also check out Chapter 8 for tips on dealing with background clean-up work around hair and fur.

✔ **To reveal hidden areas of the original image layer:** If your selection outline in Step 1 was too small and left some of the original subject pixels behind, use the Eraser on the new background layer to reveal them.

If you want to add a shadow behind the subject (which the next section explains how to do), you need to take an additional step or the shadow process won't work correctly. The shadow won't appear behind the subject areas that you made visible by erasing. See the following section for details.

Casting a shadow on the new background

If you want your subject to cast a shadow on the new background, your subject layer must be positioned directly above the new background layer. You then can apply a drop shadow effect to the subject layer using the technique outlined in Chapter 7.

Assuming that you created your new background as detailed in the preceding section, your subject layer and new background layer are already in the proper positions. However, as I alluded to a few paragraphs ago, if you erased a portion of your new background layer to reveal additional areas of the original image, those areas won't receive a shadow unless you do some clean-up work first. You must copy those areas onto the new subject layer so that they, too, reside above the new background layer.

To do this, follow these steps in Elements:

1. **Ctrl+click (⌘+click) the new background layer name in the Layers palette to select all filled areas on that layer.**

2. **Choose Select⇨Inverse to select only the areas that you erased instead.**

3. **Click the original image layer name in the Layers palette.**

4. **Press Ctrl+C (⌘+C) to copy the selected areas to the Clipboard.**

5. **Click the new subject layer name in the Layers palette.**

6. **Press Ctrl+V (⌘+V) to paste the copied pixels onto a new layer immediately above the new subject layer.**

7. **Choose Layer↷Merge down to merge the new subject layer and the layer that contains the newly copied pixels.**

Now you can add your shadow to the subject layer as usual.

After you add the shadow, you can eliminate the original photo layer — the one that contains both the subject and the original background — if you want to reduce the image file size. Just drag the layer to the Trash button in the Layers palette.

Creating a gradient background

Most photo editors offer a tool that fills an area with a gradient (band of colors). The specifics of using the tool vary from program to program, but in general, you select the colors you want to include in the gradient, choose the direction and design of the gradient, and then drag across the image to create the band of color.

In some programs, you're limited to two-color gradients or prefab gradients that include a particular spectrum of colors. In other programs, including Elements, you can take advantage of prefab gradients or design your own, custom gradients.

For background purposes, a simple gradient usually works best, so I won't get into the topic of creating a many-colored or complicated custom gradient. The following steps show you how to use the Elements Gradient tool to fill a selected area with a subtle, two-color gradient that fades gradually from the foreground color to the background color, like the example shown in the top right image of Color Plate 9-3.

After creating your new background layer as described earlier, in the section "Replacing a background," select the entire layer. Then fill the layer with the gradient like so:

1. **Set the foreground and background colors to the lightest and darkest colors that you want the gradient to contain.**

If you want to imply a natural lighting condition, as in the example photo, choose two shades of the same color. For example, in Color Plate 9-3, I set the foreground color to a medium brown and the background color to a dark brown.

2. **Activate the Gradient tool, labeled in Figure 9-16.**

The Options bar changes to offer you a variety of gradient controls, as shown in the figure.

Linear Gradient icon

Gradient tool   Start of drag

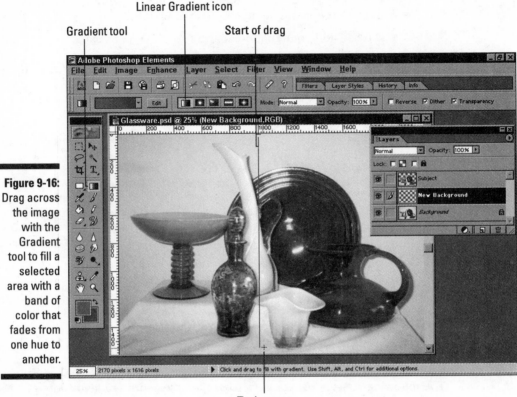

Figure 9-16:
Drag across
the image
with the
Gradient
tool to fill a
selected
area with a
band of
color that
fades from
one hue to
another.

Tool cursor

3. **Click the Linear Gradient icon, labeled in Figure 9-16, to specify the style of the gradient.**

4. **Set the Opacity, Normal, Transparency, Dither, and Reverse options as shown in Figure 9-16.**

5. **Open the Gradient Picker and click the Foreground to Background thumbnail.**

    The Gradient Picker, which contains thumbnails that represent a variety of gradient styles, lives at the left end of the Options bar. To open the Gradient Picker, click the triangle labeled in Figure 9-17. Then click the very first gradient, which is the Foreground to Background gradient, as shown in Figure 9-17.

6. **Shift+drag from the top of your image to the bottom, as shown in Figure 9-17.**

    Pressing Shift as you drag creates a gradient that has a perfect vertical alignment. If you want to create a horizontally oriented gradient, Shift+ drag from left to right instead of from top to bottom. Either way, the program creates the gradient using the foreground and background colors.

Click to display Gradient Picker

Figure 9-17:
Choose
the first
gradient
option in the
Gradient
Picker to
create a
two-color
gradient.

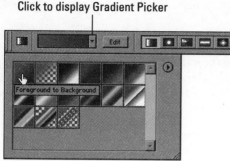

If you need to adjust the color of the gradient, you can use the Hue/Saturation command, discussed in the upcoming section "Changing the Color of an Object" or just redraw the gradient after establishing new foreground and background colors. Changing the point at where you stop and start your drag will also alter the gradient. In addition, you can use the Levels command, covered in Chapter 5, to tweak the brightness of a gradient after you create it.

Adding texture to a plain background

By adding a slight texture or pattern to a plain or gradient background, you can make the background look like one you'd see if you shot the picture in a room in your home or office — in other words, against a wall. In the lower images in Color Plate 9-3, I applied two different special effects filters found in Elements to the two-tone gradient used in the upper-right image.

After creating your new background as discussed in the earlier section, "Replacing the background," take the following steps to add the texture effect shown in the lower-left image of the color plate:

1. **Select the layer that holds the new background.**

2. **Duplicate the layer.**

   Just to be safe, you should apply the special effect to a copy of the background.

3. **Choose Filter⇨Texture⇨Texturizer to display the dialog box shown in Figure 9-18.**

4. **Use the dialog box controls to design a custom texture.**

   For the background in Color Plate 9-3, I selected Canvas from the Texture drop-down list in the dialog box, as shown in Figure 9-18. After selecting a Texture option, tweak the effect by using the other controls in the dialog box. For the most natural results, match the Light Direction setting to the direction of the original light in your photo. The thumbnail preview in the dialog box shows you how the texture will look when applied to your image.

5. Click OK or press Enter to apply the effect.

If you don't like the effect, you can use the undo options discussed in Chapter 2 to remove the filter. Or you can just trash the filtered layer. Additionally, you can modify the strength of the effect by lowering the opacity of the filtered layer.

Figure 9-18:
You can replicate the texture found in canvas, burlap, sandstone, and other materials using the Texturizer filter.

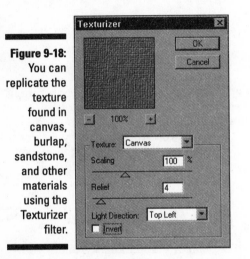

To create the effect shown in the lower-right example in Color Plate 9-3, follow the same steps but choose Filter⇨Texture⇨Grain in Step 3. I discuss the Grain filter in Chapter 8, so check there if you need help using it. I chose Vertical from the Grain Type drop-down list to get the striated look shown in the color plate.

If you're working with Elements, you may find some additional suitable texture effects in the Effects browser. For the most part, these effects allow you to create with one click results that you can get by applying two or more of the filters found on the Filters menu, one after the other. But hey, why not save some time if you can? To display the browser, choose Window⇨Show Effects Browser. (In Elements 2.0, it's just Window⇨Effects.) Scroll through the effect thumbnails, and if you see one you like, click it and then click the Apply button. After adding the effect, the program gives you a chance to accept or reject the change.

Filling the background with clouds

If you want to copy the cloud-and-sky background idea shown in Color Plate 9-2 — really, I don't mind one bit — the following steps show you how. The technique described here involves the Clouds special effects filter available in Elements. Many programs have this same filter, although it may go by a different name.

As with the other background recipes, this one assumes that you created a new layer to hold the new background. If you need help with that bit of business, refer to the earlier section "Replacing the background."

1. **Set the foreground and background colors to the color of sky and clouds you want to create.**

   You'll get the most natural results if you choose a medium blue for the sky and a very, very light blue, instead of pure white, for the clouds. Set the foreground color to the sky color and the background color to the cloud color.

   See Chapter 4 for help setting the foreground and background colors.

2. **Select the layer that contains your new background.**

3. **Choose Filter⇨Render⇨Clouds.**

   There you go, instant cloudy sky. The filter creates the effect using the foreground and background colors you established in Step 1.

If you want a more intense sky and less diffuse clouds, undo the filter and then reapply it, this time holding down the Alt (Option) key as you choose the command. For more diffuse clouds, apply the filter a second time without the Alt (Option) key.

You also can increase the size of the clouds by using the Free Transform command on the clouds layer. Press Ctrl+T (⌘+T) to display transformation handles around the layer and then drag a corner handle to enlarge the layer.

Chapter 7 explains the Free Transform command in detail.

Aging a Picture in Seconds

In Chapter 4, I discuss ways to remove an unwanted color cast such as the sepia tinge that you see in Color Plate 4-7. For that image, which was originally a black-and-white photo, removing the color cast was a simple matter of desaturating the picture.

Some people like the discolored-with-age look, however. In fact, many digital cameras now offer a feature that automatically creates this effect after you shoot a picture. Talk about instant antiques!

To give your photo an overall tint, whatever the color, you can use the same process outlined earlier in this chapter in the section "Creating a hand-tinted photo effect." Desaturate the photo, create a new layer to hold the paint, and paint the entire image with the same color, adjusting the opacity and blending mode of the paint layer as needed.

However, depending on your photo editing program, you may have access to features that make the job a little easier than manually painting on a tint.

✔ Some programs offer an automatic filter, usually called a Colorize or Tint filter, that desaturates and tints your image in one step. In Elements, this filter resides in the Hue/Saturation dialog box, shown in Figure 9-11, earlier in this chapter (and again in the upcoming Figure 9-21).

The great thing about the Colorize filter in Elements is that you can apply the effect via a Hue/Saturation adjustment layer. That means that you can use the layer blending mode and layer opacity controls to further tweak the effect and, more important, that you don't permanently alter your original image until you decide to merge all your image layers. See Chapter 4 to find out how to create a Hue/Saturation adjustment layer.

Before you create the adjustment layer, though, set the foreground color to the approximate tint color you want. After you add the adjustment layer, the program opens the Hue/Saturation dialog box. Select the Colorize check box inside the dialog box to apply the initial tint. Drag the Hue slider to adjust the tint color; drag the Saturation slider to control the intensity of the tint.

✔ If you don't have access to an automatic tint feature and you have to use the hand-painted photo technique, look for a Fill command when you get to the part where you apply the tint color.

The Fill command fills a selected area with a single color — usually, the current foreground color. See your software's Help system to find out where this command lives. (In Elements, Fill lives on the Edit menu.) Fill saves you the excruciating labor involved in dragging all over your image with the paint brush to tint the entire photo. You can read more about the Fill command in the next section. Remember to add the fill to a new image layer at the top of the layer stack.

Changing the Color of an Object

You can change the color of an object using a variety of techniques, including the tinting process explained in the preceding section. The one thing that doesn't work is to simply paint over the photo with solid color, which you might quite naturally assume would be the right approach.

When you paint with solid color, you wind up with an expanse of flat color without any detail. It's similar to rolling latex paint on a wallpapered wall, except that in this case, you don't even see the roller texture or any of the bumps or divots that may exist on the wallpaper surface. While that may be fine for home decorating, it's unnatural in a photograph, which rarely contains significant areas of a single color. Even a blue sky has subtle color variations that give the image depth.

To realistically alter the color of an object, first select the object that you want to change and copy the selection to a new layer. Then try the following techniques, applying the change to the new layer only. I used some of these tricks to change the color of the tablecloth in the product shot shown in Color Plate 9-3.

> ✔ **Apply the Fill command in conjunction with layer blending mode and opacity options.** After setting the foreground color to the color you want the object to have, choose the Fill command, available in just about every photo editor. In Elements, choose Edit⇨Fill to display the dialog box shown in Figure 9-19. Select Foreground Color from the Use drop-down list at the top of the dialog box. Leave the other options at their default settings, as shown in the figure.

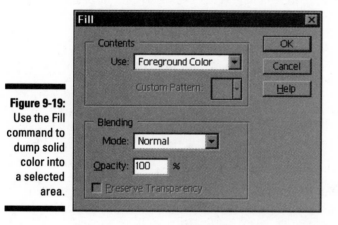

Figure 9-19: Use the Fill command to dump solid color into a selected area.

After you click OK or press Enter, the dialog box closes and the selected area is filled with the foreground color. As you can see, I just had you create that solid expanse of flat color I said earlier was no good. To bring back the highlights and shadows from the underlying image, change the blending mode of the filled layer to Color, Hue, or Overlay. You also can adjust the layer's opacity value to increase or decrease the intensity of the color. At a low opacity, the Normal blending mode may also do the trick.

Which mode delivers the results you want depends on the original image and the fill color you chose. In the top-right example in Color Plate 9-3, for example, I filled the tablecloth with a copper color and set the layer blending mode to Overlay.

Have brain space left for more keyboard shortcuts? If so, here are two that you can use to avoid having to open the Fill dialog box. Just press Alt+ Backspace (Option+Delete) to fill the area with the current foreground color; press Ctrl+Backspace (⌘+Delete) to fill the area with the current background color.

✔ **Use the Paintbrush and other paint tools in conjunction with layer blending and opacity controls.** Everything I just said about the Fill command works for any tool that paints color on an image. For a practical application of this technique, see the sections related to painting away red eye and adding skin color in Chapter 8.

✔ **Desaturate the object and use the Levels command to adjust the resulting gray values.** To turn the tablecloth gray in the lower left example in Color Plate 9-3, I just desaturated it. Then I used the Levels command to darken the shadows a little.

For details on how to desaturate a part of your photo, see the earlier section "Creating a hand-tinted photo effect." Chapter 5 explains the Levels command.

✔ **Desaturate specific image colors only.** In Color Plate 9-4, I took a different approach to desaturating. Instead of selecting everything but the water areas and then doing a wholesale desaturation, I took advantage of the fact that the Elements Hue/Saturation filter enables you to apply changes just to particular color ranges.

To try out this technique, create a Hue/Saturation adjustment layer as explained in Chapter 4. In the Hue/Saturation dialog box, shown in Figure 9-20, select a color range from the Edit drop-down list — your options are Reds, Yellows, Greens, Cyans, Blues, Magentas. Then drag the Saturation slider all the way to the left, as shown in the figure, to change colors in the selected range to shades of gray. To create the right image in Color Plate 9-4, I desaturated the reds, yellows, greens, and magentas, leaving only the blues and cyans intact.

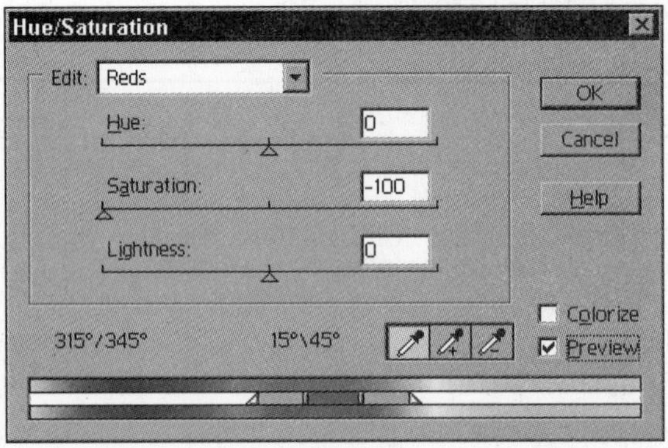

Figure 9-20:
In Elements,
you can
desaturate
or adjust the
hue of a
single color
range.

✔ **Use the Colorize option in the Hue/Saturation dialog box.** I introduced this technique in the preceding section when showing you how to tint a grayscale image. You can use the Colorize option to make a stronger color statement, though, as I did to create the blue version of the tablecloth shown in the lower-right image in Color Plate 9-3. Just adjust the

Saturation and Lightness controls to vary the intensity and shade of the new color. I used the settings shown in Figure 9-21 to turn the white table-cloth blue.

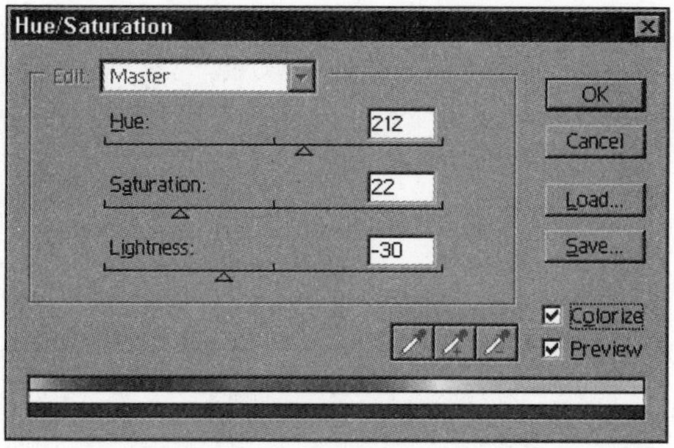

Figure 9-21:
To turn the tablecloth in Color Plate 9-3 from white to blue, I applied the Hue/ Saturation filter using these settings.

✔ **Change the Hue value to spin the object around the color wheel.** If you're starting with a colored object — one that's anything but white, black, or a shade of gray — you can deselect the Colorize option in the Hue/Saturation dialog box and just raise or lower the Hue value to change the object's color. When you raise the value, you spin the object clockwise around the color wheel, which is shown in Color Plate 4-2. When you lower the value, you send the object in the other direction. So if you start out with, say, a red vase, and you raise the Hue value 120 degrees, you turn the vase green. If you lower the value 120 degrees, you wind up with a blue vase.

Before closing out this color-shifting discussion, I want to alert you to some subtle differences in these techniques that you may not otherwise notice:

✔ Some techniques change the color of shadows cast on the object you're adjusting, while others preserve the shadow color. Notice that when I used the Overlay fill technique to change the color of the tablecloth in the upper right image of Color Plate 9-3, the shadow underneath the red pitcher retains a reddish cast, as it had in the original image. With the other two methods, that color cast was lost.

If that kind of detail bothers you — which it really should — compare your original photo with the altered one and then tint the shadows accordingly to fix the problem. You can create a new image layer and paint in the tint, adjusting the blending mode and opacity of the tint layer to get the look of the shadow just right. Don't forget, too, to adjust the shadows cast by an object whose color you've altered. You don't want a red pitcher that casts a green shadow, for example.

✔ If you want to change multiple objects that have different original colors to the same color — for example, to turn both a red vase and a green vase blue — use the Colorize option in the Hue/Saturation dialog box. That technique is far easier than trying to use the other methods, which require you to use different settings to achieve the same final color range for each object.

Chapter 10

Preserving and Sharing Your Photos

*W*hether you spent minutes or hours getting your photo in shape, the steps you take to print or electronically distribute the finished product are as important as any retouching or restoration work you can do. Make a wrong decision, and you can make your picture look worse than when you started.

Okay, maybe that intro was just a hair overdramatic. The sky probably won't come crashing down if you screw up the output part of the editing process. But the sky in your picture really *can* turn a little ugly, as can the faces, flowers, and anything else in the scene.

This chapter helps you avoid trashing all your hard work by explaining the precautions you should take when preparing your picture for printing or electronic distribution. Among other things, you can find out how to establish print size and resolution, size pictures for screen display, and compress image files to reduce the time required to download them over the Web. Because all that stuff can be a little dry, I added some creative spice to the discussion by including a section on using special effects to add a digital matte to your photo.

Setting Print Size and Output Resolution

When you open a digital image in a photo editor, the program assigns a default output resolution. That value, in turn, establishes the default print size. Before you print your picture, you need to check both values and adjust them if necessary. The next few sections discuss this important step in putting your photos on paper.

Reviewing resolution

Chapter 2 introduces the concept of output resolution, but to refresh your memory, here's a brief review of the important points:

- A digital image is built out of tiny squares of color called *pixels*.

- Every image starts out with a specific number of pixels, which is determined by the *input resolution* setting you use when you scan the photo or capture it with a digital camera. See Chapter 2 for details about establishing input resolution.

- *Output resolution* refers to how many pixels are squeezed into each linear inch when the photo is printed. A 1 x 1-inch picture with an output resolution of 300 pixels per inch (ppi) has 300 pixels across and 300 pixels down.

- Don't confuse output resolution with *printer* resolution. Printer resolution refers to the number of ink dots a printer generates to reproduce each inch of your photo. Depending on the printer technology, the machine may lay down multiple dots of ink to reproduce *each pixel*. Printer resolution is measured in *dots per inch*, or dpi. For more about printer resolution, see the upcoming section "Choosing a photo printer."

The more pixels that you pack into each inch of your image, the better the print quality. Why? Two reasons:

- More pixels means smaller pixels. (If you spread 300 pixels across one linear inch, the pixels must be smaller than if you spread them across two inches.)

    To get a clear view of how output resolution affects pixel size, notice the borders around the two images in Figure 10-1 and the top two photos in Color Plate 10-1. I applied a one-pixel black border around each picture in my photo editor. But the border on the low-resolution image on the right is thicker because one pixel is larger at 75 ppi than it is at 300 ppi.

    When pixels get too big, the block-based nature of the image becomes apparent, as illustrated by the low-resolution image in Figure 10-1 and Color Plate 10-1. The problem is especially noticeable along the edges of diagonal and curved lines, such as the collar of the boy's shirt. The edges look jagged, a phenomenon that some people refer to as *stair-stepping*.

✔ More pixels also means more blocks of color with which to create the image. That results in better rendering of details in the photograph.

Imagine trying to create a picture of someone's face with 2,000 colored tiles and then attempting the same thing with only 500 tiles. Your second picture would have to be less complex because each tile must represent a larger area of the face. The inset areas in Figure 10-1 and the top row of Color Plate 10-1 provide a close-up look at the difference in image detail between a high-resolution image (left) and a low-resolution image (right).

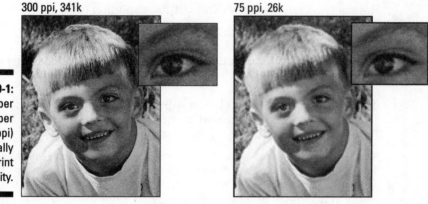

300 ppi, 341k   75 ppi, 26k

Figure 10-1: The number of pixels per inch (ppi) dramatically affects print quality.

A high pixel population has a down side, however. Every pixel increases the size of the image file. The high-resolution image in Figure 10-1 has a file size of 341K; the high-resolution color version, 723K. (Color data also increases the size of an image file.) By contrast, the low-resolution grayscale image in Figure 10-1 has a file size of just 26K; the color version, 50K.

Large files require more of your computer's resources to process, which can slow down your photo editor's performance. In addition, the larger the image file, the longer it takes to send or receive the image online. See "Saving a JPEG copy of your photo," later in this chapter, for information about compressing a file to reduce the file size without dumping pixels.

Determining the right output resolution

For most images, an output resolution of between 200 to 300 ppi delivers good print quality. Anything more than 300 ppi is usually overkill because most printers can't handle more than 300 ppi and just toss out the overage when they encounter it.

Your printer manual may indicate what output resolution you should use to get the best results. If not, do some test prints at a few different settings and make your own judgment. If you're sending your photo to a lab or commercial printer for output, consult with the printer technicians to find out what output resolution is appropriate.

Balancing resolution, size, and quality

Print size, output resolution, and pixel dimensions (the number of horizontal and vertical pixels) are always dependent on each other. You can think of this relationship in terms of simple mathematical formulas:

Horizontal pixels ÷ print width = output resolution (ppi)

Vertical pixels ÷ print height = output resolution (ppi)

If you change the output resolution, one of the other two values must change, as follows:

✔ If you raise the output resolution without changing the number of image pixels, the print size is reduced. If you lower output resolution and keep the pixel count constant, your print dimensions grow.

Both images in Figure 10-2, for example, contain 933 pixels across and 500 pixels down. But I set the output resolution of the top image to 200 ppi; the bottom image, to 300 ppi. Although the 200 ppi image looks pretty good, the higher resolution image is slightly superior in terms of sharpness and detail. (Again, notice that the one-pixel border that I placed around the 200 ppi image is slightly thicker than the one-pixel border around the 300 ppi image.)

✔ If you change the output resolution without changing the print dimensions, you must add or delete pixels to get the desired number of pixels per inch. I used this approach to convert the high-resolution image shown in Figure 10-1 and Color Plate 10-1 to the 75-ppi version. I dumped roughly three-quarters of the original pixels from the 300-ppi image to create the low-resolution image.

When you talk about adding or deleting pixels, by the way, use the term *resampling* if you want to sound like an imaging expert. Some people say *upsampling* when referring to adding pixels and *downsampling* when speaking of eliminating pixels.

You typically can eliminate excess pixels without noticeably affecting image quality, assuming that you keep the output resolution at 200 ppi or higher. (You would never want to lower the output resolution as much as I did in the figure and color plate.) However, I suggest that you perform your pixel surgery on a copy of the original image. You may want to print your photo at a larger size someday, in which case you'll need more of those original pixels.

933 x 500 pixels, 200ppi

Figure 10-2:
Raising the
output
resolution
without
adding
pixels
reduces the
print size
and may
improve
print quality.

933 x 500 pixels, 300ppi

Adding pixels, however, usually lowers image quality. The photo editor does its best to decide on the right color and placement of the new pixels, but you rarely wind up with the same image quality you would have if you had captured those extra pixels when you shot or scanned the picture. So again, add pixels to a copy of the original image. After adding pixels, do a test print of the altered photo and the original. You may find that you get a better print from the original, lower-resolution file than you do from the pixels-added version.

In Figure 10-3, for example, I started with the 75 ppi image shown on the right side of Figure 10-1. I added enough pixels to up the output resolution to 300 ppi. You can see that the result, shown on the right side of Figure 10-3, doesn't even come close to the quality of the original 300-ppi image shown on the left side of Figure 10-1. In fact, the resampled image doesn't really look any better than its 75 ppi counterpart.

75 ppi   Resampled to 300 ppi

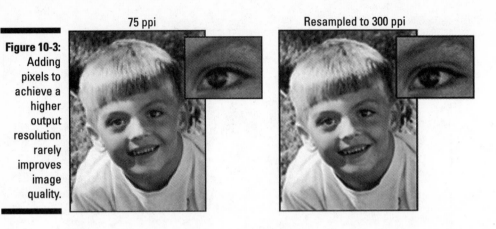

Figure 10-3: Adding pixels to achieve a higher output resolution rarely improves image quality.

Comparing the borders around the two images provides a clear illustration of the results of resampling. The process of adding pixels blurred the edges of the border — and other image details as well. That's because the photo editor attempts to add pixels between image edges (areas of contrast) by averaging the colors of existing pixels.

So what are you supposed to do if you don't have enough pixels to get both the size and output resolution you want? Unfortunately, you just have to compromise. Decide which aspect of the photo is most important — size or picture quality — and move on. For future pictures, be sure to think about your final output resolution when you set the input resolution on your scanner or digital camera. Chapter 2 provides some information to help you calculate input resolution for output at various sizes.

You can sometimes improve the look of a low-resolution image by applying a small bit of sharpening; see Chapter 5 for information on how to sharpen an image.

Adjusting print size and output resolution

As I mentioned near the beginning of this chapter, your photo editor establishes a starting point for output resolution and print size when you open an image. You can change these values whenever you want, however.

The following steps show you how to get the job done in Photoshop Elements. Things work similarly in all professional and mid-level photo editors, although the command names and dialog box involved may be different.

1. **Choose Image➪Resize➪Image Size to open the Image Size dialog box, shown in Figure 10-4.**

Figure 10-4:
To avoid adding or deleting pixels when setting print size or output resolution, turn the Resample Image check box off.

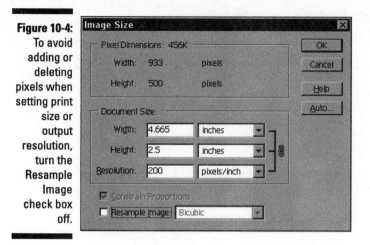

2. **To change size and resolution without resampling, deselect the Resample Image check box, as shown in the figure.**

   Notice the little line to the right of the Width, Height, and Resolution values in Figure 10-4? And the little link icon next to the line? Those symbols remind you that when you change one value, the other two automatically change as well. See the preceding section for details.

3. **To add or delete pixels in order to achieve the desired print size or output resolution, select the Resample Image check box.**

   The dialog box changes to make a few additional options available to you, as shown in Figure 10-5.

   Be sure to turn on the Constrain Proportions check box at the bottom of the dialog box, as shown in the figure, to retain the original proportions of the picture when you change the width or height. Also, select Bicubic from the drop-down list to the right of the Resample Image box. This setting enables you to choose from several algorithms the program can use when resampling the image; Bicubic produces the best results.

4. **Adjust the output size or resolution as desired.**

   You can change the unit of measure for the Width or Height by selecting a different option from the adjacent drop-down lists.

   The Columns unit of measurement enables you to match output width to a specified column size, which can be helpful if you're preparing a picture for use in a publication such as a newsletter. To establish the column width, exit the Image Size dialog box and choose Edit➪Preferences➪ Units and Rulers. Use the Column Size options to set the column width and gutter width (space between columns). When you reopen the Image Size dialog box, select Columns as the Width unit of measurement and enter the number of columns that you want the image to cover.

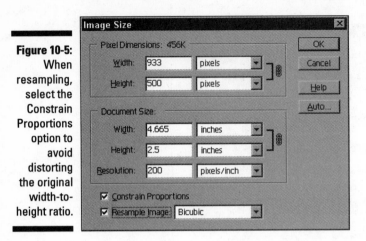

Figure 10-5:
When
resampling,
select the
Constrain
Proportions
option to
avoid
distorting
the original
width-to-
height ratio.

If the Resample Image option is turned on, the top set of Width and Height controls, which reflect the pixel counts, change automatically when you change the lower set of Width and Height values or the Resolution value. If you prefer, you can enter the new pixel dimensions using those top Width and Height boxes.

As for that Auto button found in the Elements 1.0 dialog box, ignore it. It's designed to automatically select the right resolution after you enter a printer specification known as the *line screen* value. This value comes into play only for traditional commercial printers. In fact, the Auto option is gone from Elements 2.0. If you're having your photo professionally printed, just ask the printer technician what output resolution to use and enter that value in the Resolution box.

5. Click OK or press Enter to apply your changes and close the dialog box.

Depending on what view setting you're using in your photo editor, the on-screen image may not appear to change size. But if you display the window rulers, you can confirm that the program did in fact resize the photo according to the values you entered in the Image Size dialog box. To display and hide the rulers, press Ctrl+R (⌘+R) or choose the Show/ Hide Rulers command from the View menu. You also can choose View⇨ Print Size to see the approximate print size of the image; just keep in mind that this display isn't 100 percent accurate.

If you are using an entry-level photo editor, your software may automatically add or delete pixels when you change the resolution or print size. Check your program's Help system for details on this issue. Remember that you can tell whether a program is resampling the photo by comparing the image file size before and after you adjust the resolution or print size. If the file size changes, the image was resampled.

Note that the image file size that's shown at the top of the Image Size dialog box in Elements reflects the amount of system memory that's tied up while the picture is open. This value is not the actual size of the image file. You can check the actual file size in the Open dialog box (File➪Open) or in a file-management tool (Windows Explorer, for example). In the Open dialog box, you may have to change the dialog box preferences to display file sizes.

Adding a Digital Matte

Because the film industry long ago agreed upon a set of standard sizes for film prints — 4 x 6, 5 x 7, 8 x 10, and so on — the framing industry did the same. That presents a dilemma for us digital-imaging enthusiasts who want to frame our photos.

First, the aspect ratio of images produced by most digital cameras is geared toward computer monitors and other screen devices, which use a different aspect ratio than standard film prints and frames. If you scan a film print in its entirety, of course, you preserve the original aspect ratio, in which case there's no problem. You can also take care to crop to a specific aspect ratio when you edit the photo, a technique you can read about in Chapter 7. But that cropping technique doesn't always create the composition you want, in which case your aspect ratio problem is back.

You can always have a framing shop cut a custom matte for the picture so that you can put the image in a standard-size frame. But that can get expensive, not to mention inconvenient. It wasn't long after I started framing some of my work for commercial sale that I figured out that I could save lots of time and money by investing in my own matte cutter. I haven't yet figured out a good way to store all the matte scraps and other framing paraphernalia, but that's another story.

If you're not inclined to invest in a professionally-cut matte or do your own matte-cutting, you can add a digital matte to your picture in your photo editor to enlarge the image size to standard photo dimensions. All you need to do is enlarge the image canvas and then fill the empty areas of the new canvas with a solid color, or, for a more interesting look, a textured or patterned fill, as shown in Figure 10-6. In this example, I even added a bevel effect around the matte to create the illusion of depth.

Note that even if you add a digital matte, you should still use a regular matte board to separate your printed image from the glass in your picture frame. Buy a frame that's one size larger than your finished photo with its digital matte. You can then use a standard precut matte between the print and the glass.

Figure 10-6:
As an alternative to a custom matte, you can create a digital matte by expanding the canvas and filling the empty areas with color or texture.

The following steps show you how to add the matte shown in Figure 10-6 in Photoshop Elements. You can use the same general approach to add a matte in any photo editor that offers layers and similar special effects.

1. **If your image has multiple layers, duplicate and flatten the image.**

   Just save a copy of your image under a new name and then choose Layer⇨Flatten Image to merge all image layers. After you flatten the image, it should just have one layer, called Background.

2. **Duplicate the background layer.**

   The quickest way to do this is to drag the layer to the New Layer button at the bottom of the Layers palette. (Refer to the upcoming Figure 10-8.)

   The program names your new layer Background Copy; you may want to rename the layer Photo Layer to avoid confusion later on. To do this in Elements 1.0, double-click the layer name in the Layers palette to display the Layer Properties dialog box and enter a new layer name. In Elements 2.0, double-click the layer name, type the new name directly in the Layers palette, and click outside the layer name. Or double-click the layer thumbnail to rename the layer using the dialog box, if you prefer.

3. **Expand the image canvas to match the final picture size you want.**

   Choose Image⇨Resize⇨Canvas Size to open the Canvas Size dialog box, shown in Figure 10-7, and set the Width and Height values to match the desired final print dimensions. Click the center anchor square inside the dialog box so that you center the image on the expanded canvas. If you're using Elements 2.0, deselect the Relative check box before changing the Width and Height values.

After you click OK to close the Canvas Size dialog box, the program adds the new canvas area and fills it with the current background color.

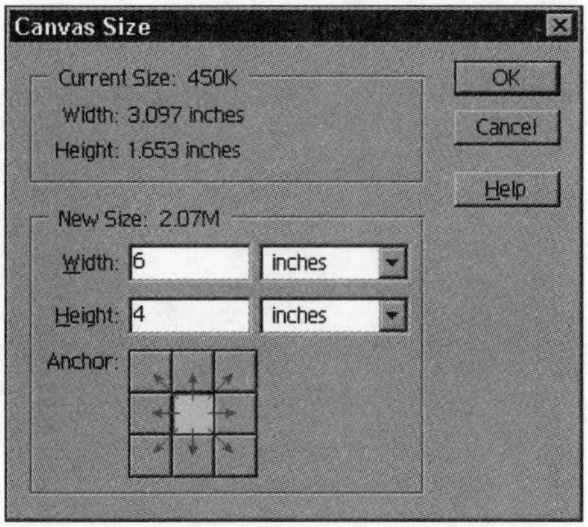

Figure 10-7:
Set the new canvas width and height to the final print dimensions you want.

Canvas Size	☒
Current Size: 450K	OK
Width: 3.097 inches	Cancel
Height: 1.653 inches	Help

New Size: 2.07M

Width: 6   inches

Height: 4   inches

Anchor:

4. **Select and delete everything on the bottom image layer.**

   Click the layer in the Layers palette, press Ctrl+A (⌘+A), and then press the Delete key. The entire layer should now be filled with the background color. In the upper layer, which shall heretofore be known as the photo layer, the new canvas areas you added in Step 3 are transparent, as indicated by the checkerboard pattern in the Layers palette.

   The appearance of transparent areas depends on the setting on the Transparency panel of the Preferences dialog box. To change the setting, choose Edit➪Preferences➪Transparency.

5. **Fill the background layer with a solid color, texture, or pattern to create the matte.**

   For a solid color matte, you can skip this step by setting the background color to the matte color you want before you take Step 4.

   To create the matte shown in Figure 10-6, open the Elements Effects browser, shown in Figure 10-8, by choosing Window➪Show Effects Browser (Window➪Effects in Version 2.0). Select Textures from the drop-down list at the top of the browser, click the Rusted Metal thumbnail, and click Apply. When the program asks whether you want to keep the effect, click Yes.

   Note that Elements automatically creates a new layer, called Layer 1, to hold the texture effect, as shown in the Layers palette in Figure 10-8. I renamed this layer Matte Layer in the figure. You can ignore the original background layer or hide it, but don't trash it or merge it with the new matte layer yet.

Effects browser

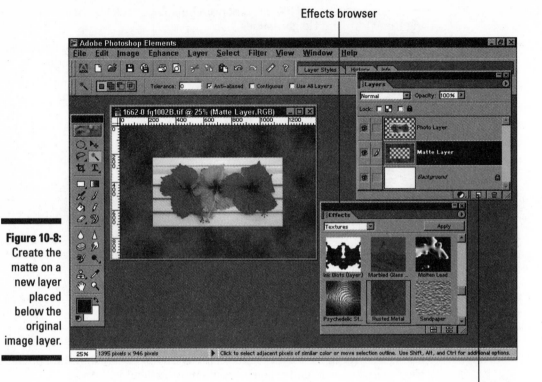

New Layer button

Figure 10-8:
Create the
matte on a
new layer
placed
below the
original
image layer.

6. To bevel the inside edge of the matte, first delete the portion of the matte layer that's covered by the photo.

To do this, you first need to select the non-transparent areas of the photo layer. In Elements, Ctrl+click (⌘+click) the photo layer in the Layers palette to create the selection outline quickly. Next, click the matte layer in the Layers palette to transfer the selection outline to that layer. Then press the Delete key to delete the interior of the matte layer. Your matte layer should look like the one shown in the Layers palette in Figure 10-8 — that is, transparent in the middle.

7. Press Ctrl+D (⌘+D) to get rid of the selection outline.

8. Apply a bevel layer style to the matte layer.

In Elements, display the Layer Styles palette, shown in Figure 10-9, by clicking its tab in the palette well or choosing Window⇨Show Layer Styles (Window⇨Layer Styles in Version 2.0). Choose Bevels from the drop-down list at the top of the palette and click the Simple Sharp Pillow Emboss thumbnail, as shown in the figure.

Layer Styles palette

Figure 10-9:
To bevel the
inside edge
of the matte
as well as
the outside
edge, you
must first
delete the
interior of
the matte.

The effect names don't display in their entirety at the default palette settings. Click the List View button at the bottom of the palette to switch to a display that features small previews but shows the entire effect name. The List View button is the leftmost button at the bottom of the palette.

To tweak the bevel effect, choose Layer⇨Layer Style⇨Style Settings. Play with the controls in the resulting dialog box to adjust the lighting angle, bevel size, and direction of the bevel.

9. Flatten the image (optional).

After you merge the layers, you can no longer tweak the bevel layer style that you applied in Step 7. So you may want to save a backup copy of the layered image before flattening the image. To flatten the image, choose Layer⇨Flatten Image. Even if you choose not to flatten the image, you can now delete the background layer if you like.

Using these same basic steps, you can create an endless variety of matte designs. Try filling your matte with a gradient or using any of the artistic effects your photo editor may offer to create a random pattern or color effect. You can also fill the matte with another photo. For example, you might surround a photo of your family at the beach with a close-up photo of sand or water.

This kind of creative experimentation is the real fun of digital imaging — at least, it is for me. And because you're working on a backup copy of your original photo and creating the matte as a separate image layer, you can easily get rid of any effects you don't like.

Adding a Plain Border

To add a simple, plain border around an image, use either of these techniques:

✔ Set the background color to the border color you want. Then enlarge the image canvas, adding double the dimensions of the border to both the width and height boxes. For example, if you want a quarter-inch border all around, raise the Width and Height values both by one-half inch.

In Elements, make this change via the Canvas Size dialog box, covered in Chapter 7. Be sure to click the center anchor square to position the image in the center of the enlarged canvas.

✔ Select the entire image and apply a *stroke,* which is the digital geek's way of saying *border.* In Elements, select the entire image and then choose Edit⇨Stroke. In the resulting dialog box, you can choose the color, width, and select the placement of the border.

Be sure to enter the abbreviation for the unit of measurement after the stroke width — pixels (px), inches (in), and so on. (See the Elements Help system for other abbreviations.) Remember also that if you set the border size in pixels, the actual printed size of the border depends on the output resolution you use, as illustrated by the top two images in Figure 10-1 and Color Plate 10-1. For more information, read the earlier section "Reviewing resolution."

You can position the border inside the selection outline, outside the outline, or straddling the outline. However, for the latter two options to work, you first must enlarge the canvas size to accommodate the border pixels. Otherwise, the program doesn't have anywhere to put the border. And of course, if you put the stroke inside the outline, the border covers up part of your image.

Your photo editor may also offer a way to apply a border during the printing process only. In Elements, you can apply the border via the Print Options dialog box, discussed in the next section. You also can print a colored background around your picture via the Print Options dialog box. Neither option permanently affects your image file; the program adds the border or background to the printed picture only.

Making Your Own Photo Prints

Many of the steps and options involved in printing photographs are the same as when you print anything from your computer, whether it's a Web page or letter that you created in a word processor. But you may encounter some photo-printing options that are new to you if you haven't worked with digital images before. I'm sure you could easily master these options on your own, but because you were kind enough to put down good money for this book, the next several sections provide some guidance to get you up to speed more quickly.

Printing options vary widely depending on the photo software and printer model; the information I present here concentrates on the most common printing controls and problem issues. For more details on printing, check your software and printer manuals so that you can get the best performance from your system.

Setting up and previewing the print job

Your photo editor offers one or more commands that enable you to specify certain aspects of how you want the picture printed, such as how to position the picture on the page, the paper size, the number of copies, and print orientation. Look for these commands on the File menu, home of the official Print command.

The following steps provide a general overview of the process of setting up your print job, with specific instructions for doing so in Photoshop Elements on Windows-based and Macintosh computers.

1. **Choose a printer.**

    - Windows: Choose File⇨Page Setup. In Elements 1.0, you see the dialog box shown in Figure 10-10. Select a printer from the Name drop-down list at the top of the dialog box. In Elements 2.0, the dialog box offers a different set of controls (more about those momentarily). Click the Printer button at the bottom of the dialog box to display the options shown in the top half of Figure 10-10 and choose your printer. Click OK to return to the first dialog box.

    - Macintosh: Select a printer via the Chooser, which you access via the Apple menu.

2. **Specify the paper size and print orientation (landscape or portrait).**

    - Windows: In Elements 1.0, click the Properties button in the Page Setup dialog box to display a second dialog box, which offers options specific to your selected printer. No matter what printer you're using, you'll find controls for selecting a paper size and specifying whether you want your picture to be printed in portrait or landscape orientation. (You may need to dig through two or more tabs in the dialog box to find these options.) Click OK to close this second dialog box and return to the Page Setup dialog box.

Page Setup

Printer

Name: HP DeskJet 890C Series (3)   Properties...

Status: Default printer; Ready
Type: HP DeskJet 890C Series
Where: LPT1:
Comment:

Background... ☐ Corner Crop Marks ☐ Caption

Border...

OK   Cancel

Portrait orientation prints the photo in normal, upright position; *landscape* orientation turns the photo sideways on the page.

In Elements 2.0, the paper size and orientation options are now found in the dialog box that first appeared when you chose the Page Setup command in Step 1.

 • Macintosh: Choose File➪Page Setup to display a dialog box similar to the one in Figure 10-11. The options in the dialog box depend on your printer and the version of the Macintosh operating system you use.

3. Click OK to close the Page Setup dialog box.

4. Preview the print job and specify additional print options.

For this step, the process is the same for both Macintosh and Windows-based computers. Choose File➪Print Preview to display the options shown in Figure 10-12. (The Macintosh dialog box looks a little different, but offers the same options.) The list following these steps explains the most important options found in this dialog box.

5. Click Print to send the photo to the printer.

When you click Print, your printer's main dialog box reappears, and you can then make any additional changes to the final print settings, such as print quality and paper type. Click OK or press Enter to wrap things up.

Figure 10-11:
On my Macintosh computer, the Page Setup command displays this dialog box, where I can select the paper size and print orientation.

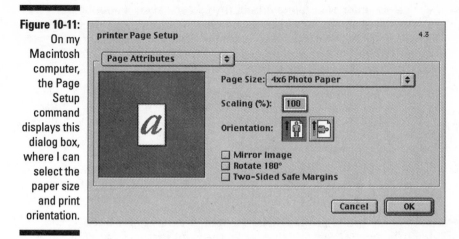

Figure 10-12:
In Elements, choose the Print Preview command to display this dialog box and access additional print options.

The options in the Photoshop Elements Print Preview dialog box are pretty self-explanatory, but I want to share a few tips about some of them:

✔ Select the Show More Options box underneath the image preview to display options that are otherwise hidden. When you select Output from the list underneath the check box, you access the options shown in Figure 10-12.

✔ If you select Color Management from the list, you access options that control how the program translates the colors in your image when sending the picture to the printer. Unless you know what you're doing, leave these options at their default settings. See the upcoming section "Matching screen and print colors" for information about these options.

✔ You can use the Scaled Print Size options to change the output size of the image, but remember that enlarging the photo may lower picture quality, just as when you enlarge a picture through the Image Size dialog box. Select the Show Bounding Box check box to display handles that you can drag to resize the image.

✔ If you have an active selection outline when you open the dialog box, you can print only the selected area by turning on the Print Selected Area check box.

✔ The Caption option prints comments that you may enter into the File Info dialog box. After canceling out of the Print Preview dialog box, choose File⇨File Info to display the File Info dialog box and type your caption or anything else that you want to print with the image.

✔ All the options found in the Print Preview dialog box affect the current print only; they don't permanently alter your image file.

Matching screen and print colors

Over the past few years, the quality of consumer and small-office photo printers and photo paper has soared, to the point that few people can distinguish a print made from a good photo printer from one done at a commercial photo lab. In fact, the prints that I make from my photo printers are *more* vibrant than those that I get when take my pictures to a professional imaging lab for output on traditional photo paper. (You can read about this service in the sidebar "Exploring professional printing options," later in this chapter.)

One aspect of photo printing remains problematic, however: getting printed colors and screen colors to match. This sounds like it should be easy to do, but remember that colors in digital images are produced by mixing red, green, and blue light. Printed colors, on the other hand, are created by mixing cyan, magenta, yellow, and black ink. No matter how sophisticated the printer, you just can't reproduce with ink the entire spectrum of colors that you can create with light. That's why colors that appear very vibrant on-screen usually look duller when printed.

Complicating the problem further, basic ink colors vary slightly from printer to printer, and inks from a single printer produce different results depending on the paper stock. Throw in the variations in color that occur from monitor to monitor, and you've got one tough nut to crack.

Hardware and software manufacturers are working diligently to improve color matching between screen and printer, however, and things are much better than they were even a year ago. New photo printers, digital cameras, scanners, and photo software feature *color management* tools that you can use to get your input and your output better in sync. Notice that I qualified that last statement with the phrase "better" — even using all these tools, you may not be able to achieve perfect color matching, especially with photos that contain very hot, bold colors.

Because color management tools, like printer options, vary widely from product to product — and because which settings are best depend on your computer hardware — I can only give you general pointers here. If you're using Photoshop Elements, explore the manual and Help system information about color management to find out how to take advantage of the available tools. These options can be quite confusing, so if you're unsure of which options to use, just stick with the default settings. The following list provides some basic information to get you started, along with some simple, non-technical things you can do to match screen and print colors.

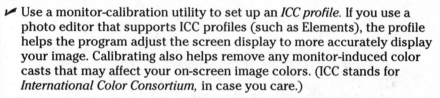

✔ Use a monitor-calibration utility to set up an *ICC profile.* If you use a photo editor that supports ICC profiles (such as Elements), the profile helps the program adjust the screen display to more accurately display your image. Calibrating also helps remove any monitor-induced color casts that may affect your on-screen image colors. (ICC stands for *International Color Consortium,* in case you care.)

Adobe provides a calibration utility called Adobe Gamma with Elements 1.0 and some of its other programs. The steps for using the utility vary depending on your operating system, so check the Elements Help system for details. In Version 2.0, the utility is provided for the Windows operating system only. If you use a Macintosh computer, click the Apple menu and then check your Control Panels submenu to see whether you have access to ColorSync, an Apple color profile utility.

✔ Inside your photo editor, experiment with different color management options by printing a test image at a variety of settings. You may find, as I do, that you get better color matching if you turn *off* color management controls. In Elements, choose Edit⇨Color Settings to open a dialog box where you can turn color management on and off.

Other color management options are available in the Print dialog box and the Print Preview dialog box. (In the Print Preview dialog box, select the Show More Options check box and then select Color Management from the drop-down list underneath the check box.)

✔ Don't forget that the quality and color settings you choose inside your printer's specific dialog box affect your output color, too. Again, experiment with different settings to see which combinations work best.

✔ When setting up your print job, be sure to select the paper type setting that corresponds to the paper you put in the printer. Photo printers output varying amounts of ink depending on the type of paper you indicate, and that can affect your print colors. If your printer requires you to change to special photo ink cartridges, be sure to select the corresponding cartridge setting. I've found that some printers even distort the image proportions when the wrong paper and ink settings are selected.

✔ With most printers, you get better color matching from high-quality photo stock than with plain paper.

✔ Remember that the ambient light in which you view your pictures on-screen and examine your prints affects your color perception.

✔ Some photo editors enable you to convert your image from RGB to the CMYK color model. (Elements doesn't.) Although that sounds like a good idea, converting to CMYK actually has a negative impact when you print using home and small-office printers, which are engineered to translate colors from RGB images.

✔ If your colors are really wacky, check your ink cartridges. One or more may need replacing.

Choosing a photo printer

Thanks to the surging interest in digital photography and photo editing, you now can buy a terrific photo printer for under $200. In fact, I daresay you can even go lower and be quite happy with your prints.

That's not to say than any printer on the market is a good choice for printing photographs. To make sure that you wind up with a winner, keep these pointers in mind if you're shopping:

✔ Get a dedicated photo printer. Some printers are engineered as all-purpose models that can handle everyday text documents as well as photos. These units do an okay, but usually not stellar, job with photographs. For the best photo quality, get a model that's engineered specifically to render digital images. Typically, manufacturers put the word "photo" in the names of these models. For example, in the Hewlett-Packard line, printers in the PhotoSmart series are geared to printing photos, while the DeskJet models are designed for general-purpose printing.

✔ Opt for inkjet or dye-sub (also known as thermal dye) technology. Both technologies can produce prints that are comparable to traditional film prints. However, dye-sub printers can print only on special glossy stock, which can be problematic if you need to print the occasional text document — not to mention expensive if you typically print several rough drafts of your photo before making a final print.

✔ Don't be a sucker for resolution hype. Most people think that a higher printer resolution means better print quality. But that's just not true. A good 600-dpi inkjet printer can output just as good a print as a model that offers twice the resolution, and a dye-sub printer that has a resolution of only 300 dpi can match the highest-resolution inkjet. For a real indication of print quality, compare print samples and read product reviews. (Computer and digital photography magazines print such reviews regularly.)

✔ Don't assume that you get better quality as you move up the price curve. In most cases, the different models in a manufacturer's line of printers all have the same print engine. The higher priced models offer features such as faster print speed, the ability to print on wider paper, or slots that enable you to print directly from a digital camera memory card.

✔ Look for a six-color or four-color model. Six ink colors usually means truer color rendition than four ink colors. Avoid models that use only three ink colors (cyan, magenta, and yellow); these models can't reproduce shadows well.

✔ One printer manufacturer, Epson, offers a specialty printer, the Epson Stylus Photo 2000P, which uses special archival inks. When used in conjunction with archival Epson paper, this printer is estimated to provide a print life of 200 years. Unfortunately, the inks aren't capable of producing quite the same vivid colors as printers that use non-archival inks. As I write this, however, Epson is planning a new version of the printer with an improved inkset to address this issue.

✔ Finally, consider the cost of ink cartridges and paper when you're making your final decision. Over the course of the printer's life, you'll likely spend just as much on these so-called *consumables* as you will for the printer itself. Figuring out consumables cost is tough because ink usage varies depending on the size and colors in a particular photo. But the manufacturer should provide a general ink-per-print cost, and some digital imaging and computer magazines regularly publish cost comparison charts.

✔ You can save money with a model that offers individual ink cartridges; printers that put multiple colors in one cartridge require you to buy a new cartridge when a single color is gone, even if other colors aren't yet depleted.

Printing multiple images on one page

In the old days of digital imaging — about five years ago — printing multiple pictures on one sheet of paper was a pain. You had to copy and paste all the photos into one document, which resulted in a huge image file that often caused your computer to crash. Even if you just wanted to print several copies of the same picture on the page, you had to go through this process.

Exploring professional printing options

If you can't afford a top-notch photo printer, want a print size that your printer can't produce, or just don't feel like sitting at your computer while the printer spits out your latest pictures, you can take your image files to a photo lab for printing. For everyday prints, you can take your files to any retail photo lab, even ones found in the corner drugstore. Pictures are output on traditional film photo paper, and you shouldn't have to pay much more, if anything, than you do for reprints from a film negative.

For special pictures, ask a photographer friend to recommend a professional imaging lab in your neighborhood. Local camera stores also usually know what labs do the best job with this kind of output; the store may even have its own lab. You may pay more for your prints, but you

typically get a higher quality of output and service. For example, if I have a picture that I plan to sell, I take it to a commercial imaging lab for output on archival photographic paper, and I pay about $12 for a 5 x 7 print. But that fee includes color matching to a color proof that I make on my inkjet printer — something that you don't normally get from a retail lab.

Online printing services, such as Ofoto, offer another option. You can e-mail your pictures to the Ofoto Web site (www.Ofoto.com) and have your prints mailed to you, or to anyone, for that matter. Ofoto also enables you to store and share photos online so that acquaintances can view your pictures in their Web browsers and order their own prints. Prices for prints are about the same as what you'd pay in a retail lab.

You can still use this method to print multiple photos on a page; just enlarge the canvas size to hold all the pictures and copy and paste as outlined in the collage-building section of Chapter 9. Remember, though, that when you paste a picture into another document, the pasted picture is automatically converted to the output resolution of the new document, which means that the print size may change. So if you want to gang pictures with different output resolutions on the same page, I recommend that you save copies of the images in the TIFF file format and import the TIFF versions into a word-processing or publishing program for printing. (See Chapter 2 to find out how to save in the TIFF format.)

However, before you go to all this trouble, check to see whether your photo editor offers a utility that simplifies the job. Many programs do, especially those aimed at the novice. Some printers and scanners also ship with this kind of software.

If you don't already have a good printing utility, you can buy a separate program such as PrintStation ($20, from PicMeta, www.picmeta.com) to do the job. The CD at the back of this book includes a trial copy of PicMeta, by the way. Figure 10-13 gives you a look at the layout tools found in the program.

Figure 10-13:
Printing utilities such as PicMeta simplify the job of printing multiple images on one page.

Photoshop Elements offers a very limited printing utility, which you can launch by choosing File⇨Automate⇨Picture Package (in Version 2.0, choose File⇨Print Layouts⇨Picture Package). However, I'm not a fan of the Elements version of this tool. First, you're limited to printing multiple copies of the same image. On top of that restriction, the interface isn't very intuitive, and adding or removing pictures from the page layout isn't possible.

When you use any printing utility, the software may automatically alter the sizes of the pictures to fit the layout that you choose. Usually, programs don't enlarge a photo unless you request that change, but they do typically shrink the photo size if needed. So be sure to set up the layout so that it has enough space to accommodate your pictures at the print size you want. In any case, the changes to print size affect only the printout — your image files aren't permanently changed.

Preparing Images for On-Screen Use

Earlier sections of this chapter spend a good deal of time talking about the importance of output resolution — the number of pixels per inch in a printed photo. Well, you can forget output resolution entirely if you're getting an image ready for use in a Web page, multimedia presentation, or any other purpose where the picture will be viewed on-screen.

Why no output resolution issues when you're working with screen images? Because pixels per inch affects your image size *only* when you print photos.

As you already know if you studied Chapter 2, which introduces the concept of resolution, a computer monitor or other display device devotes one of its screen pixels to reproduce each pixel in your image. Always. No matter what. You can set the output resolution of the image to 72 or 7200, and you still get one screen pixel used for each image pixel. Changing the output resolution of the image doesn't affect the display size of the image at all.

What does affect the display size is the screen resolution of the monitor on which the image is viewed. Most computers, for example, enable you to set the monitor to a variety of screen resolutions, each of which results in a different number of screen pixels. Typical screen resolution settings include 640 x 480, 800 x 600, and 1280 x 960 pixels, with the horizontal pixel count always listed first. (How you adjust this setting depends on your operating system and video card.)

Given the one-to-one relationship between image pixels and screen pixels, it follows that raising the screen resolution makes the image display size go down. The image still requires the same amount of screen pixels, but now those pixels are smaller, so the image appears smaller. Lower the screen resolution, and the image display size goes up.

Perhaps an example will make all of this a bit clearer. Figure 10-14 shows a screen shot of my Windows desktop as it appears on my 17-inch monitor when the screen resolution setting is 800 x 600. Using the Windows Desktop Properties feature (right-click the desktop and choose Properties), I selected a sunset picture to serve as my desktop background. But because I sized the photo to 640 x 480 pixels, it doesn't cover the entire desktop. It occupies a 640 x 480-pixel area smack dab in the center of the screen, surrounded by the Windows taskbar and program icons. Desktop areas that the photo doesn't cover have a plain gray background (because that's the default background color I selected for my system).

Figure 10-15 shows the exact same desktop design when I lower the screen resolution to 640 x 480. Now the photo covers the entire background. Notice that everything on the screen appears larger, not just the photo.

The upshot is that all you need to do to set your image display size is to figure out how much of the screen you want your picture to consume and then set the horizontal and vertical pixel counts accordingly. (The next section shows you how.)

Of course, if you're sharing your picture with other people, perhaps on a Web site or via e-mail, you have no way of knowing or controlling what screen resolution will be in force when they view your image. Most people set their screens to one of the three resolutions mentioned earlier. But if you want to ensure that most people will be able to view your image without scrolling the screen display, assume the lowest common denominator — 640 x 480 — when setting your image size.

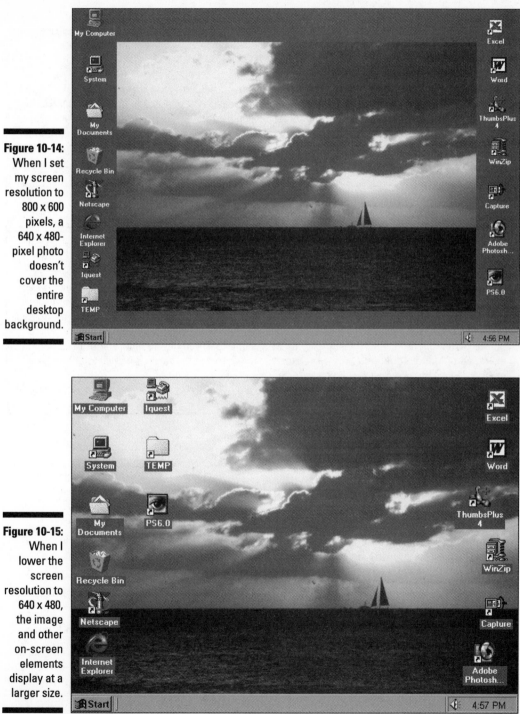

Figure 10-14:
When I set
my screen
resolution to
800 x 600
pixels, a
640 x 480-
pixel photo
doesn't
cover the
entire
desktop
background.

Figure 10-15:
When I
lower the
screen
resolution to
640 x 480,
the image
and other
on-screen
elements
display at a
larger size.

But the guy on the Internet said 72 ppi!

Somewhere along the way to this book, you may have heard that you should use an output resolution of 72 ppi or 96 ppi for screen pictures. With all due respect to the person who passed along this misinformation, it simply isn't true.

Way, way back in the infancy of digital graphics and the Internet, some experts did suggest that an output resolution of 72 – 96 ppi was appropriate for screen images. Those numbers were based on the fact that the standard Macintosh monitor of the day left the factory set at a default screen resolution that resulted in 72 screen pixels per inch, based on the viewable area of the monitor screen. The standard PC setting delivered 96 screen pixels per inch. So if you used your photo editor to establish an output size of, oh, say 1 inch by 1 inch, and set the output resolution to 72 ppi, it would display at exactly one inch by one inch on a Macintosh monitor. If you set the output resolution to 96 ppi, the picture would appear at one inch by one

inch on a PC monitor. However, the 72 or 96 ppi setting didn't have anything to do with how the monitor thought about the picture — it always just used one of its screen pixels to reproduce each image pixel.

Today, monitors come in many different sizes, and people have a choice of multiple screen resolutions. So there is no standard number of screen pixels per inch, which means that the 72/96-ppi thing is totally off base. For some reason, though, this old chiphead's tale remains a popular one, especially in Internet newsgroups that discuss digital imaging. Call it mass confusion — sort of like what happened when we thought platform shoes and big hair were cool in the 80s. I trust that you will help enlighten the world by sharing what you know, in the same way you gently pointed out to your best friend that perhaps one's hair shouldn't be twice as tall as one's head.

Setting the display size

To establish the screen display size of a photo, take these steps:

1. **Save a copy of your original image under a new name.**

   You may need to add or delete pixels to get the image display size you want, and after you do so, you can't get the original pixels back. So always save a copy of your photo in its original form.

2. **Working with the duplicate image, add or delete pixels as needed to achieve the screen dimensions you want.**

   In Elements, you do this in the Image Size dialog box, shown in Figure 10-16. To open the dialog box, choose Image⇨Resize⇨Image Size.

   Select the Constrain Proportions box and the Resample Image boxes, as shown in the figure, and select Bicubic from the drop-down list next to the Resample Image box.

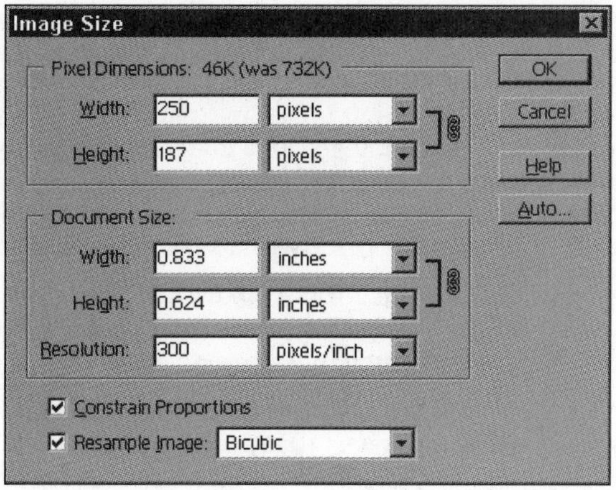

Figure 10-16:
To set
screen
display size,
enter the
new pixel
dimensions
in the top
set of Width
and Height
boxes.

The drop-down list enables you to select from different formulas that the program can use when resampling an image. Bicubic, the default setting, works best.

If by some chance the original pixel dimensions serve your purposes just fine, click Cancel or press Esc to close the dialog box without making any changes. Otherwise, enter the new pixel dimensions in the Width and Height boxes at the top of the dialog box and press Enter or click OK.

3. Save your image.

For most screen uses, you should save the picture in the JPEG file format, as explained in the next section.

For more details about the Image Size dialog box, see the section "Adjusting print size and output resolution, earlier in this chapter."

To view your resized image at its new display size in Elements, choose View⇨Actual Pixels. Remember, though, that the image will display at this same size only on monitors set to the same screen resolution as yours.

Saving photos in a screen-friendly format

If you want to use your photos on a Web site or share them via e-mail, you must save the file in a format that Web browsers and e-mail programs can open. Currently, you have three format choices:

✔ **JPEG:** Pronounced *jay-peg*, this format offers the best choice for online photo sharing. JPEG can save full-color images and grayscale photos, and when you save to this format, you can *compress* the file to make it smaller. Smaller files mean shorter download times for people who want to view your photos.

On the downside, JPEG compression sacrifices some image data to achieve the smaller file size. If you compress a file too much, you start to see *JPEG artifacts* — random blocks of color in areas that should look smooth and detailed. The lower-left image in Color Plate 10-1 shows an example of an overcompressed image. This image has as many pixels as its high-resolution, uncompressed TIFF counterpart directly above. By applying a high amount of JPEG compression, I reduced the file size from 723K to a mere 47K, but paid the price with lousy image quality.

✔ **GIF:** Some people pronounce this format *gif,* with a hard *g,* while others say *jif,* like the peanut butter. I vote for the former, because GIF stands for Graphics (with a hard *g*) Interchange Format.

Web designers use GIF mainly to create small, animated graphics, such as those annoying blinking messages that pop up on some Web sites. These so-called *GIF animations* are really a series of images saved within a single image file. GIF also enables you to make a part of an image transparent, so that the Web page background shows through and the picture appears to float on the page. In addition, GIF gives you smaller file sizes without the artifact problem that can occur with heavy JPEG compression, although GIF can't get the file size down quite as low as JPEG.

GIF has a serious downside, however: It can store a measly 256 colors. That's not a problem with simple graphics or text banners that contain only a handful of colors. But the limitation makes GIF unsuitable for full-color photos, as you can see from the lower-right image in Color Plate 10-1, which I saved in the GIF format. Not only is the image splotchy looking due to the color limitation, but the file size is about twice that of the compressed JPEG version to the left. Again, both images have the same number of pixels; the file size and quality differences are strictly due to the file format.

If you've converted your image from RGB to the grayscale color mode, your photo only has 256 colors, so GIF is an option in that scenario. However, I suggest that you stick with JPEG for grayscale pictures anyway. It's simply better at handling photographic images.

✔ **PNG:** Pronounced *ping,* PNG stands for Portable Network Graphics. PNG is one day supposed to provide the benefits of both GIF and JPEG without the drawbacks. Unfortunately, it's not ready for prime time yet, in large part because older Web browsers can't open PNG images. Stay away for now.

Hmm, I guess you really have only one good choice after all. The next section shows you the ins and outs of saving files in the JPEG format.

Saving a JPEG copy of your photo

WARNING!

The following steps explain the various options that you encounter when you save a file to the JPEG format. Before you go ahead, though, a few pre-save precautions are in order:

✔ JPEG is a *lossy* file format, which means that it destroys some image data. Every time you open, edit, and resave a JPEG image, you do further damage.

✔ Remember that when you save to JPEG, any independent image layers are merged into one.

✔ For both these reasons, save to this format only after you're completely finished editing your image and only if you want to share the picture online or use it for some other screen purpose that requires JPEG, such as a multimedia presentation.

✔ Before saving to JPEG, save the image in a format that supports all the image features and retains all image data. Your best bet is your photo editor's *native* (own) format; in Elements, that's PSD.

These steps give specific instructions for saving to JPEG in Photoshop Elements, but you will encounter the same format options when you save in the format in any program.

1. **Choose File⇨Save As to display the Save As dialog box.**

   Figure 10-17 shows the Windows version of the dialog box. The Mac version offers similar options.

   If your image contains layers or other features that JPEG doesn't support, a warning appears at the bottom of the dialog box, as shown in the figure.

2. **Select JPEG from the Format drop-down list in the dialog box, as shown in Figure 10-17.**

3. **Enter a name in the File Name box.**

   In an attempt to be helpful, the program automatically enters the existing image name and adds the word *copy*. But you don't have to use this name. Just double-click the box and type whatever filename you want.

   You also can choose from several other standard file-saving options, including one that enables you to embed a color profile in the image file. (*Color profiles* are part of the color management system introduced earlier in this chapter.) I recommend that you don't embed profiles unless someone — like a boss or client — specifically asks you to do so.

4. **Select a storage location for the file as you usually do.**

TIP

Just to avoid confusion — I'm easily confused — I store my original and print-ready images in a separate folder from the screen versions. This setup also makes sending a batch of photos over the Internet simple because they're all in one location.

5. **Click Save.**

   The program presents the JPEG Options dialog box, shown in Figure 10-18.

6. **If your image background contains transparent areas, select a Matte option to fill those areas.**

   This option is available only if the lowest layer in your image contains transparent areas, and only if flattening the image doesn't fill those transparent areas. When you save to JPEG, you must fill the transparent areas with a solid color, which you can specify via the Matte drop-down list at the top of the dialog box.

TIP

If you want the transparent areas to appear as though they're still transparent when you place the picture on a Web page or on a slide in a multimedia presentation, match the Matte color to the background color of the Web page or slide. Choose Custom from the Matte drop-down list to open the Color Picker and select the background color you want to use. When you add the image to the Web page or slide, the matte-filled areas of the image merge invisibly with the background. Around the edges of the matted areas, the program blends the existing pixels with the matte color to create a smoother color transition.

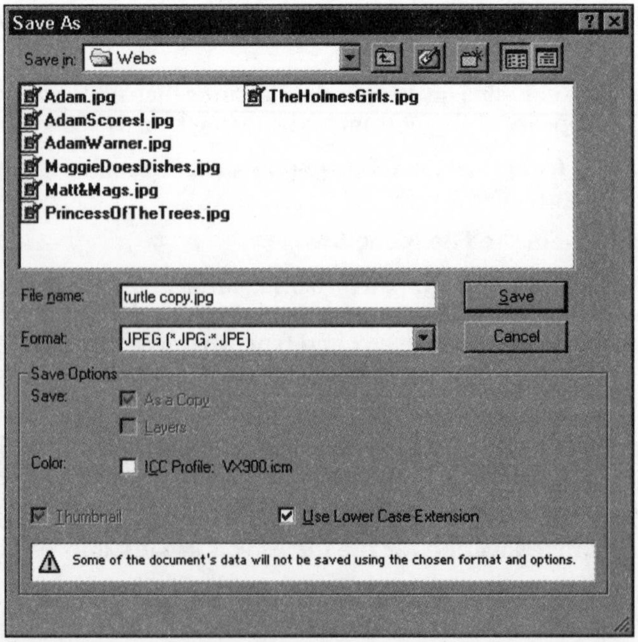

Figure 10-17:
JPEG
doesn't
support
independent
image
layers and
some other
features
found in
high-end
imaging
programs.

Save As	? X

Save in: 🗀 Webs

📄 Adam.jpg   📄 TheHolmesGirls.jpg
📄 AdamScores!.jpg
📄 AdamWarner.jpg
📄 MaggieDoesDishes.jpg
📄 Matt&Mags.jpg
📄 PrincessOfTheTrees.jpg

File name: turtle copy.jpg   **Save**

Format: JPEG (*.JPG;*.JPE)   Cancel

Save Options
Save: ☑ As a Copy
        ☐ Layers

Color: ☐ ICC Profile: VX900.icm

☑ Thumbnail   ☑ Use Lower Case Extension

⚠ Some of the document's data will not be saved using the chosen format and options.

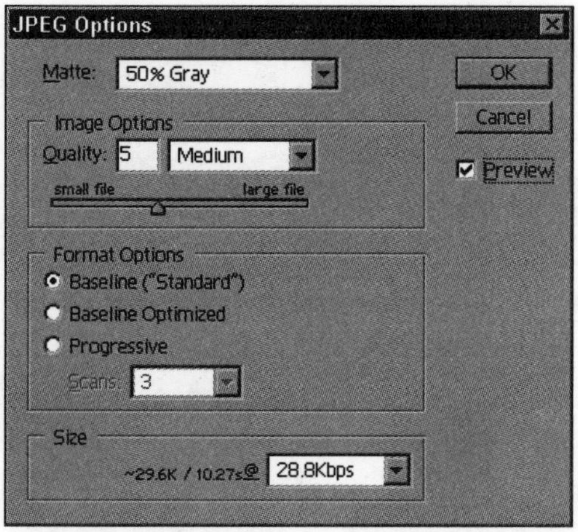

Figure 10-18:
You can
specify how
much
compression
you want to
apply.

Figure 10-19 shows a Web page that illustrates this trick. The two pitcher images are identical except that I selected white as the Matte color when saving the left image and matched the Matte color to the Web page background when saving the right image.

While you're selecting a Matte option, turn on the Preview check box in the JPEG Options dialog box to view the matte color in the image window.

7. Set the compression amount.

The Quality options determine how much image compression the program applies when you save the file. The higher the Quality setting, the *less* you compress the image, and the larger the image file.

To apply heavy compression, lower the Quality setting; to apply minimal compression, raise the Quality setting. You can select Low, Medium, Maximum, or High from the Quality drop-down list or get more specific and enter a value from 1 through 12 in the neighboring box. If you prefer, you can also drag the slider underneath the boxes to set the compression amount. Drag to the left to increase compression; drag to the right to lower the compression amount.

If the Preview box is selected, the Size area at the bottom of the dialog box shows you the approximate file size and download time at various modem speeds as you adjust the compression amount. However, the image window preview does not show the impact of the compression on your image quality. resulting change to the photo.

I usually start out with a Medium or High setting if I'm e-mailing pictures to friends; and High or Maximum if I'm posting a photo in an online album. The Low settings are typically too destructive for my taste.

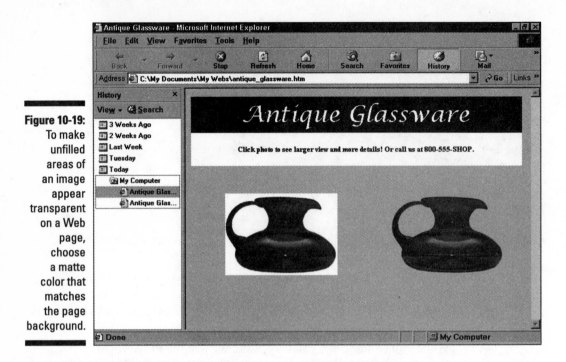

Figure 10-19:
To make
unfilled
areas of
an image
appear
transparent
on a Web
page,
choose
a matte
color that
matches
the page
background.

8. **Select a format option.**

   For screen images, choose Baseline ("Standard"), as shown in Figure
   10-18. If you choose Progressive and place the image on a Web page, the
   Web browser downloads a low-quality version of the image first and
   then gradually adds more image data until the file is complete. This
   makes the image appear to load faster on the page, but the entire file
   actually takes longer to download. In addition, some Web browsers don't
   play nice with progressive JPEG images. So I suggest that you stick to
   the Baseline ("Standard").

9. **Click OK to close the dialog box and complete the save.**

After you create your JPEG version of the photo, close the image and then
reopen it and see whether you've gone too far with compression and created
artifacting. (You typically can't see the effects of compression until after you
close and reopen the image.) If the picture simply looks a little blurry, try
applying a small amount of sharpening and then resave the file. Don't do this
more than once, however — as I said before, each time you open and edit the
file, the compression does more damage to the image.

If you want to be able to see how the compression affects your image while
you're in the process of saving the image, abandon the Save As dialog box
and use a Web optimization tool, described next.

Using Web optimization tools

Finding the right balance between file size and image quality when you save to the JPEG file format can be time-consuming if you stick with your photo editor's standard Save As dialog box to make the JPEG file. Most photo editors don't provide a live image preview via the dialog box to help you make your decision.

If you use Elements, however, you can take advantage of a special tool that enables you to preview your image at a variety of JPEG compression settings as well as in the 256-colors or less GIF format. Many other programs offer this feature, which we tech-heads refer to as a *Web optimization* tool. You can also find shareware and free optimization utilities on the Web.

To try out the Elements Web optimization feature, open the image you want to save in the JPEG format and then choose File⇨Save for Web. In Elements 1.0, the dialog box shown in Figure 10-20 appears.

Click to display Preview menu

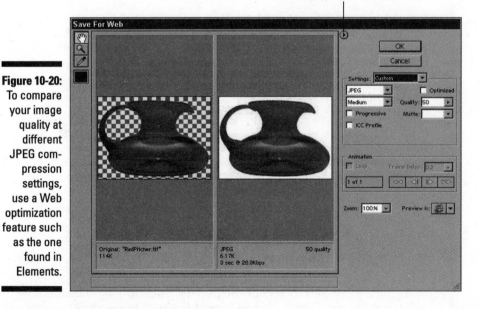

Figure 10-20: To compare your image quality at different JPEG compression settings, use a Web optimization feature such as the one found in Elements.

In Version 2.0, the dialog box also includes options that enable you to add or delete pixels to set the display size without heading off to the Image Size dialog box, which is a great new feature.

I don't have room in this book to do a full-scale exploration of the Save for Web dialog box, which is packed with features to make the Web-imaging geek's heart soar. But here are the highlights as they relate to saving a picture in the JPEG format:

✔ The left preview shows your original image; the right view shows the image as it will appear when saved using the options shown in the Settings area of the dialog box.

✔ Choose JPEG as your file format from the drop-down list in the Settings area, as shown in Figure 10-20. Then specify an image quality by using the Quality options, just as in the regular JPEG Options dialog box. The Matte and Progressive options also work as explained in the preceding section, and the ICC Profile option is the same as found in the Save As dialog box. (On the Macintosh platform, the option is named Embed Color Profile in the Save As dialog box.)

✔ The Optimized option applies a special compression algorithm that's supposed to deliver better image quality at a smaller file size than is available through the standard JPEG compression option. However, because some Web browsers can't display images saved in this fashion, you should avoid it for now.

✔ Instead of going through the backbreaking process of choosing your own JPEG settings, you can select Low, Medium, or High from the Settings drop-down list. The program then chooses all the other JPEG options for you.

Remember that Low, Medium, and so on refer to *image quality,* not the amount of image compression.

✔ Each time you change the compression settings, the preview updates to show the effect on your image. Beneath the preview, the program display the image file size and the approximate file download time at a specified modem speed. You can select a different modem speed by clicking the Preview Menu arrow, labeled in Figure 10-20, and selecting the speed from the resulting pop-up menu.

I urge you, however, to stick with the default modem speed setting, which is 28.8 kbps (kilobytes per second). You may have a superfast cable modem or DSL line, but unless you're sending pictures to someone with the same advantage, assume the lowest common denominator, 28.8 kpbs.

✔ To zoom in on the preview, click the Zoom button in the top-right corner of the dialog box and then click the preview. Alt (Option) click the preview to zoom out. Click the Hand button (located below the Zoom button) and then drag in the preview window to shift the display so that you can see a hidden area of the image.

✔ In the left preview, transparent areas of your picture appear in the same checkerboard pattern that's used in the regular Elements window (assuming the default setting for transparency in the Preferences dialog box). The right preview shows the image as it will appear when the transparent areas are filled with the selected matte color.

TECHNICAL STUFF

What's JPEG 2000?

If you're working with a recently released photo editor, including Photoshop Elements 2.0, you may have the option of saving files in the regular JPEG format and in a variation of that format known as JPEG 2000. A group of imaging experts got together to develop this updated JPEG format in hopes of finding a way to achieve the tiny file sizes that ordinary JPEG compression offers without significantly lowering image quality.

Despite the fact that this format has been in the works for a couple of years (that's why it's called

JPEG 2000) it's not yet fully finalized or supported by enough programs to make it a good choice for saving your digital photos.

If you want at look inside the minds of the format's designers, though, point your Web browser to www.jpeg.org. Reading through all the documentation provided by the committee developing the format is guaranteed to make your head spin — it's like a trip to a graduate level mathematics or physics course.

✔ If color accuracy is very important for the image, you can preview the photo as it will appear when viewed on a Macintosh system or on a Windows system. Click the Preview Menu triangle (labeled in Figure 10-20) and select Macintosh or Windows from the pop-up menu.

This preview is primarily important for GIF images. For JPEG images, the main difference that you will see is in apparent image brightness. Assuming default monitor settings, images appear brighter on a Mac than they do on a Windows-based computer. However, I don't really think you can assume that everyone sticks with default settings, so whether or not you want to base the optimum image brightness on this preview is your call. If the picture looks seriously dark or too bright, I would cancel out of the dialog box and tweak the image exposure a little.

✔ After you've tweaked the settings, click OK to open the Save As dialog box. You can then name your image and select a storage location. JPEG is automatically selected as the file type.

Sharing Photos the Digital Way

When you're ready to show off your finished pictures, you can go the old-fashioned route and print and mail copies to everyone on your distribution list. Or you can save a few trees — and reduce your stamp budget — and share pictures via digital means.

If you want to send out just one or two images to people who have e-mail accounts, you can attach the image to an e-mail message, following the instructions in your e-mail software's Help system. Remember to save the image in the JPEG format and set the size appropriately for screen display, as explained earlier in this chapter.

Because the e-mail program window eats up a good portion of the screen, I usually limit e-mail pictures to a maximum width of 300 pixels and a maximum height of 350 pixels.

For times when you want to share a collection of images, however, e-mail is inefficient. Consider these other alternatives for digital distribution of your photos:

✔ Join an online photo-sharing community, such as Ofoto, which is owned by Kodak. Membership in photo-sharing sites is typically free. After joining, you can create online photo albums and then invite other people to view the albums. Best of all, people who want prints of the pictures can order them from the Web site (this is how such sites make a profit).

Figure 10-21 gives you a look at the Ofoto Web site, and the CD at the back of the book includes a free copy of a utility that you can use to create and upload albums to the site. Be sure to also check out the similar photo-sharing features at NikonNet (www.nikonnet.com), Fujifilm.net (www.fujifilm.net), and Epson Photo Center (www.photo.epson.com).

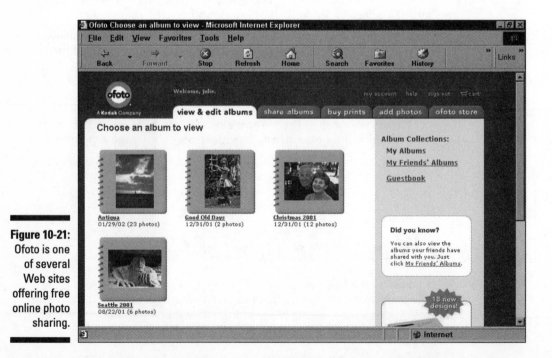

Figure 10-21:
Ofoto is one of several Web sites offering free online photo sharing.

✔ If you have a Web site of your own, you can use a tool such as the Web Photo Gallery feature found in Photoshop Elements to create a collection of pictures on your site. To open the Web Photo Gallery dialog box, shown in Figure 10-22, choose File⇨Automate⇨Web Photo Gallery in Elements 1.0 and File⇨Create Web Photo Gallery in Version 2.0. The Version 2.0 dialog box sports a new design and a few new options, but the basic controls are the same as in Version 1.0.

The Web Photo Gallery creates a Web page that includes thumbnail images that visitors can click to see a larger view of the picture. You can choose from several different layouts and designs.

Don't have an official Web site? Check with your Internet provider to see whether it makes free pages available to account holders — most do. In most cases, the amount of space you're provided at no cost is limited, but you should be able to post small collections of images.

✔ To share pictures with people who don't have Web or e-mail access or just to create a long-lasting archive of photos related to a special occasion, create a photo album on CD-ROM. Programs such as FlipAlbum, introduced in Chapter 1, make this project easy by including everything that people need to view the pictures on the CD that you create.

You can experiment with FlipAlbum and other album programs by installing the trial versions on the bonus CD that accompanies this book.

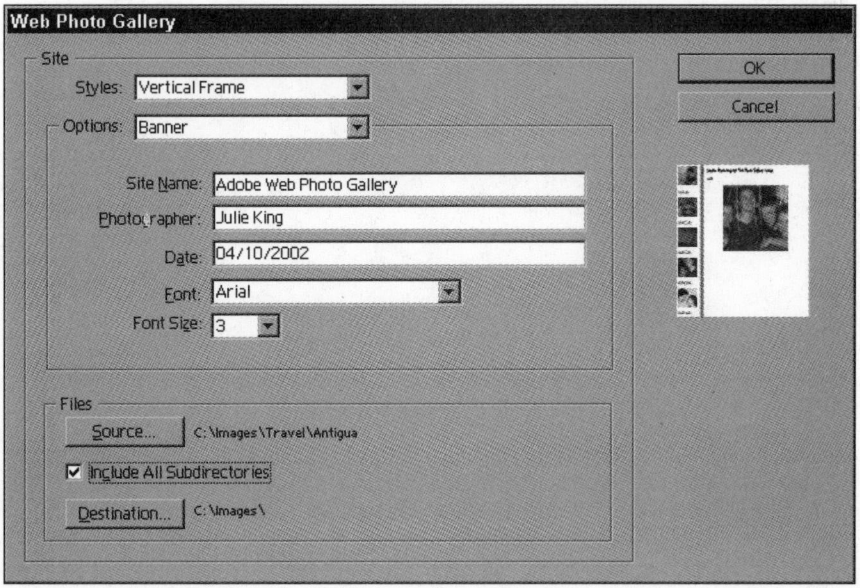

Figure 10-22: The Elements Web Photo Gallery utility simplifies the job of posting a group of pictures on a Web page.

Part IV
The Part of Tens

The 5th Wave   By Rich Tennant

"...and here's me with Cindy Crawford. And this is me with Madonna and Celine Dion..."

In this part . . .

Chapters in this part of the book are small in size but packed with information.

To help you better understand what's being said when you overhear discussions about digital imaging, Chapter 11 explains the top ten technical terms related to photo editing. Chapter 12 shares ten secrets for getting more professional-looking results even when you're brand new to the game, and Chapter 13 offers ten tips for protecting your photographs from environmental damage, accidental digital disposal, and other unfortunate events.

Chapter 11

Ten Techie Terms You Should Know

*W*hen you travel to a foreign country, it's a good idea to master a few basic phrases in that country's native tongue before you go. I find that I get along better on my trips, for example, if I know how to say, "Please," "Thank you," and "Why are those people pointing at me and laughing?"

The same advice holds true when you start exploring digital photo retouching and restoring. You're able to get where you need to go faster and with fewer headaches if you get acquainted with the basic lingo. To that end, this chapter defines what I consider to be the ten most important terms that you encounter during your adventures in the sometimes baffling land of digital imaging.

Pixel

A pixel, pronounced *picks-el,* is short for *picture element.* Pixels are the tiny, colored squares that digital devices use to create pictures. You can think of pixels as similar to tiles in a mosaic, except that all pixels in a digital image are the same size. In addition, each pixel can be only one color, whereas a mosaic tile may include several different hues.

For a close-up look at a pixel, see Chapter 2.

Pixels per Inch (ppi)

Pixels per inch, or ppi, is a measurement of the number of pixels packed into each linear inch of a printed photograph. You establish this value in your photo editor before sending the picture to the printer.

For good print quality, you need somewhere between 200 and 300 pixels per inch. (The optimum number varies depending on the printer.) If you don't have the right number of pixels, you can add or delete them in your photo editor. This process is known as *resampling*. However, adding pixels usually degrades image quality.

Chapter 10 explains this aspect of preparing your pictures for printing.

Dots per Inch (dpi)

Dots per inch, or dpi, is a measurement of how many dots of color a printer lays down per linear inch of paper.

Dpi is *not* the same thing as *ppi*, even though you may hear people (incorrectly) describe their printer's capabilities in terms of ppi. A printer may use several dots to reproduce each pixel in a digital image. I repeat: *dpi and ppi are two different things.* Also note that a higher dpi doesn't necessarily translate to better print quality.

For more on this subject and other aspects of print quality, check out Chapter 10.

RGB Color Model

Digital cameras, scanners, computer monitors, and digital projectors produce colors by mixing red, green, and blue light. This process of blending two or more primary colors to create a spectrum of colors is known as a *color model* or *color mode.* The color model based on red, green, and blue light is known as the RGB color model, for what I hope are obvious reasons.

You can read more about RGB and its close cousin, HSB (Hue, Saturation, Brightness) in Chapter 4.

CMYK Color Model

CMYK stands for *cyan, magenta, yellow,* and *black,* which are the primary ink colors used by most printers. (Some lower-end printers eliminate the black, which usually results in a lower quality photographic print.)

Printed colors usually look a little duller than their onscreen counterparts because the spectrum of colors that you can create with CMYK inks is smaller than what you can produce with RGB. The range of colors that a color model can produce is known as its *gamut* (say *gam-mutt.*) RGB colors that CMYK can't reproduce are said to be *out-of-gamut*.

Chapter 10 discusses ways that you can get the closest possible match between the RGB colors you see on your computer screen and the colors in your printed photos.

Layers

An invaluable feature found in mid-range to high-end photo editing programs, as well as in a few entry-level programs, layers are similar to the sheets of transparent acetate that people use to create presentations for an overhead projector.

By placing different photographic elements on different layers, you can make changes to everything on one layer without affecting the other layers. You also can use layer *blending modes* and *layer opacity* controls to alter the way that two layers mix together. These options come in handy for brightening image colors, adding color density, and creating special effects, among other things.

For the full story on layers, start with Chapter 3. Chapter 4 introduces you to layer blending modes and other layer tricks. Also see Chapter 7 to find out how layers make altering the composition of a photograph easier.

Clone Tool

A *Clone tool,* found in most photo editors, enables you to copy pixels from one area of an image to another. This tool is ideal for covering up small blemishes in an image.

After clicking on some "good" pixels to establish the *clone source* — the pixels you want to copy — you click or drag over the flawed pixels. As you move your cursor, the program keeps lifting pixels from the clone source and pasting the clones over the "bad" pixels.

Chapter 6 gives you a thorough introduction to the Clone tool and shares some tips for adjusting the tool to make your repair job undetectable. Chapter 8 discusses some special tricks for using the Clone tool to retouch skin.

TIFF

TIFF, which stands for *Tagged Image File Format,* is a universal file format used for digital photographs that are destined for the printer.

If you need to import your finished photograph into a word-processing, page layout, or any text-based document that you plan to print, save a copy of your photo in this format. TIFF files can be opened both on Windows-based computers and Macintosh systems.

While you're working on your photograph, however, save the picture file in your photo editor's *native format* — that is, the program's own format. In Photoshop Elements, that's the PSD format, for example. The program can process your edits more quickly on a file in its native format, and TIFF (and other formats) may not be able to preserve all the special image features, such as independent layers, that the native format supports. In fact, there isn't any reason to save your picture in TIFF or any other format unless you need to open the file in a program that doesn't accept the photo-editor's native format.

Chapter 2 explains how to save a file in the TIFF format.

JPEG

If you want to add your photo to a Web page or attach it to an e-mail message, you need to save a copy of the file in the JPEG format.

JPEG — say it *jay-peg* — is one of three image formats that Web browsers and e-mail programs can open. JPEG is a better choice for photographs than the other two formats, GIF and PNG. You may also need to create a JPEG version of your image if you need to import it into a multimedia presentation program.

When you save your file, you can apply JPEG *compression,* which shrinks the size of the image file. Keep reading to find out the good and bad sides of this option.

For complete instructions on how to save in the JPEG format, see Chapter 10.

Compression

Compression refers to a process that reduces the size of a digital image file during the file-saving process. Several formats, including TIFF and JPEG, offer file compression as an option.

Although smaller files are great, especially for files that need to be transferred over the Internet, compression achieves the size reduction by tossing away image data. If the file format uses *lossless* compression, only extraneous data gets dumped, so no detectable damage is done to the image quality. TIFF uses lossless compression. (However, because some programs can't open compressed TIFF files, taking advantage of this feature isn't always a good idea.)

Lossy compression, which is applied by the JPEG format, is less discriminating. You can reduce file size much more dramatically with lossy compression than with lossless compression, but you pay the price in terms of image quality.

Chapter 10 discusses JPEG compression in more detail; Chapter 2 tells you more about the TIFF format.

Chapter 12

Ten Tips for More Professional Results

*B*ecoming skilled at photo editing takes patience and practice. Don't be discouraged if your first efforts look a little clumsy — in time, you'll master all the tools your program offers.

If you want to enjoy more professional results from the start, however, keep in mind the pointers provided in this chapter as you work on your pictures. By following these tips, you can avoid mistakes that result in amateurish, poor-quality images.

Step Lightly on the Sharpening Pedal

Almost every digital image can benefit from a small amount of sharpening. A careful application of the Unsharp Mask filter, explained in Chapter 5, can create the illusion of better focus and bring out image details.

Too much sharpening, however, creates ugly color halos along the borders between light and dark areas. You can see an example in the lower-right image in Color Plate 5-1.

Remember that even the heftiest dose of sharpening doesn't make blurry pictures come into focus. So all you do when you over-sharpen is make matters worse — you wind up with poor focus *and* sharpening halos.

Select with Care

Before you make any change to a photograph, you must first draw a selection outline to tell your photo editor what part of the picture you want to alter. Drawing precise selection outlines is perhaps one of the most important things you can do to ensure that your edits aren't obvious.

Sloppy selection outlines are especially problematic when you copy and paste a subject from one photo to another. If you're not careful, you can grab some of the background pixels in the selection outline. When you then paste the subject into its new home, you see a ring of background pixels around the pasted object — a dead giveaway that the object isn't in its original surroundings.

To find out how to get the best results with your selection tools, read Chapter 3. Follow up with a trip to Chapter 8, which offers tips for selecting hair and fur, which are among the most difficult things to select with precision.

Pay Attention to Lighting

When combining pictures or shifting objects around within a picture, make sure that you maintain consistent lighting throughout the scene. Refer to the original image to see the placement of the original highlights and shadows. If necessary, use the techniques outlined in Chapter 5 to adjust exposure and Chapter 7 to rebuild shadows.

Remember, too, that if you change the color of an object or its background, you may also need to change the color of the shadows cast by that object. Chapter 9 discusses this issue.

Learn to Love Levels

Every photo editor, from the most basic to the most advanced, offers a Brightness/Contrast filter. Newcomers to photo editing naturally assume that this control offers the fix for underexposed, overexposed, or low-contrast images.

Because of the way that Brightness/Contrast works, however, it actually is destructive to your images. You can read about this problem in Chapter 5, which also discusses the Levels filter, a much better tool for correcting exposure and contrast. With Levels, you can adjust image shadows, highlights, and midtones independently and, in some programs, correct color-balance problems at the same time.

Take Advantage of Layers

For extra editing flexibility and security, get acquainted with your photo editor's layers controls. If your software doesn't offer layers, seriously consider moving up to a program that does — layers are among the most useful tools you can have.

Before you make a major change to your picture, duplicate the layer that contains the pixels you want to adjust. Then apply the edit to the duplicate layer. That way, if you decide later that the change was a mistake, you can just delete the duplicate layer; your original image remains untouched. Or you can lower the opacity of the duplicate layer to reduce the impact of the edit.

Some programs, including Elements, offer *adjustment layers,* which enable you to apply color and exposure changes to a whole stack of image layers at the same time, without permanently affecting the original image. You can explore this valuable layer option in Chapter 4.

Also become familiar with Layer blending modes, which control how the pixels in one layer mix with pixels in the underlying layer. The Multiply and Screen modes are helpful for intensifying and lightening image colors, as discussed in Chapters 4 and 5. The Color and Overlay modes enable you to realistically alter the color of an object, a topic addressed in Chapter 9.

Match Textures When Making Repairs

When you patch a hole in a wall in your house, you have to be careful to recreate the texture found in the surrounding area. Otherwise, when you apply touch-up paint to the repaired area, the patch becomes obvious because of the change in texture.

The same holds true when you cover up bad spots in an image. If you're working with a brush-based tool, such as the Clone tool, match the softness of the brush to the surrounding area. In most cases, a medium-softness setting works best, as illustrated in Color Plate 8-2.

After you make your repair, use your software's noise or grain filters to build texture in the altered areas if necessary. Chapter 8 shows you how.

Get a Grip on Resolution

No matter how adept you become with your photo editor's tools, you simply can't produce quality prints unless your image contains enough pixels to achieve an adequate output resolution (pixels per inch). And to wind up with the right number of pixels, you have to choose the correct input resolution when you scan or shoot the original photo.

Chapter 2 provides you with the background information you need to make the right resolution decision at the input stage, and Chapter 10 explains how to establish output resolution.

If you're preparing pictures to share over the Internet or for some other onscreen use, on the other hand, remember to *ignore* resolution. All that matters is the total number of horizontal and vertical pixels, not pixels per inch. Again, see Chapters 2 and 10 for details.

Apply Limited JPEG Compression

You should save pictures in the JPEG file format if you want to place them on a Web page or attach them to an e-mail message. All Web browsers and e-mail programs can open JPEG files.

When you save your image in the JPEG format, you can apply compression to reduce the size of the image file. Smaller file sizes reduce the amount of storage space the file uses on the Web server and the length of time the image takes to download.

Unfortunately, JPEG compression eliminates image data in its quest for slimmer files. Too much compression creates weird color-blocking effects, known as *artifacts,* as illustrated by the lower-left example in Color Plate 10-1.

The exact amount of compression you can apply before you do serious damage to your image depends on the photo, but typically you can get away with a medium compression setting. See Chapter 10 for more information about compression and other JPEG file-saving options.

Use Special Effects Sparingly

Your photo editor likely offers a dozen or more special effects. Some effects mimic traditional artistic styles, while others produce bizarre, psychedelic images.

Playing around with special effects is a gas, and certainly much more fun than doing ordinary retouching tasks such as removing dust specks from a scanned image. So go ahead and enjoy yourself — heck, spend all day exploring special effects if you want. As illustrated by Color Plate 9-1, some effects can help you preserve a treasured memory while disguising the flaws in the original photo.

Don't get in the habit of applying effects to every picture, however. And if you do decide to apply effects, stick with the subtle ones. Many effects call too much attention to themselves, which takes away from the subject of your photo.

Invest in Quality Paper and Printing

You can enjoy a huge improvement in your printed images by coughing up the cash for a good printer. If your current printer is a few years old or is an all-purpose office printer, you'll be amazed at how much better your pictures will look when output on one of today's photo printers. Of course, the paper you use makes a big difference, too; for important pictures, buy high-quality photo stock.

In case you're in the mood to go printer shopping, Chapter 10 offers some buying tips. If a new printer isn't in the cards, the same chapter provides information about affordable professional printing alternatives.

Chapter 13

Ten Ways to Protect Your Pictures

• •

In This Chapter

▶ Scan important pictures now

▶ Work on copies, not originals

▶ Save in a lossless format

▶ Archive images on CD

▶ Catalog your image files

▶ Print on archival paper

▶ Protect prints from the environment

▶ Use a matte with framed images

▶ Display photos out of direct light

▶ Keep your mitts off!

• •

*W*hen asked to name the belongings they'd take if suddenly forced to leave their homes because of a fire, flood, or alien invasion, most people put their family photographs at the top of the list. Our pictures provide a visual record of our lives, and those images usually can't be replaced if lost.

If flames, floodwaters, or space creatures appear at your door, I trust you'll have the presence of mind to grab at least a few of your photos as you're running away. In the meantime, this chapter discusses things you can do to protect your photographs from environmental decay, digital destruction, and other, more common mishaps that can ruin your pictures.

These guidelines apply to business photographs, too, by the way. Although the loss of commercial images may not have a huge emotional impact, it certainly can be costly in financial terms.

Scan Important Pictures Now

Take steps now to get the most important pictures in your collection into digital form. Follow the guidelines presented in Chapter 2 to scan your pictures, or find a commercial imaging lab that can scan them for you. You can have a picture scanned to CD for about $1 an image, which is a small price to pay for peace of mind. Your scanned pictures provide a digital "negative" from which you can always create new prints in the future if needed.

Whether you do the job yourself or pay someone else, don't wait until the photos start to fade or discolor to get started. Scan while the pictures are still in good shape, and you save yourself the trouble of restoring them later.

Work on Copies, Not Originals

Always work on a copy of your original picture file. That way, if you mess up, you haven't ruined everything. You can just open the original image, make another copy, and start again. Of course, you should save the work-in-progress image often during an editing session to preserve your changes.

For safety's sake, I store my original image files in a folder separate from the copies. I even add the word *Original* to the file name so that I'm reminded not to make alterations to that version of the picture.

Save in a Lossless Format

As discussed in Chapter 2, you can save a digital picture in several different file formats. To preserve all original image data as you work on a picture, be sure to select a *lossless* format when you save the file. Your photo editor's native file format likely fits the bill, as does the TIFF format. Chapter 2 explains the options that you may encounter when you save a TIFF file.

Two other common formats for digital images, JPEG and GIF, destroy some of the image data during the file-saving process. For that reason, you should save in JPEG or GIF only after you're completely done editing, and only if you want to use the picture for some purpose that requires one of these formats.

Note that if you took your pictures with a digital camera that stores images in JPEG, you don't do any harm to the images by simply opening and viewing them. But if you decide to edit the picture, work on a copy saved in TIFF or another lossless format.

Archive Images on CD

Computer hard drives serve as digital storage cabinets for the programs that you install as well as for data files that you create. However, files stored only on a hard drive can be at risk.

If your computer crashes during an image-editing session, you lose all the changes that you made since the last time you saved the image. In most cases, the original image file remains intact, and you can just open the image and start over after you re-boot your computer. But for various reasons, hard drives can and do fail completely, in which case your image files may be unrecoverable.

To protect yourself from this disastrous scenario, use a CD recorder to copy important image files to an archival CD. If you're really paranoid, like me, make two copies of each disc and send one copy to a friend or relative for safekeeping.

Be sure to use a high-quality CD-R disc, which prevents anyone (including you) from erasing the files after they're copied to the CD.

If you don't have a CD recorder, you can take your images to a commercial imaging lab for copying to CD. You can also archive image files to magnetic media such as a Zip disk, but remember that data on this type of storage may degrade in as few as 10 years, while CD-R discs have a life span of about 100 years.

Catalog Your Image Files

No matter how large your image collection, cataloging and organizing your files is a must. After all, having your pictures in digital form does you no good if you can't remember where you stored a particular image a few years down the road.

To make your cataloging job easy, I recommend that you invest in a specialized image-management program such as ThumbsPlus, from Cerious Software, or ACDSee, from ACD Systems. These programs not only make organizing your image collection simple, they enable you to assign keywords to each image and then search for images by keyword. In addition, you can print catalog pages that show thumbnail views of each image along with information about the picture, such as the date you last edited it.

The CD at the back of this book includes trial versions of ThumbsPlus and ACDSee, as well as other cataloging and album programs.

Print on Archival Paper

All photographic prints degrade over time. But you can prevent rapid demise of your photos by printing them on paper that's designed to preserve them as long as possible.

Several manufacturers now produce so-called *archival* photo paper for use with consumer photo printers. These papers typically claim a life span of 25 years. Because the printer ink plays a big role in the life of the print, these life-expectancy figures assume that you use the paper with a printer approved by the paper manufacturer.

For a bit longer life span, you can have your photograph printed on traditional, archival photo paper at a professional lab. Your picture then should last as long as a print from a film camera, which can be as much as 60 years. You can also consider the archival Epson Stylus Photo 2000P printer, which uses special inks that researchers predict will provide a life expectancy of 200 plus years. The downside is that the archival inks typically have a smaller color gamut than standard inkjets, so prints may appear a little duller.

Keep in mind, though, that all these life-span ratings are simply estimates. How long a photo actually lasts before you notice degradation of the image can vary wildly depending on the environmental conditions to which you expose the print. The good news is that because you have your original image file archived in a safe spot, you can make a new print if the current one starts to show signs of age.

Protect Prints from the Environment

Photographic prints are finicky beasts. They don't respond well to humidity, dirt, dust, or the chemicals that waft through our air. Exposure to any of these factors can shorten the life span of a print.

The best way to protect your photos is to frame them and then display them in a low-humidity environment. Make sure to seal the back of the frame so that moisture and other contaminants can't get in.

Store pictures that you don't frame in archival photo boxes or albums, and keep those treasure chests out of the attic, basement, and garage. (You don't need squirrels and bugs nibbling at your pictures on top of everything else.)

Ask the salespeople at your local camera store to guide you to suitable storage materials. If you don't have a retail outlet in your area, try online and catalog photo-supply companies such as Light Impressions (www.lightimpressionsdirect.com).

Use a Matte with Framed Images

For framed photos, always place a matte between the picture and glass, even if you add a digital matte to fill an image out to a standard photo size, a trick explained in Chapter 10. Otherwise, if you later try to remove the picture from the frame, you may find that the picture is stuck to the glass.

Be sure that you use archival, acid-free matte board. Non-archival matte materials release chemicals that can discolor a photograph.

On a related note, never glue a photograph to a mounting board, because the glue can seep through the print. Instead, use archival tape to attach the edges of the print to the matte. You can buy this type of tape in most craft and art-supply stores.

Display Photos Out of Direct Light

You know how sunlight coming through a window can fade your carpet or furniture? It has the same effect on photographic prints, even framed ones. Fluorescent light can suck the life out of a print, too.

To preserve your image colors as long as possible, display the picture in a location that doesn't get doused with strong light for hours each day. For framed photos, special UV-filtering glass can help, too.

Keep Your Mitts Off!

When handling prints and negatives, avoid touching the surface of the picture. Even if your hands are absolutely clean, the oil from your fingers can leave thumbprints that may be difficult to remove. If your hands are moist, you may even smudge inkjet prints.

If you do your own scanning and picture-framing, I suggest that you invest in a pair of lint-free, cotton gloves to wear while you work. You can buy gloves specially made for this purpose at your local photography-supply outlet or through online stores.

Part V
Appendixes

The 5th Wave   By Rich Tennant

"THAT'S A LOVELY SCANNED IMAGE OF YOUR SISTER'S PORTRAIT. NOW TAKE IT OFF THE BODY OF THAT PIT VIPER BEFORE SHE COMES IN THE ROOM."

In this part . . .

*I*f you're using Jasc Paint Shop Pro, Adobe Photoshop, or Ulead PhotoImpact to edit your photographs, the charts in Appendix A will help you translate the instructions that I give throughout this book to your software.

For those readers who haven't selected a photo-editing program yet, the bonus CD included with this book offers trial versions of some of the best programs available, as well as trials of cataloging and album software, printing utilities, and more. Appendix B provides a list of the CD contents and explains how to install the programs on your computer.

Appendix A

Software Translators

• •

*T*o help you adapt the Photoshop Elements instructions and information discussed in this book to your software, this appendix contains translation charts for three other leading photo-editing programs: Jasc Paint Shop Pro, Ulead PhotoImpact, and Adobe Photoshop. Of course, some tools and features work slightly differently from program to program, so use these tables in conjunction with your software's manual or Help system as you work on your photographs.

If you haven't yet selected a photo-editing program, the CD included at the back of this book provides you with an excellent way to sample some of the best options. Appendix B provides instructions for installing programs from the CD.

Jasc Paint Shop Pro 7

The following tables cover Version 7 of Paint Shop Pro. However, if you're using an older version of the program, many items are the same as in Version 7. For more information about Paint Shop Pro, visit the Jasc Software web site, www.jasc.com. This program is available for Windows only.

Photoshop Elements	Jasc Paint Shop Pro
Focus Adjustments	
Unsharp Mask filter	Effects⇨Sharpen⇨Unsharp Mask
Unsharp Mask Amount control	Strength control
Unsharp Mask Radius control	Radius control
Unsharp Mask Threshold control	Clipping control
Sharpen tool	Retouch tool in Sharpen mode
Gaussian Blur filter	Effects⇨Blur⇨Gaussian Blur
Blur tool	Retouch tool in Soften mode

(continued)

Photoshop Elements	Jasc Paint Shop Pro
Exposure and Color Adjustments	
Levels adjustment layer	Layers⇨New Adjustment Layer⇨Levels
Levels filter	Colors⇨Adjust⇨Levels
Screen/Multiply layer blending	Screen/Multiply (set in Layer palette) modes
Dodge tool	Retouch tool in Lighten RGB or Dodge mode
Burn tool	Retouch tool in Darken RGB or Burn mode
Variations filter	Colors⇨Adjust⇨Color Balance
Hue/Saturation filter	Colors⇨Adjust⇨Hue/Saturation/Lightness
Hue/Saturation adjustment layer	Layers⇨New Adjustment Layer⇨Hue/Saturation/Lightness
Colorize option in Hue/Saturation dialog box	Colors⇨Colorize
Selection Tools and Techniques	
Establish tool options	Use controls in Tool Options palette; display palette by choosing View⇨Toolbars⇨Tool Options palette
Rectangular, Elliptical Marquees	Selection tool; set shape in Tool Options palette
Lasso	Freehand tool in Freehand mode
Polygonal Lasso	Freehand tool in Point to Point mode
Magnetic Lasso	Freehand tool in Smart Edge mode
Magic Wand	Magic Wand; set Match Mode to RGB
Feather existing selection outline	Selections⇨Modify⇨Feather
Invert a selection outline	Selections⇨Invert
Add to a selection outline	Shift+drag or Shift+click with Freehand, Selection, or Magic Wand tool
Subtract from a selection outline	Ctrl+drag or Ctrl+click with Freehand, Selection, or Magic Wand tool
Reposition a selection outline	Select Mover tool, right-click inside selection outline, and drag

Selection Tools and Techniques

Select everything on active layer	Ctrl+A
Deselect everything	Ctrl+D

Layer Features

Layers palette	View⇨Toolbars, select Layer palette
Copy selection to new layer	Selections⇨Promote to Layer
Create new empty layer	Layers⇨New Raster Layer or click New Layer icon in Layer palette
Create new adjustment layer	Layers⇨New Adjustment Layer
Make layer active	Click layer in Layer palette
Show/hide layer	Click eyeglass icon in Layer palette
Delete layer	Layers⇨Delete or drag layer to Trash icon in Layer palette
Set layer opacity and blending mode	Use Layer palette controls or choose Layers⇨Properties
Merge visible layers only	Layers⇨Merge⇨Merge Visible
Flatten image	Layers⇨Merge⇨Merge All

Size and Transformation Features

Image Size command	Image⇨Resize
Canvas Size command	Image⇨Canvas Size
Image⇨Crop command	Image⇨Crop to Selection
Free Transform command	Deformation tool (cannot be applied to background layer)
Rotate	Image⇨Rotate

Paint and Edit Tools

Paintbrush	Paint Brush
Clone tool	Clone Brush
Eyedropper	Dropper
Smudge tool	Retouch tool; Smudge mode

(continued)

Photoshop Elements	Jasc Paint Shop Pro
Paint and Edit Tools	
Set tool options	Use controls in Tool Options palette; display palette by choosing View⇨Toolbars⇨Tool Options palette
Fill command	Activate Flood Fill tool (toolbox icon looks like a paint can.) Set fill contents via the foreground Styles and Textures controls in Color palette. Then click inside selection outline.
Gradient tool	Activate Flood Fill tool and set the foreground Styles control (in the Color palette) to Gradient. Click Styles box to set gradient style; use foreground Textures option to add/remove texture. Then click inside selection outline.
Display Color Picker	Click Foreground or Background color swatch in Color palette; can also click foreground or background Styles box when control is set to Solid

Ulead PhotoImpact 7

The following tables cover Version 7 of PhotoImpact. However, if you're using an older version of the program, many items are the same as in Version 7. For more information about PhotoImpact, visit the Ulead Systems Web site, www.ulead.com. This program is available for Windows only.

Note that layers work slightly differently in PhotoImpact than in Photoshop Elements. You can create a new layer, called an *object* in PhotoImpact, by copying a selection or by using the Paint, Clone, and Retouch tools in Paint as Object mode. You can't create an empty layer. Also, you can't select part of an object; you can select only the entire object. To make a portion of an object transparent, use either the Object Paint Eraser or Object Magic Eraser.

Photoshop Elements	Ulead PhotoImpact
Focus Adjustments	
Unsharp Mask filter	Effect⇨Blur & Sharpen⇨Unsharp Mask; click Options to access filter controls
Unsharp Mask Amount control	Sharpen Factor control

Focus Adjustments

Unsharp Mask Radius control	Aperture Radius control
Unsharp Mask Threshold control	None
Sharpen tool	Retouch tool in Sharpen mode
Gaussian Blur filter	Effect⇨Blur & Sharpen⇨Gaussian Blur; click Options to adjust filter impact
Blur tool	Retouch tool in Blur mode

Exposure and Color Adjustments

Levels adjustment layer	Not available
Levels filter	Format⇨Highlight Midtone Shadow
Screen/Multiply layer blending modes	Inverse of Multiply/Multiply (set in Layer Manager)
Dodge tool	Retouch tool in Dodge mode
Burn tool	Retouch tool in Burn mode
Variations filter	Format⇨Color Balance or use color adjustment buttons on Tool panel
Hue/Saturation filter	Format⇨Hue & Saturation
Hue/Saturation adjustment layer	Not available
Colorize option in Hue/Saturation dialog box	Colorize option in Hue & Saturation dialog box

Selection Tools and Techniques

Establish tool options	Use controls on Attribute toolbar; display by choosing View⇨Toolbars⇨Attribute Toolbar.
Rectangular, Elliptical Marquees	Standard selection tool; set shape on Attributes toolbar
Lasso	Lasso tool (on flyout menu with Standard selection tool)
Polygonal Lasso	Click with Lasso tool
Magnetic Lasso	Lasso tool with Snap to Edges option
Magic Wand	Magic Wand tool (on flyout menu with Standard selection tool)
Feather existing selection outline	Selection⇨Soften

(continued)

Photoshop Elements	Ulead PhotoImpact
Selection Tools and Techniques	
Invert a selection outline	Selection⇨Invert
Add to a selection outline	Press A while clicking or dragging with selection tool; or set Mode option on Attributes toolbar to Add.
Subtract from a selection outline	Press S while clicking or dragging with selection tool or set Mode option on Attributes tool bar to Subtract.
Reposition a selection outline	Drag inside outline with Pick tool
Select everything on active layer	Click layer name in Layer Manager; to select background image, press Ctrl+A
Deselect everything	Shift+G
Layer Features	
Layers palette	Click Layer Manager icon on Panel Manager. Choose View⇨Toolbars⇨Panel Manager to show/hide Panel Manager.
Copy selection to new layer	Selection⇨Convert to Object
Create new empty layer	Not available
Create new adjustment layer	Not available
Make layer active	Click layer in Layer Manager
Show/hide layer	Click eyeball icon in Layer Manager
Delete layer	Object⇨Delete or drag layer to click Delete icon in Layer Manager (icon looks like the letter X).
Set layer opacity and blending mode	Use Layer Manager controls or choose Object⇨Properties (blending modes are called *merge modes*)
Merge visible layers only	Not available; however, Object⇨Merge merges currently selected layer with background layer; Object⇨Merge as Single Object combines multiple selected layers into one layer
Flatten image	Object⇨Merge All

Size and Transformation Features	
Image Size command	Format⇨Image Size
Canvas Size command	Format⇨Expand Canvas Size
Image⇨Crop command	Edit⇨Crop
Free Transform command	Transform tool in Transform mode (select transformation style on Attribute toolbar)
Rotate	Edit⇨Rotate & Flip or Transform tool in Rotate & Flip mode
Paint and Edit Tools	
Paintbrush	Paint tool
Clone tool	Clone tool
Eyedropper	Eyedropper
Smudge tool	Retouch tool; Smudge mode
Set tool options	Use controls on Attribute toolbar; display by choosing View⇨Toolbars⇨Attribute Toolbar
Fill command	Edit⇨Fill
Gradient tool	Edit⇨Fill; set gradient options in Fill dialog box. Or use Bucket Fill tool in any gradient mode.
Display Color Picker	Click Foreground or Background color swatch in Tool panel

Adobe Photoshop 6 and 7

Because Photoshop Elements was derived from its famous sibling, Photoshop, many features are the same in both programs. I've trimmed this table to include only those features that work differently.

This information applies to Photoshop 6 and 7; however, if you're using an earlier version of the program, some items will be the same. Also, if you are working with Photoshop 7, information provided for Elements 2.0 in the body of the book applies (where Photoshop offers a corresponding feature). Also note that in Photoshop 7, the Image⇨Adjust submenu was renamed Image⇨ Adjustments. For more information about Photoshop, visit the Adobe Web site, www.adobe.com.

Photoshop Elements	Photoshop 6/7
Levels filter	Image⇨Adjust⇨Levels
Variations filter	Image⇨Adjust⇨Variations
Hue/Saturation filter	Image⇨Adjust⇨Hue and Saturation
Image Size command	Image⇨Image Size
Canvas Size command	Image⇨Canvas Size
Free Transform command	Edit⇨Free Transform

Appendix B

Exploring the Bonus CD

• •

In This Appendix

▶ System requirements for using the CD that accompanies this book

▶ Instructions for using the CD with Windows-based PCs and Macintosh computers

▶ Descriptions of content provided on the CD

▶ Troubleshooting tips

• •

*W*alk though your local computer store, and you can find dozens of programs related to photo editing. To help you pick the right products for your needs, the CD at the back of this book provides try-before-you-buy versions of those programs that I think are among the best available. In most cases, you have 30 days to experiment with the program before you have to ante up the purchase price.

For more details about any of these programs, visit the Web site listed in the product description.

System Requirements

Make sure that your computer meets the minimum system requirements shown in the following list. If your computer doesn't match up to most of these requirements, you may have problems using the software and files on the CD.

✔ A PC with a Pentium II or faster processor and 300+ MHz; or a Power Mac G3 OS computer or faster processor

✔ Microsoft Windows 98, 2000, NT, ME, or XP; or Mac OS system software 9.1, 9.2.1, or OS 10.1

✔ At least 64MB of available RAM on your computer; for best performance, we recommend at least 128MB

✔ At least 200MB of available hard drive space if you want to install all the software from this CD; you'll need less space if you don't install every program

✔ A CD-ROM drive

✔ A sound card for PCs; Mac OS computers have built-in sound support

✔ A monitor capable of displaying at least 256 colors or grayscale

✔ A modem with a speed of at least 14,400 bps

If you need more information on the basics, check out these books published by Wiley Publishing, Inc.: *PCs For Dummies,* by Dan Gookin; *Macs For Dummies,* by David Pogue; *iMacs For Dummies* by David Pogue; *Windows 95 For Dummies, Windows 98 For Dummies, Windows 2000 Professional For Dummies, Microsoft Windows ME Millennium Edition For Dummies,* all by Andy Rathbone.

How to Use the CD Using Microsoft Windows

To install the items from the CD to your hard drive, follow these steps.

1. **Insert the CD into your computer's CD-ROM drive.**

2. **Choose Start⇨Run.**

3. **In the dialog box that appears, type** D:\Setup.EXE.

   Replace *D* with the proper drive letter if your CD-ROM drive uses a different letter. (If you don't know the letter, see how your CD-ROM drive is listed under My Computer.)

4. **Click OK.**

   A license agreement window appears.

5. **Read through the license agreement, nod your head, and then click the Accept button if you want to use the CD — after you click Accept, you'll never be bothered by the License Agreement window again.**

   The CD interface Welcome screen appears. The interface is a little program that shows you what's on the CD and coordinates installing the programs and running the demos. The interface basically enables you to click a button or two to make things happen.

6. **Click anywhere on the Welcome screen to enter the interface.**

   Now you're getting to the action. This next screen lists categories for the software on the CD.

7. **To view the items within a category, just click the category's name.**

   A list of programs in the category appears.

8. **For more information about a program, click the program's name.**

Be sure to read the information that appears. Sometimes a program has its own system requirements or requires you to do a few tricks on your computer before you can install or run the program, and this screen tells you what you may need to do, if necessary.

9. **If you don't want to install the program, click the Back button to return to the previous screen.**

   You can always return to the previous screen by clicking the Back button. This feature allows you to browse the different categories and products and decide what you want to install.

10. **To install a program, click the appropriate Install button.**

    The CD interface drops to the background while the CD installs the program you chose.

11. **To install other items, repeat Steps 7–10.**

12. **When you've finished installing programs, click the Quit button to close the interface.**

    You can eject the CD now. Carefully place it back in the plastic jacket of the book for safekeeping.

How to Use the CD Using a Mac OS Computer

To install the items from the CD to your hard drive, follow these steps.

1. **Insert the CD into your computer's CD-ROM drive.**

   In a moment, an icon representing the CD you just inserted appears on your Mac desktop. Chances are, the icon looks like a CD-ROM.

2. **Double-click the CD icon to show the CD's contents.**

3. **Double-click the License Agreement icon.**

   This is the license that you are agreeing to by using the CD. You can close this window once you've looked over the agreement.

4. **Double-click the Read Me First icon.**

   The Read Me First text file contains information about the CD's programs and any last-minute instructions you may need in order to correctly install them.

5. **To install most programs, open the program folder and double-click the icon called "Install" or "Installer."**

   Sometimes the installers are actually self-extracting archives, which just means that the program files have been bundled up into a single archive file, and a self-extractor tool unbundles the files and places them on your hard drive. This kind of program often has the letters .sea in its name. Double-click anything with .sea in the title, and it will run just like an installer.

6. **Some programs don't come with installers. For those, just drag the program's folder from the CD window and drop it on your hard drive icon.**

What's on the CD?

The following sections provide a summary of the goodies included on this CD. You can install the programs by following the instructions provided in the preceding sections of this appendix.

Before you install a program, though, be sure to check out the information provided for each program and the Read Me file that may be included as part of the installation screen. (Read Me files contain late-breaking news that may be important to the installation process.)

Most programs on the CD are *trial, demo,* or *evaluation* versions of software, which means that the programs are limited either by time or functionality. For example, you may not be able to save a project after you create it. (Software companies assign their try-before-you-buy offerings these various labels, which the publisher is required to use.)

Image-editing software

The programs in the following list offer most or all of the photo-editing features discussed in this book. (Appendix A provides translation charts to help you convert the instructions I give for Photoshop Elements to the other programs.)

- **Paint Shop Pro, from JASC, Inc.:** Evaluation version for Windows; www.jasc.com.

- **PhotoImpact, from Ulead Systems:** Trial version for Windows; www.ulead.com.

- **Photoshop, from Adobe Systems, Inc.:** The CD provides a trial version of Photoshop 6.0; QuickTime movie previews are available at the Adobe Web site (www.adobe.com).

- **Photoshop Elements, from Adobe Systems, Inc.:** Trial version for Windows and Macintosh; www.adobe.com.

For novice photo-editors who want just the basics, the following programs are good choices. However, these programs don't offer some of the advanced retouching tools found in their more sophisticated cousins.

- ✔ **AfterShot, from JASC, Inc.:** Trial version for Windows; www.jasc.com.

- ✔ **FotoCanvas, from ACD Systems Ltd.:** Trial version for Windows; www.acdsystems.com

- ✔ **PhotoExpress, from Ulead Systems:** Trial version for Windows. www.ulead.com.

Specialty software

In addition to the image-editing programs listed in the preceding section, the CD also includes the following special-purpose programs:

- ✔ **ACDZip, from ACD Systems Ltd.:** Zip/unzip utility for packaging multiple images in one file. (This product is similar to the popular PKZip, WinZip, and StuffIt utilities, but offers thumbnail previews of zipped files). Trial version for Windows; www.acdsystems.com.

- ✔ **FotoSlate, from ACD Systems Ltd.:** Printing utility. Trial version for Windows; www.acdsystems.com.

- ✔ **nik Sharpener Pro! Complete, from nik multimedia, Inc.:** Image-sharpening plug-in filter for Photoshop and compatible programs (including Photoshop Elements). Demo version for Windows and Mac; www.nikmultimedia.com.

- ✔ **nik Color Efex Pro! Complete Edition, nik multimedia, Inc.:** Special-effects plug-in filters for Photoshop and compatible programs (including Photoshop Elements). Demo version for Windows and Macintosh; www.nikmultimedia.com.

- ✔ **OfotoNow, from Ofoto, Inc.:** Free software for Windows and Macintosh. Use this browser to easily upload photos to an online album at the Ofoto Web site, www.Ofoto.com.

- ✔ **Print Station, from PicMeta:** Printing utility. Evaluation version for Windows; www.picmeta.com.

- ✔ **SilverFast SE, from LaserSoft Imaging:** Scanning utility. Trial version for Windows and Macintosh; www.lasersoft-imaging.com.

  Note: The CD includes Windows and Macintosh copies of four different versions of this software. Each version supports select scanner models from a specific manufacturer (Hewlett-Packard, Microtek, Umax, or Epson). Please read the information provided for each version to see whether your scanner is supported before installing the software. Be sure to install the version provided for your scanner manufacturer and operating system.

✔ **VueScan, from Hamrick Software:** Scanning utility. Trial version for Windows and Macintosh; www.hamrick.com.

Cataloging and album programs

The following programs provide you with different approaches to keeping track of your digital image files:

✔ **ACDSee, from ACD Systems Ltd.:** Image browser and cataloging software. Trial version for Windows and Macintosh; www.acdsystems.com.

✔ **FlipAlbum Suite, from E-Book Systems, Inc.:** Album software. Trial version for Windows; www.flipalbum.com. (A free utility for viewing albums is available for download from the Web site.)

✔ **PhotoExplorer, from Ulead Systems:** Image browser and cataloging software. Trial version for Windows; www.ulead.com.

✔ **Picture Information Extractor, from PicMeta:** Image browser and cataloging software. Evaluation version for Windows; www.picmeta.com.

✔ **ThumbsPlus, from Cerious Software, Inc.:** Image browser and cataloging software. Evaluation version for Windows; www.thumbsplus.com.

✔ **Virtual Album, from Radar Software, Inc.:** Album software. Trial version for Windows; www.albumsoftware.inc.

Images on the CD

So that you can work along with the steps discussed throughout this book, I've provided low-resolution versions of some images featured in the examples. Figure B-1 provides thumbnail views of the sample photos.

To work with these images, open the Sample Photos folder on the CD as you would open any other folder inside your photo editor. If you use a Windows-based system, the files have the file extension .JPG.

Please note, however, that these are copyrighted images made available just for your use while you're exploring this book. Using them on your Web site, in a print publication, or any other purpose is verboten.

Web links page

While you're browsing the Web, you can bring up this page to connect quickly to the software companies that provided products for the CD. Put the

CD in your CD-ROM drive and then choose File⇨Open inside your Web browser. Select the file named Links.htm and click OK to display the page. Then just click a link to jump to the corresponding Web site.

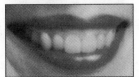

Figure B-1:
You can find these images in the Sample Photos folder on the CD.

And one last thing . . . .

The CD also includes a copy of **Acrobat Reader from Adobe Systems, Inc.** This free program enables you to view and print Portable Document Format, or PDF files. Some programs on this CD include manuals in PDF format.

For more information about Acrobat Reader, visit the Adobe Web site at www.adobe.com.

If You've Got Problems (Of the CD Kind)

I tried my best to compile programs that work on most computers with the minimum system requirements. Alas, your computer may differ, and some programs may not work properly for some reason.

The two likeliest problems are that you don't have enough memory (RAM) for the programs you want to use, or you have other programs running that are affecting installation or running of a program. If you get error messages saying that your computer's out of memory or the Setup program can't continue, try one or more of these methods and then try using the software again:

- ✔ **Turn off any antivirus software that you have on your computer.** Installers sometimes mimic virus activity and may make your computer incorrectly believe that it is being infected by a virus.

- ✔ **Close all running programs.** The more programs you're running, the less memory is available to other programs. Installers also typically update files and programs. So if you keep other programs running, installation may not work properly.

- ✔ **In Windows, close the CD interface and run demos or installations directly from Windows Explorer.** The interface itself can tie up system memory or even conflict with certain kinds of interactive demos. Use Windows Explorer to browse the files on the CD and launch installers or demos.

- ✔ **Have your local computer store add more RAM to your computer.** This is, admittedly, a drastic and somewhat expensive step. However, adding more memory can really help the speed of your computer and allow more programs to run at the same time.

If you still have trouble installing the items from the CD, please call the Wiley Publishing Customer Service phone number: 800-762-2974 (outside the United States: 317-572-3993) or send email to techsupdum@wiley.com.

Index

• *M* •

Wiley Publishing, Inc.
End-User License Agreement

READ THIS. You should carefully read these terms and conditions before opening the software packet(s) included with this book ("Book"). This is a license agreement ("Agreement") between you and Wiley Publishing, Inc. ("WPI"). By opening the accompanying software packet(s), you acknowledge that you have read and accept the following terms and conditions. If you do not agree and do not want to be bound by such terms and conditions, promptly return the Book and the unopened software packet(s) to the place you obtained them for a full refund.

1. **License Grant.** WPI grants to you (either an individual or entity) a nonexclusive license to use one copy of the enclosed software program(s) (collectively, the "Software") solely for your own personal or business purposes on a single computer (whether a standard computer or a workstation component of a multi-user network). The Software is in use on a computer when it is loaded into temporary memory (RAM) or installed into permanent memory (hard disk, CD-ROM, or other storage device). WPI reserves all rights not expressly granted herein.

2. **Ownership.** WPI is the owner of all right, title, and interest, including copyright, in and to the compilation of the Software recorded on the disk(s) or CD-ROM ("Software Media"). Copyright to the individual programs recorded on the Software Media is owned by the author or other authorized copyright owner of each program. Ownership of the Software and all proprietary rights relating thereto remain with WPI and its licensers.

3. **Restrictions On Use and Transfer.**

   (a) You may only (i) make one copy of the Software for backup or archival purposes, or (ii) transfer the Software to a single hard disk, provided that you keep the original for backup or archival purposes. You may not (i) rent or lease the Software, (ii) copy or reproduce the Software through a LAN or other network system or through any computer subscriber system or bulletin-board system, or (iii) modify, adapt, or create derivative works based on the Software.

   (b) You may not reverse engineer, decompile, or disassemble the Software. You may transfer the Software and user documentation on a permanent basis, provided that the transferee agrees to accept the terms and conditions of this Agreement and you retain no copies. If the Software is an update or has been updated, any transfer must include the most recent update and all prior versions.

4. **Restrictions on Use of Individual Programs.** You must follow the individual requirements and restrictions detailed for each individual program in Appendix B of this Book. These limitations are also contained in the individual license agreements recorded on the Software Media. These limitations may include a requirement that after using the program for a specified period of time, the user must pay a registration fee or discontinue use. By opening the Software packet(s), you will be agreeing to abide by the licenses and restrictions for these individual programs that are detailed in Appendix B and on the Software Media. None of the material on this Software Media or listed in this Book may ever be redistributed, in original or modified form, for commercial purposes.